Geschenk der Eheleute Wallmeyer

in Taunusstein-Hahn

im Mai 1991

(Gedächtnisstiftung Uwe Wallmeyer)

Design of Distributed Operating Systems

Paul J. Fortier

Intertext Publications, Inc.
McGraw-Hill, Inc. New York, NY

DESIGN OF DISTRIBUTED OPERATING SYSTEMS
INTERNATIONAL EDITION

Copyright © 1988
Exclusive rights by McGraw-Hill Book Co. - Singapore
for manufacture and export. This book cannot be re-exported
from the country to which it is consigned by McGraw-Hill.

1st Printing 1988

Copyright © 1986 by Intertext Pulications. Inc. All rights reserved.
Except as permitted under the United States Copyright Act of 1976, no
part of this book may be reproduced or distributed in any form or
by any means, or stored in a data base or retrieval system, without the
prior written permission of the publisher.

Library of Congress Cataloging-in-Publication Data

Ada is a registered trademark of the United States Department of Defense
(Ada Joint Program Office).
UNIX is a registered trademark of Bell Laboratories.

When ordering this title use ISBN 0-07-100433-5

Printed and bound in Singapore by Chong Moh Offset Printing Pte Ltd.

Table of Contents

Preface

1. Introduction 1
1.1   Introduction 1
1.1.1 History of Operating Systems 1
1.2   Distributed Operating Systems 6
1.2.1 Process Model 7
1.2.2 Object Model 8
1.3   Overview of Text 11

2. Introduction to Operating Systems 15
2.1   Introduction: Componemts of Operating Systems 15
2.1.1 Hardware Architectures 15
2.2   Traditional Operating Systems 26
2.2.1 Single User Operating Systems 27
2.2.2 Batch Operating Systems 28
2.2.3 Real-time Operating Systems 29
2.2.4 Multiprocessing Operating Systems 31
2.2.5 Time-sharing Operating Systems 31
2.2.6 Distributed Operating Systems 32
2.3   Components of Traditional Operating Systems 33
2.3.1 Process Management 34
2.3.2 Memory Management 42
2.3.3 I/O and Device Management 54
2.3.4 File Management 62
2.4   Summary 65

3. Distributed Computing 66
3.1   Introduction 66
3.2   Control Protocols 68
3.3   Routing 69

3.4	Flow Control	73
3.5	Addressing	74
3.6	Reliability	76
3.7	Security	77
3.8	Resource Sharing and Distributed Processing	77
3.9	Models of Computation	79
3.9.1	Hierarchical Model	79
3.9.2	Federated Model	81
3.9.3	Resource-sharing Model	81
3.9.4	Homogeneous Model	82
3.9.5	Data-flow Model	82
3.10	Local Area Networks	83
3.10.1	Topology	84
3.10.2	Protocols	89
3.10.3	Processing Devices	91
3.11	Operating Systems	91
3.12	Services	92
3.13	Languages	93
3.14	Synchronization	95
3.15	Summary	96
4.	**Introduction to Distributed Operating Systems**	**97**
4.1	Introduction	97
4.2	Process Management	101
4.3	Communications Management	104
4.4	Device Management	106
4.5	Memory Management	108
4.6	File Management	108
4.7	Event Management	112
4.8	Models of DOS Design	113
4.8.1	The Process-oriented Model	114
4.8.2	The Object-oriented Model	115
4.9	Summary	118
5.	**The Process Model**	**119**
5.1	Introduction	119
5.2	History and Motivation	125
5.3	Process Model	131
5.3.1	Processes	132
5.3.2	Ports	134

5.3.3	Messages	141
5.3.4	Synchronization	142
5.4	Process Management	144
5.5	Device Management	147
5.6	I/O Management	150
5.7	Memory Management	151
5.8	Network Management	151
5.9	Summary	153

6. The Object Model ... 154
6.1	Introduction	154
6.2	Object Model	156
6.2.1	Objects	156
6.2.2	Operations	157
6.2.3	Capabilities	167
6.2.4	Synchronization	173
6.3	Process Management	176
6.4	Memory Management	180
6.5	Device Management	181
6.6	I/O Management	187
6.7	Network Management	188
6.8	Summary	191

7. Process-Based Distributed Operating Systems ... 192
7.1	Introduction	192
7.2	Chorus	193
7.2.1	Concepts	196
7.2.2	Communications	197
7.2.3	Actor Architecture	199
7.2.4	Processing Structures	203
7.2.5	Synchronization	204
7.2.6	Process Management	207
7.2.7	Memory Management	208
7.2.8	Device Management	208
7.2.9	I/O Management	210
7.2.10	File Management	211
7.2.11	Network Management	211
7.3	Thoth/Hermes	213
7.3.1	Concepts	213
7.3.2	Process Management	215

7.3.3	I/O Management	218
7.3.4	Memory Management	219
7.4	Basic Operating System (BOS)	223
7.4.1	Processes	224
7.4.2	Communications	226
7.4.3	Architecture	226
7.4.4	Supervisor	227
7.5	RTDOS	229
7.5.1	Processes	230
7.5.2	Ports	234
7.5.3	System Management	238
7.6	Summary	246

8. Object-Based Distributed Operating Systems ... 248

8.1	Introduction	248
8.2	MIKE	249
8.2.1	Introduction	250
8.2.2	Basic Concepts	251
8.2.3	Structure of MIKE	251
8.2.4	Objects	252
8.2.5	Object Interaction	258
8.3	ARCHOS	265
8.3.1	Introduction	265
8.3.2	Arobjects	266
8.3.3	Arobject Processes	267
8.3.4	Communications	268
8.3.5	Transactions	269
8.3.6	Synchronization	270
8.3.7	Process Management	271
8.3.8	Communications Management	275
8.3.9	File Management	277
8.3.10	I/O and Device Management	278
8.3.11	Time Management	278
8.3.12	Policy Management	279
8.3.13	System View	280
8.4	Clouds	281
8.4.1	Introduction	281
8.4.2	Memory Management	286
8.4.3	Process Management	287
8.4.4	Network Management	288

8.5	SODS/OS	288
8.5.1	Introduction to SODS/OS	288
8.5.2	Architecture	292
8.5.3	Systems Calls	293
8.5.4	Process Management	295
8.5.5	I/O Management	295
8.6	Summary	295
8.7	Other Systems	296

Appendix 298

References 309

Index 318

Preface

This text is the outgrowth of work I have been performing in specification analysis and the design of distributed operating systems for real-time control environments and for advanced software engineering tools. My interests in this area grew out of my dissertation research, which led from the data-base world back into the operating system world and revealed the tight synergism that exists between the operating system and all other components of a distributed system. Through these investigations, I discovered a lack of any text that tried to bring together the concepts embodied in distributed systems management. These factors provided the impetus to produce this book. The writing of this text could not have been realized without the support of my publisher, Alan Rose, and even more so that of my wife, Kathleen Fortier, who provided me with unending encouragement during this endeavor. I also wish to extend my gratitude to Lloyd Watts of Portsmouth, Rhode Island, for the preparation and editing of my manuscript. His tireless efforts made possible a finished product as opposed to a crude presentation. My children have always been an inspiration and this one is for them: Nicole, Brian, and Daniel.

Paul J. Fortier
Portsmouth, R.I.
May, 1986

1. Introduction

1.1 Introduction

The operation of any computer system relies on the use of some form of operating system to transform the lifeless hardware into a usable machine. The operating system of any computer or collection of computers represents the point within the system that provides the user with his view of its capabilities and interfaces.

Operating systems evolved over a long period of time. As the environment of use for computers changed and new problems arose, researchers met the challenges with new solutions.

1.1.1 History of Operating Systems

In the beginning, there existed few tools to enhance the usefulness of the computer, and it was relegated to use by a select few who could trudge through the translation of real problems into sequences of adds, subtracts, multiplies, etc. Operation of the early machines was performed by the coders, because only they could figure out a problem or even recognize that one existed. As this was very inefficient, work was begun to rectify the situation.

The first problem tackled by systems programmers was how to make easy transitions from job to job without the many headaches involved with system setup and breakdown. The monitor or batch system provided the solution. Early operating system structures allowed operators to load several jobs at one time; the computer swapped them in, let them run, and swapped them out upon completion. Although this was a step in the right direction, the expensive equipment still was not being efficiently utilized. New devices were being developed to aid in I/O and storage, but the control mechanisms to use them efficiently still were not there.

The next major evolutionary step was based on the need to better utilize the I/O devices. The concept that arose was that of an executive program. This provided a means for programs to run concurrently with I/O under the control of a watchful eye, the executive. It provided the management of the interaction between the I/O devices and the running program. This solution was adequate for a while, but it did not provide for multiple users simultaneously using the system; this would follow.

The advent of the development of a supervisor program was the next step. This program took over more functions from the operators and coders, and ushered in the "swapping" of programs based on time slices.

Following this major breakthrough came true operating systems. The IBM System/360 operating system ushered in the present era. Many of the services provided in today's systems trace their basis or inception to early OS/360 facilities.

The goals of these developments had one thing in common. They were striving to facilitate the more efficient use of computers. They were meant to provide convenient interfaces to users while hiding the bare machine's computational complexities. They provided transparent use of resources, thereby relieving users from the burden of needing to know configuration of the particular system. They offered users and systems programmers protection from accidental or malicious destruction, theft, or unauthorized disclosure.

The most obvious accomplishments of an operating system are the hiding of the machine's details and the optimal use of the resources. Users need not know the particular device they are using, only that they need one of a certain class: they can ask for a "printer" or "tape," and not need the exact name and number of the device. This shields users from the problems of down components. If it were necessary to specify a particular device that was not available, work might not be able to go on; if the user can specify a class of device, any one of that type can meet the need, increasing the ability of the user to get the job done.

The systems programmers and the hardware and software researchers did not end their quest for perfection here. There were more areas to look at and many more problems to solve.

Sharing introduced its own new set of problems. As systems became more usable, still more uses were envisioned and implemented. Systems began to meet the raw processing capacity boundaries of the machines. Designers looked at a way to solve this dilemma. To provide more processing cycles for applications, software developers tried to streamline and improve the performance and computational complexity of operating systems. These improvements provided some relief, but it was only temporary. Hardware designers improved the computational power of the singular CPU systems through pipelining of instruction execution and other hardware improvements. These, too, provided only a limited increase in performance.

The research and development community began to look at ways to improve performance within the bounds of fixed or marginally increasing processor performance. The concept that was initially embraced looked at multiprocessor configurations, which represented a divergence from contemporary systems in a simple way. The multiple processors could each run their own executive programs, needing to be augmented only to provide system calls for synchronizing their autonomous actions. This was accomplished through system calls for semaphore-type operations. Utilizing these extensions, the operating systems and/or the users could synchronize the operation of two or more machines, thereby providing increased performance. However, this still was not a panacea. The overall system performance was bounded by the level of interaction in the shared memory and, additionally, by the distribution of the processing of complicated programming.

Research continued toward the goal of connecting computers spread over geographic distances to provide the view of a large "virtual" machine to the user community. Thus was created the world of distributed computers and processing. Early work dealt more with developing technology so that the machines could converse, than with with total control.

Big problems existed with providing robust intercomputer communications hardware that was reliable. Once hardware was developed, the systems designers began to look at improvements to make it more usable. The early machines required users to be cognizant of the distribution and of the intricacies of their location and usage. The first improvements dealt with providing protocols to provide reliable, error-free communications. These were then refined with techniques and mechanisms to provide location transparency to users. This was provided mainly through logical naming schemes rather than physical ones. This gave users the ability to utilize simple primitives, such as: send message to name, receive message from name, and reply message to name.

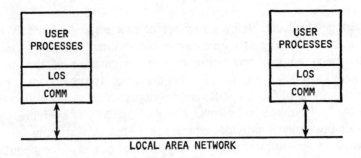

Figure 1.1 **Early Communications Services**

Name could be either a single device or process designator, or one representing multiple devices or processes. What we had at that point (fig. 1.1) was a system comprised of traditional cooperating user processes, operating under a local operating system (LOS). These communicated to and interacted with each other via a simple communications sublayer that provided the network transparency to users. This was analogous to the early operating systems that provided a monitor to users that protected them from the hardware dependencies. The evolution continued in an attempt to provide a more integrated, unified view of the distributed system. Efforts in this area have been referred to as NOS (network operating system) designs. The NOS provided more transparent use of distributed assets beyond the mere communications. NOS designs began to look at global resource allocation and management, global process management, and total or nearly total transparency of network assets for the users and local operating systems. A NOS environment (fig. 1.2) is comprised of four layers. The communications layer provides the reliable transfer of messages between devices. It provides all interactions for disjointed devices.

The NOS layer provides the transparency of system to all the users and the local operating system. It provides the ability to accept a request for, say, processing or data not available locally, and determines where the assets are, how to initiate its operation based on the request, and how to return the appropriate service, all transparent, to the users and local environments. The local environment views the action as having been performed locally with no reservations. The NOS handles the interfacing and coordination of the remote actions and communications between local operating systems. It maintains cognizance of the state and location of all entities in the system.

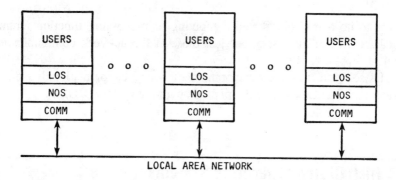

Figure 1.2 **NOS Hierarchy**

The NOS receives service requests from the local operating systems and provides them with status as if it were the actual wanted entity responding.

The LOS is a traditional operating system in all senses except one. If it is asked to perform some task (say, to execute a process to do data reduction), it will try to schedule it. If the process is in its local cognizance it will schedule and execute the task; otherwise, it will tell NOS to run it. To the local operating system, the NOS is the actual server performing the task, while in reality it is just the agent for the actual task.

The final layer is made up of the users. They operate oblivious to all distribution and interactions. They view the system as one large uniprocessor with all the processes and resources it needs local to its domain. This simplifies the view the users need to have and the complexity of their job.

This environment was sufficient when only increased overall throughput was wanted, but researchers and coders got smarter. They wished to utilize the distribution to perform each job more quickly; that is, they wanted parallel execution of jobs. Thus dawned the the era of distributed processing or computing. When the goal is to change the way we think about coding systems (from sequential to parallel or distributed processing), the emphasis falls on redefining how we solve problems; from sequential solutions, we move to something different (for example, divide and conquer, and massively parallel data flow). With this shift in emphasis came a whole new raft of problems; the NOS environments did not worry about or consider process management, I/O management, memory management, device management, or information management from a global viewpoint, but as autonomous local functions that must interact but that do not steer each other. The problem is that to do a true distributed computing or processing function required global control of all assets, not just those at the network communications level.

The solution was the development of concepts for a global operating system (GOS), also called a distributed operating system (DOS).

1.2 Distributed Operating Systems

To meet the more robust requirements for future distributed environments, workers in research and development have embarked on the development of the next generation of operating system, the distributed operating system.

A distributed operating system represents a total view and structure for control and management across multiple computer systems. The goal of a distributed operating system is to provide an environment devoid of local dependencies. The operating system makes management decisions based on the return to the entire system rather than a singular processor. Management is a cooperative process encompassing all resources and involving all sites. The DOS environment is comprised of cooperating peers that strive toward the system management and performance goals (fig. 1.3).

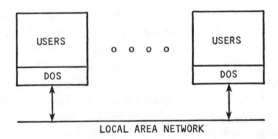

Figure 1.3 **DOS View of System**

A distributed operating system is built on top of the bare machine; it is not an add-on to existing software. This allows the DOS to encompass all resources without interference from old software. Therefore, a distributed operating system is comprised of the same management components as traditional systems, yet it has a wider range of view. The components of a DOS must have the following as a minimum:

> Process or object management
> Memory management
> I/O Management
> Device Management
> Network Management

Each of these management components provides global control and management of their entrusted resource(s). These components typically are broken up into cooperating peers on the physical systems. Details will be described later.

Distributed operating systems research has headed down two major paths. Each path is in essence a parallel of the other; that is, the capability of one path is similar to that of the other path. These paths of research deal with two models of design: the process model and the object model.

1.2.1. Process Model

The main elements of the process model are processes and messages. All actions in the system, whether user applications or system management functions, are performed by processes; that is, any job to be done in the system (such as memory management, process management, scheduling, I/O management, device management, or network management) will be constructed as a collection of cooperating processes. Processes interact and direct each other by means of messages. This is strictly adhered to in the pure model. For example, for a running process to input data from a disk unit, it would need to send a request message to the disk manager process, which would then interpret this message, act accordingly to find the data, extract it from the media, and then form a response message to return the proper data to the requestor. Similarly, in any other interaction, whether between user processes or system processes or a combination thereof, messages would be used as the only means to interact and control the system's operations (fig. 1.4). Systems of this type tend to have few processes with much functionality built into each one.

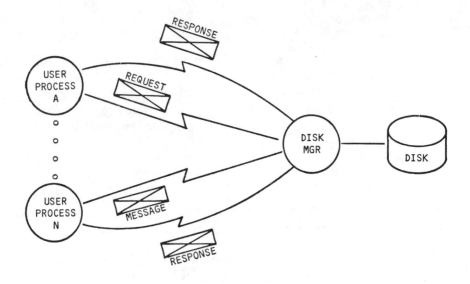

Figure 1.4 **Example of Process Interaction**

1.2.2 Object Model

The object model has similar overall functionality, although its operations and concepts are different. The object model provides a basic structure called an object. An object is comprised of a specification, or external part, and a body, or internal part. An object provides its entire "state" information within itself. It does not require extra information to determine its state. An object, as shown in fig. 1.5a, provides a means to encapsulate the internal details from the outside (the concept of hiding information).

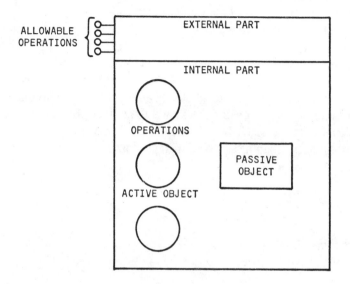

Figure 1.5a **An Object**

Objects are totally specified and autonomous. They can change their state, but only through the use of a specific set of operations (actions) on the object's structure. Objects are viewed as abstract data types that keep hidden any internal details that may cause problems to users. For example, a stack object can have only two operations, push and pop, visible to the outside, although internally it would have procedures to implement the push and pop on an internal data structure. Additionally, internal private operations could exist that would be used by the push and pop operations in doing their jobs. For example, before we pop an item from the stack, it should be checked to see if there is anything on it. This could be represented by a private operation on the object, called empty. The object model of DOS design utilizes these basic objects plus another, to structure systems. (Be sure to keep in mind that only operations that make sense to an object's type can be allowed.) But how is this done and, additionally, how do we guarantee that only the right people are allowed to access objects? A concept referred to as protection domains is utilized. This concept provides a mechanism that dynamically checks on users. Rights to objects are stored in areas of memory separate from the object. These rights, called capabilities, can best be viewed as being tickets that, once purchased (acquired), provide a particular right or group of rights. The object model embraces this concept in protecting objects; that is, for an object to use another (perform an operation on it), it must process a capability (ticket) that indicates the object and the rights to that object. In the previous stack example, we may wish to give to one object the capability to pop items off the stack, and to another object the capability to push items onto the stack (fig. 1.5b). Object A has a capability, among its list of acquired capabilities, to push items onto the stack object, whereas object B has the capability to pop items off the stack.

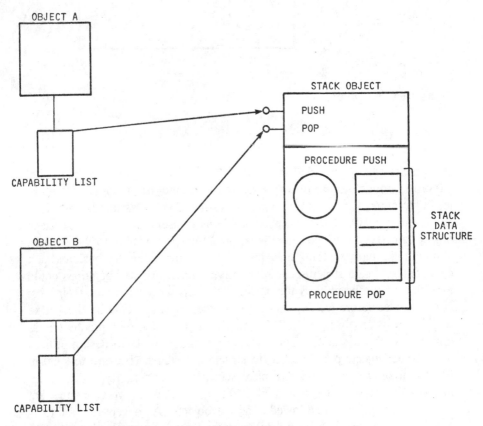

Figure 1.5b **Stack Object**

Using this basic notion of objects, operations, and capabilities, the object model can be used to structure operating systems or any user applications. This is the notion behind the object-based approach to DOS design, as will be seen later in this text.

1.3 Overview of Text

The goal of this text is to provide an understanding and appreciation of the concept and technology associated with constructing distributed operating systems. In particular, the emphasis is on distributed operating systems for local area networks [FOR86], [FORT83]. The text is structured to provide an overview of the concepts involved in operating systems.

Chapter 2 introduces the notions associated with and concepts utilized in contemporary operating systems and provides the reader with an in-depth review of contemporary operating systems structure. The concepts for memory management, process management, I/O and device management, and file management are covered in depth.

The section on process management is concerned with how to create processes, manage them within the system, and how to destroy them once they are no longer needed. The discussion views the active states of processes (ready, running, waiting) and elaborates on their meaning and usage in managing processes.

The section on memory management looks at the problems of contemporary operating systems in providing memory assets to processes when needed. The discussion covers issues in memory allocation, deallocation, and cleanup. Notions of a working set of active "virtual" pages are introduced, as are concepts for paging systems, segmentation systems, and hybrid systems.

The section on I/O management deals with the software mechanisms necessary to provide transparent I/O to processes, the allocation of and usage of buffers, and their interaction in actual performance of the low-level I/O task. Additional discussions cover methods utilized in traditional systems, such as programmed I/O and dedicated I/O devices.

The section on device management sets out to review the concepts, mechanisms, and operations associated with peripheral device management. Covered are the methods used to hide the device dependencies from the higher-level support software as well as a definition of the usage for specific high-interest devices.

Finally, Chapter 2 addresses the issues associated with interrupt management and how operating systems operate in fulfilling this function.

The purpose of Chapter 2 is to delineate the present state of operating systems technology for uniprocessor systems. This description is essential since the concepts associated with specific portions at this level are used and expanded on for distributed systems.

Chapter 3 strives to introduce concepts required to understand the essence of distributed computing, or processing, as it has become known. The chapter begins by addressing issues on sharing of resources among disjointed computers, such as is seen in the Arpanet. The concepts of what constitutes a distributed computer system are covered. The chapter looks at the level of distribution, the extent of control, and the extent of interaction as primary considerations. A distributed computer system is a set of loosely connected computing devices that have been brought together via an overlying operating environment and that operate on unified systems goals; this generalized description is particularized in Chapter 3. The extent of sharing exhibited by these systems is of utmost importance in defining their usefulness in performing specific tasks. For example, if two computers are linked together in a strictly master/slave configuration (fig. 1.6), then they can be used only in strictly controlled predecessor-related processing. The slave does not do for itself; it must obey what the master tells it. On the other hand, if two computers with total distribution of hardware and software exist within a unified control environment (distributed operating system), then they can be used as if they were a single CPU, but one with immensely more

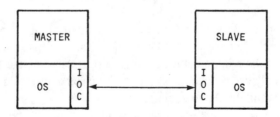

Figure 1.6 **Master/Slave Computer System**

power. The interrelationships among their processing jobs can vary widely. They can support predefined sequencing of processing, totally autonomous computing, tightly coupled coprocesses, or loosely coupled interprocess sharing. The extent of their interaction and operations is dependent on the problem being formulated.

Chapter 3 covers local area networks. This section addresses issues in topology selection and characteristics, control protocol mechanism for media access, flow control, routing, and transfer of messages over the network. The chapter ends by indicating some of the features desirable in distributed systems for management of user applications over a local area network of computers.

Chapter 4 introduces the major issues to be covered in the remainder of the text. The goal of this chapter is to provide an overview of the service mechanisms needed for distributed operating systems, namely:

> Process (object) management
> Device management
> Memory management
> File management
> Event management
> Communications management

The discussion begins by addressing what a distributed system is expected to provide in support of the user. It provides an introduction to and model of the distributed operating system's design. The chapter discusses how these aid in the construction, comprehension, and use of operating systems for distributed computer systems.

Chapter 5 provides an in-depth view of the process model and its use in structuring distributed operating systems. The chapter discusses basic concepts for the model (processes, messages, and ports) and how such mechanisms can be applied to the solution of:

> Synchronization
> Process management
> Device management
> I/O management
> Memory management
> Network management

Examples are provided of how the process model can be used to solve the issues arising in each of the management categories.

Chapter 6 provides the reader with an investigation into the concepts, mechanisms, and operations embraced within the object model of structuring systems. In particular, this model is introduced as the structuring tool for building distributed operating systems. The chapter addresses the basic notion of what constitutes the object model (objects, operations, and capabilities) and the methods for application of this technique to the solution of:

>   Synchronization
>   Object (process) management
>   Memory management
>   Device management
>   I/O management
>   Network management
>   Protection

The discussion provides thorough examples of how this structuring tool can be used to address the issues encompassed in providing the aforementioned management and interaction mechanisms. Additionally, it shows how user-object applications can operate within such a model.

Chapter 7, using examples of systems developed or being researched, focuses on the basic concepts embodied in Chapter 5, which deals with the process model. The selected systems are meant to a cross-section of systems exhibiting the major features of the model. The example systems are examined as to their basic computational model, the method(s) they use to promote the process model, and how they provide the basic services of process management, device management, I/O management, event control, memory management, synchronization, and protection, if relevant. The scope of the coverage is intended more to fully emphasize the basic structure than to constitute a complete treatise on the operating system's implementations.

Chapter 8 provides a similar overview of four major efforts that run the gamut from a loose application of the object model (SODS/OS) to strict adherence (CLOUDS or ARCHOS) to the model. Again, the presentation is meant to solidify concepts and strengthen understanding of the composition of distributed operating systems.

References brought out during the discussions will help readers to follow up on more specific details of implementations.

A final note: To truly comprehend the scope and magnitude of these systems, interested readers should get involved with them. The best way to knowledge is through understanding, which is best accomplished by action. Experiment with the concepts, try out the ideas, and discover the truth.

2. Introduction to Operating Systems

2.1 Introduction: Components of Operating Systems

To understand the function of an operating system for any computer system, we must first comprehend the operation of the hardware associated with traditionally controlled computer systems and the control that is required to operate these devices in a noninterfering fashion.

A computer system is comprised of a complex configuration of low-level hardware components controlled by either microcode (firmware) or software. Looked at from a macro view, these low-level components form five major elements that, when taken together, form the basis of all computers of the Von Neumann class: an ALU (arithmetic logic unit), a control unit, memory, input, and output. Taken together and provided the proper sequence of commands, a computer system becomes operational.

2.1.1 Hardware Architectures

The basic Von Neumann architecture (fig. 2.1) has not changed much since its conception in the 1940s. Most contemporary architectures are still developed around these basic elements, although they may have been slowed down, speeded up, or connected slightly differently. The building blocks used to construct the basic architecture exhibit characteristics as follow.

The ALU is the element of the computer that performs the actual work of computation. It acquires data from memory and provides it back, once it completes its operations, performing the addition, subtraction, multiplication, and division, as well as the comparison, of operands. In short, it is the calculator, translator, or workhorse, element of the machine. This element is the control site where all information flows that is being acted upon.

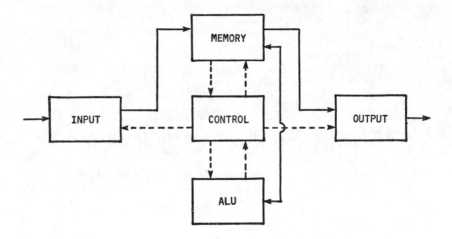

Figure 2.1 **Basic Von Neumann Architecture**

The ALU acts on data in various ways, the most common being to take data (the operands) from two places (using the ALU temporary registers) and perform the stated function (operation) on the operands. For example, the assembly code which is shown below describes typical operations. Let's say we wish to execute a simple function such as taking two items from memory, adding them together, multiplying them by a third, and storing them in a fourth location. Let's assume the data are stored in logical locations W, X, Y, and Z, respectively. The following code can be used to realize the function.

Mnemonic	Action
LDA W	A<--MEM[W]
LDB X	B<--MEM[X]
ADD A,B	A<--A+B
LDB Y	B<--MEM[Y]

```
MUL A,B         A<--A*B
STA Z           MEM[Z]<--A
Assembly code to realize Z = (W+X) * Y
```

The ALU, in order to perform this task, is first instructed to perform a load of ALU register A with the contents of memory location W (LDA W). It then performs the fetch of the second operand by performing a load of ALU register B with the contents of the second operand located in memory location X(LDB X). Next the ALU is instructed to perform the add operation (add A,B). This operation extracts the operands of register A and B and adds then together, using bit-oriented hardware add circuitry (figs. 2.2 and 2.3) to perform the operation.

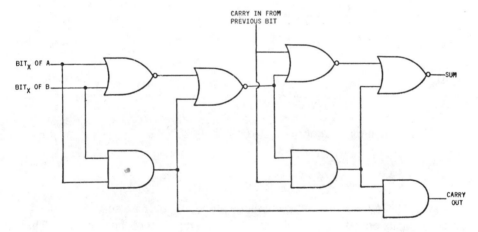

Figure 2.2 **Full Adder**

The result of this operation is stored in the A register of the ALU. Most ALU's allow for easy string operations on items to be processed.

For the next operation, the multiplication, we must first put the second operand for the operation into ALU register B. This is performed via the LDB Y instruction, which loads register B with the contents of memory location Y. Now we have the two operands for the operation (multiply) in the accumulator (ALU). We perform the multiplication by providing to the control circuitry the ALU instruction MUL A,B. This instruction, using specialized multiplication hardware, is performed by the ALU with the resultant of the process being again stored in ALU temporary register A. This result in turn is stored into memory location Z by the use of the STA Z instruction, which extracts the contents of ALU register A and stores it into the memory address supplied. We can see from this simple example that the ALU acts as the focal point of most arithmetic, logical, and transformal operations performed by a computer system.

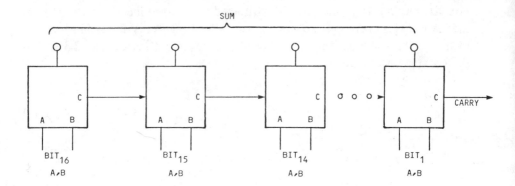

Figure 2.3 **Multiply Circuitry**

The ALU cannot perform this operation alone. It requires a source and destination of its operations, supplied by the local memory of the computer. The local memory possesses the ability to store information--data or actual software programs--for future use in the future by the remainder of the computer system. The memories of contemporary computers, mostly composed of RAM (random access memory), are constructed so that any individual word can be accessed in the same unit time delay from W. This memory can read or be written from or to, and is usually semiconductor-based in modern systems.

Memory typically is the limiting factor in the speed of present systems; that is, if the memory runs at _n_ seconds, then this becomes the limit of the machine's performance. Hardware designers have gone to great lengths to develop "whizbang" schemes to ease this bottleneck. They have developed caching systems, where the memory is comprised of a hierarchy (fig. 2.4).

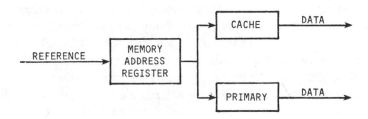

Figure 2.4 **Memory Hierarchy**

In this configuration, the address of the memory to be read is sent to both the cache and the primary memory. The cache, comprised of a collection of high-speed registers, is associatively searched (performed by hardware via a mask to all locations simultaneously), in one register cycle, which is much (about ten times) quicker than a primary memory reference cycle. If the item being looked for is in the cache, it is sent to the ALU for processing. If it is not found, the primary (slower) memory is accessed in the traditional fashion to acquire the wanted item. Other similar schemes have been developed to help speed up the process of getting the data to the ALU, where it is needed for processing. Doing this does add problems. If we adopt a memory hierarchy (cache, primary, secondary), we must also provide a means to control it. This leads to the memory management issue, which will be addressed in greater detail later in this chapter.

We now have shown two of the elements of the Von Neumann architecture. Two others, the input and output elements, are very similar in structure and operation. One controls the flow of external information into the computer system, while the other controls it going out.

From a Von Neumann standpoint, an input device is represented as merely an avenue to provide data into the computer. The avenue can be as simple as a memory port to another computer doing the input job. Input devices range from simple card readers to high-speed real-time data sensors. The range of devices is very broad, as is their complexity and control. Card readers extract the information from punched holes in a card and feed it, one unit at a time, to the CPU (memory, ALU, and control unit). The speed of such devices ranges from 10 to 250 characters per second. At the other extreme are real-time data extraction devices, such as thermal sensors or radiation sensors at nuclear plants, and sensors that feed back information from robotic construction devices in automated factories. These devices run at speeds that range from hundreds of thousands to millions of characters per second. Between these extremes are a myriad of other devices. Many computer hackers and professionals are familiar with video displays, keyboards, mouses, graphics pads, touch panels, paper tapes, magnetic tapes, floppy disks, hard disks, cassette tapes, and Teletypes. All of these devices have similar characteristics in that they all represent a means to input human requests, data, and control into a computer for processing.

Output devices operate in a similar fashion. When data is to be extracted from the computer, the output device is signaled by the CPU to ready itself. It performs this task, then accepts a block of information into its controller, which in turn provides it to the end media. The range of output devices is as wide as that of input devices and includes punched cards, paper tape, video displays, voice, magnetic tape, cassette tape, drums, hard disks, floppies, printers, graphics devices, and Teleptypes.

In modern computers, some combination of input and output devices is offered to provide a wide range of services to users. Personal computers are equipped with video displays and keyboards, minimally, and usually are purchased with some combination of floppy disk system, hard disk (high density), printer, and I/O cursor-control (mouse, joystick, or trackball) mechanism. Minicomputers are equipped with a wide range of I/O devices, including massive arrays of disks, video screens and (I/O cards to support them), tape units, graphics terminals, and printers. The type, number, and combination of I/O devices present in any computer system--whether personal computer, minicomputer, real-time supercomputer or distributed system--is determined by the volume and type of input and output.

In all cases, the basic architecture of the Von Neumann machine still exists as the hub and is the focal point of the system. The main integrating element of the architecture is the control unit. This unit provides the essence of the computer; that is, it provides the ability for the machine to extract information (data or programs) from the memory or support devices, determines what it is being asked to do, and provides the proper level of control to the slave devices that perform the desired task. The control unit singularly controls the actions of all elements in the computer.

The control section of the Von Neumann machine is required to control every cycle of execution within its control sphere. In the typical Von Neumann scheme of things, the control unit, based on the supplied clock signals, must control the actions of fetching instructions from memory, extract the meaning of the instruction via decode circuitry, and, using this decoded instructions intent, execute the proper threads of control to cause the correct sequence of actions on the involved pieces of the machine. This cycle is the same for all stored program machines of Von Neumann structure. The basic structure of the cycle comes in two flavors: the fetch, decode, execute, and the fetch, fetch, decode, execute. In these two cycles, the control unit, based on the state of its control circuitry and on the instruction pointer (fig. 2.5), will fetch the instruction from memory and based on the instruction, perform certain control functions.

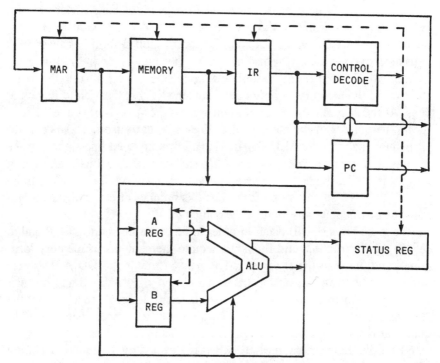

Figure 2.5 **Basic Structure of Von Neumann Computer**

Let's examine the previous example, which added two values, multiplied them by a third value, and stored the result in a destination location. We must start by bounding where the process begins; that is, we must assume a location in memory where the data and program exist. The start point (address) is assumed to reside in the control unit's program counter (PC). The address for the variables W, X, Y, and Z have been inserted for the variable representation by the compiler or assembler. Now we can begin. The program counter supplies to the memory address register (MAR) the address from which to acquire the next instruction. This value is sent to the MAR via a clock signal supplied to the PC via the control unit. Concurrently, the control unit enables the MAR to accept the input. On the next clock cycle, the control unit excites the enable signal to allow the memory to use the address supplied by the MAR to acquire the content of the location and provide this to the instruction register (IR). The instruction register now holds the instruction that is to be executed next. The contents of this register are provided to the control unit on the next clock cycle to decode the instruction. In the case of the LDA,W instruction, the control unit determines that the A register is to be loaded with the contents of the supplied address of memory location W. To do this, the control unit provides this address Y to the MAR and excites the memory to provide the contents of this location to its output lines. At the same time the control unit signals the A register of the ALU to accept the outputs of the memory data line as input to itself. This is accomplished by enabling the ALU signal. That allows the input line signals or the A register to be gated into the register's storage cells. At this point, the A register is loaded with the contents of memory location W. It took a finite number of clock signals to perform this; this number of clock signals represents the instruction cycle time of the computer.

The same process will occur in order to fetch the instruction LDB and to decode this instruction, and finally to acquire the contents of memory location X and put it in the B register. The next instruction, ADD A,B, is performed by first fetching the instruction as previously defined and by then decoding the instruction into a sequence of control signals that instruct the ALU to add the contents of register A with that of register B, using the additional hardware, and storing the result back into the A register.

Similarly, the instruction MUL A,B is performed by the proper decoding of the instruction in the control section and the excitation of the proper hardware lines in order to cause the proper set and sequence of hardware actions to be performed. The example ends with the fetching of the STA Z instruction, its decoding, and the insertion of the results into the proper memory location--all under the watchful eye of the control logic. The question arises as to how the control logic is implemented in order to bring about the ability to control all these diverse functions. Typically, control circuitry is implemented using either ROM (read only memory) or architecture based on programmed logic arrays (PLA). In ROM designs, the wanted outputs are mapped to an address where the address represents the instruction opcode in binary form. The opcode (operation code) represents the instructions for the machine to perform its particular coded function. The decoding of the instruction is performed simply by reading out the contents of the address supplied (the instruction). The output is then sent to the proper points to stimulate the proper actions in the physical devices. The problem with this approach is that it may leave many spaces in the ROM empty and therefore waste space. In the PLA approach the address (instruction) is mapped to the outputs using logic array circuitry. This design does not result in any unused locations, because of the one-to-one mapping of instructions to outputs. Other techniques applied include microprogramming, as described by Wilkes [WILK51].

A new wrinkle in recent systems developments is the connection of multiple computer systems into networks. These, too, must be controlled by an operating system, and will be described in greater detail later in the text.

In traditional designs for computers, the CPU, memory, and I/O devices (disk, tape, terminal, printer) have been combined into various organizations to form working computer systems. The major differences among these architectures are in the device that acts as the switching or interfacing element in the system. The three major types are bus control, CPU control, and memory control architectures.

The bus control architecture consists of an active or passive data/control bus that is used in connecting the various functional elements. Examples of this type of architecture are the PDP-11 family of processors (fig. 2.6).

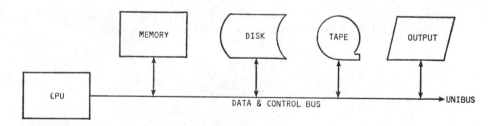

Figure 2.6 **PDP-11 Bus Central Structure**

[24] Design of Distributed Operating Systems

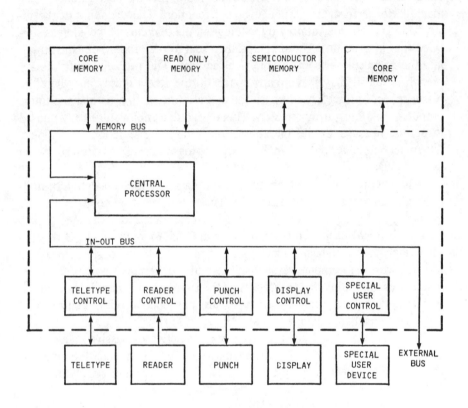

Figure 2.7 **IBM 370 CPU Central Architecture**

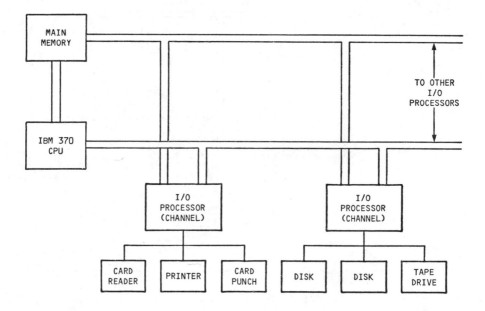

Figure 2.8 **Typical NOVA System Configuration**

In the CPU control architecture, sometimes referred to as the multibus architecture, the CPU acts as the central point through which pass all peripheral devices and memory. This structure is represented by the Data General NOVA minicomputer (fig. 2.8) and the IBM 370 systems (fig. 2.7). In these figures, note the position of the CPU in relation to the memories and I/O devices. One problem with this architecture is the need for the CPU to often control the transfers between main memory and the I/O devices.

In memory control architecture, the main memory is used as the connector between the central processing unit and the peripheral devices. This type of architecture facilitates direct transfer of blocks of storage from main memory to I/O devices and vice versa. This architecture requires that the I/O peripheral devices have the intelligence to control the data flow between themselves and the main memory. An example of this type of architecture can be seen in the CDC CYBER 70 computer (fig. 2.9).

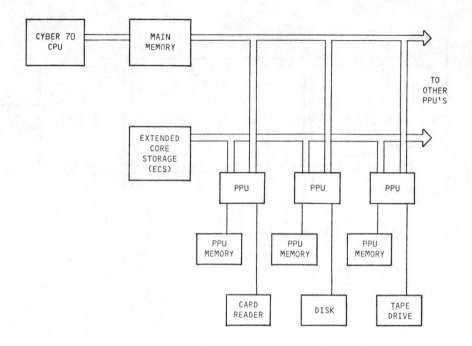

Figure 2.9 **Organization of the CDC CYPHER 70 Computer**

2.2 Traditional Operating Systems

As discussed in Chapter 1, no contemporary computer system exists without the embedding of some level of an operating system within its bowels. Operating systems primarily supply resource management services to user processes.

The primary resources controlled are the processors, storage (primary and secondary), input and output devices, and information. To perform these tasks, an operating system provides to the users features such as a meaningful interface, scheduling of resources, sharing of resources, error detection and recovery, communication amongst processors and users, I/O management, and data sharing.

Operating systems are viewed as the highest-level user in a system; as such, they have the best access and control of all features of a system's hardware, user programs, and data. This situation is the result of the evolution of operating systems to their present status. In early systems, the computer had no operating system and ran in a totally stand-alone fashion. This was referred to as the single user system. The second class of operating system was the batch, or serially shared, system. This system allowed groups of users to bundle work and execute it in a high-speed, non-human-interfered fashion. Another early operating system concept was the real-time executive. This class of operating system can be best characterized as event-driven, with constraints for hard completion of deadlines processing; it is limited to a few users per system.

The fourth class of operating system, the multiprocessing system, is characterized by the physical presence of two or more central processing units that execute instructions in parallel. They are usually configured as either tightly coupled or loosely coupled, a reference to the control they exhibit over each other.

The fifth class of operating systems, the time-sharing or multiprogramming system, is characterized by a relatively large number of users sharing the resources of the machine. The sharing is done in an attempt to provide each user the illusion of possessing a single dedicated computer system.

The sixth class, the distributed operating system, is best described as a set of computer systems networked together to form a unified system. The main goal of a distributed processing system is to provide a wider range of resources for users to utilize in doing their applications. The goal of a distributed operating system is to provide the mechanisms under which these expanded resources are available without the user being aware of the distribution.

2.2.1 Single User Operating Systems

The single user operating system (fig. 2.10a) dates back to the early days of computers. In this type of system, a user is essentially the operating system. Before he runs his job, the user must set up the initial conditions for all hardware dependencies; that is, the state of all registers, the allocation and status of all devices required, etc. In the early days, this type of system typically was a standalone system in which the user inputted a bootstrap program to initialize the system, after he had gone through the process of setting each of the initial registers, for example, with the front panel toggle switches. Once the bootstrap program (simple operating system) was in memory, the user could then set up the I/O devices as necessary and have his applications program loaded. The system then could be initiated to run the user's inputted applications. When the application was completed, the user was then required to break down the system to bring it back to the initial idle state. This was necessary so that the next user could start his program using a known initial state.

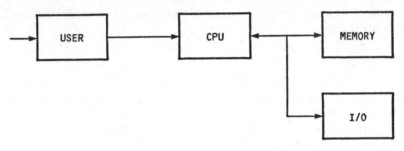

Figure 2.10a **Single User System**

2.2.2 Batch Operating Systems

The batch operating system environment was an evolutionary move forward from the single user environment (fig. 2.10b). The problem encountered in the single user system, that of the exorbitant time necessary for setup and breakdown for each job, was lessened with the advent of batch systems. In batch systems, jobs are provided to the system operators in bundles called batches. These batches of jobs are linked together into a larger single job. This single job is then set up on the computer, run to completion, and the results removed from the system. This simplified the setup and breakdown problem and allowed for more jobs to be run per unit of time.

Typical of this type of system was one that used punched cards as the input medium and printed output as user's output. The biggest problem with both this operating scheme and the previous one is the difficulty associated with debugging. The user, in order to debug a program, was required to reedit the cards on a punch machine or paper tape machine, provide the edited cards on tape to the operator, wait for the output to return (using hours

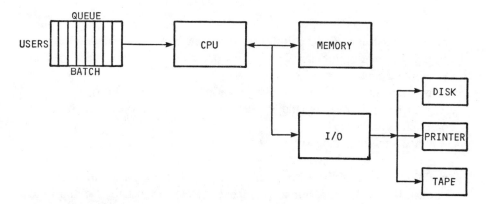

Figure 2.10b **Batch System**

for batch), and examine them. If there was an error, the user repeated the process; if the editing was correct the user submitted his code to process data as intended.

This represented an improvement in terms of the system, but still did not correct the problem from a user's viewpoint. It was deemed acceptable when computer time was much more expensive than user's time. This situation has drastically changed today.

2.2.3 Real-time Operating Systems

Real-time operating systems (fig. 2.11) arose with the advent of minicomputers and high-speed analog and digital I/O devices. Real-time systems have been built and utilized to monitor and control the actions of real-world systems. In order to provide this capability, the real-time operating system must be developed to respond to events (for example, temperature sensors exceeding some boundary value, a procedure boundary or construction of a part in automated factories). These events form the basis of control for the real-time system. An operating system built for such environments must have the capacity to receive event signals, determine which event is occurring, process the event-supplied data, and respond accordingly to the event in order to drive the state of the real-world system to that wanted by the developer. Additionally, if the real-time system is being stimulated by multiple

[30] Design of Distributed Operating Systems

inputs, it must have the capability to select one based on criticality of processing and control to determine the best one on which to operate, based on the supplied conditions.

In order to do this, the real-time operating system should possess a hierarchy of control priorities and a means to select the proper set, based on conditions supplied.

A real-time operating system is one that is developed solely for the purpose of monitoring some action, processing the conditions and data, and providing a response based on a pre-determined set of possibilities. Due to the critical processing requirements, these systems are usually limited from one to a few user processes. Usually, real-time computer systems are found embedded in other hierarchically configured operating systems, and are used as the interface to system elements requiring control on a real-time basis.

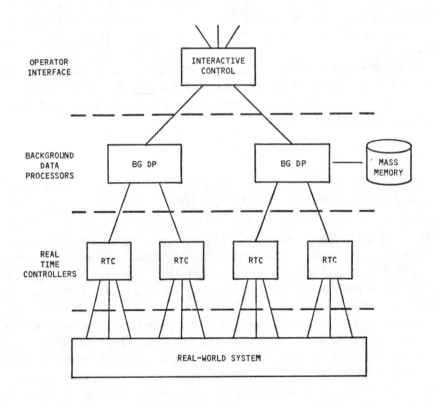

Figure 2.11 **Real-Time System Hierarchy**

2.2.4 Multiprocessing Operating Systems

Multiprocessing operating systems (fig. 2.12) are concerned with the control and sharing of multiprocessors connected together via a shared memory scheme. In such systems, the operating environment can be either tightly coupled (the goal is to have the processors synchronized very closely in performing their jobs) or loosely coupled (the synchronization is not strict, and they can be run more as autonomous machines, with the combination of the two or more processors providing higher job throughput). In either case, the main problem of an operating system in this type of configuration is to determine how to share the memory among the multiple processors and how to schedule the use of the processors based on the system criteria in place.

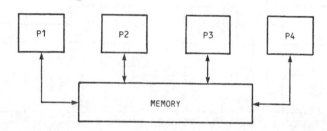

Figure 2.12 **Multiprocessor**

2.2.5 Time-sharing Operating Systems

Time-sharing (sometimes called multiprogramming) systems (fig. 2.13) represent the next phase of evolution, beyond the batch systems. In a time-sharing environment, the goal is to provide to each user the vision or illusion of having a computer system dedicated to himself. This is realized through the intelligent, time-sliced sharing of the computer resources among the active users. The users interface to time-sharing systems through interactive display devices. Therefore, the job of the operating system is to provide the users just enough interaction to make them feel that they are getting much better service. This type of service, however, has its drawbacks; it places much more responsibility for the control of resources on the operating system and complicates its job drastically. The operating system must worry about multiple processes residing in memory simultaneously. It must maintain and control their storage on secondary and primary memory resources. It must control the use of the CPU by any process in order to guarantee the fair sharing of the resource. It must provide the ability to manage and control the use of I/O devices among the active processes, as well as control the communications between the processes. These features will be covered in greater detail later in this chapter because of their important effect on temporal operating systems.

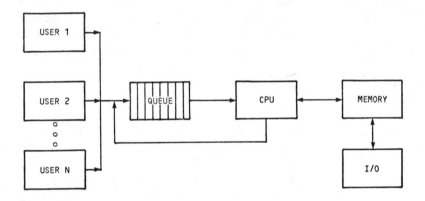

Figure 2.13 **Time Sharing Systems**

2.2.6 Distributed Operating Systems

A distributed operating system has been described as possessing multiple loci of control. Simply stated, distributed operating systems are comprised of an operating environment that has components strewn across all nodes in a system. The control of the system could be centralized (localized to one site) or distributed (no central point can be found; control is effected through the cooperative actions of all). The two major emphases in terms of the services offered in such systems are that the users have a uniform and transparent view of resources, and that global resources be allocated fairly to independent processes. The challenge for distributed processing and operating systems is for them to provide the proper level of service without extra overhead. Further details of goals and objectives for distributed systems and operational environments will follow.

2.3 Components of Traditional Operating Systems

In most contemporary operating systems, the following components or entities can be found:

> Process management
> Memory management
> I/O management
> Device management
> File management

Each of these components strives to provide a service to the users. In each case, the objectives are similar and encompass all aspects of the design and usage of operating systems. These services extend from the basic one of sharing the resources and cover a wide range. They exhibit the goals of reliability, protection, predictability, extendability, transparency, flexibility, efficiency, and convenience while providing the service of controlling and managing the interaction of the diverse set of devices that comprise the computer systems.

In process management, the problem is how to keep the CPU busy while providing a fair to good level of service to the individual users (processes) on the system; meanwhile, the processes wish to view the system as a dedicated resource to their problems.

In memory management, the problem is how to keep the memory loaded with the portions of secondary storage most likely to be accessed by the running system over a fixed period of time.

Another issue is how to control the inputting and outputting of information to the system while hiding the particulars of devices from a user process.

Conversely, the device management task is to provide the proper level of service to a device in order to control its specific method of inputting and outputting information to or from the CPU.

The last major element is the file manager, which must control the interface to externally stored data structures created by users and used by them. This area of the operating system can range from the simple, such as a simple head reader, to extremely complex data-base functions.

2.3.1 Process Management

Process management deals with the operating system's policies and mechanisms for sharing the CPU resource among N user processes. But what is a process and what constitutes its management in relation to others?

The process is typically viewed as the lowest level executable element recognized by the operating system. In other words, it is the view of a minimum program in execution on a piece of hardware. The program is one autonomous collection of instructions that perform work. This is not to say that we are limited to a fixed-size program. The program-in-execution notion could imply a main program (process), which could go off and spawn (initiate) N other related processes, or it could imply one large program that encompasses the entire memory space of the machine. The concept of process is important in the model of an operating system and particularly in process management. It allows us an entity upon which we can partition and manage the available resources within the context of time and space. In order to perform this management, the process (program in execution) must be described to the system. This is performed through the use of a process control block (PCB). This block of information is created by the operating system when the process is born and brought into the system.

The PCB contains descriptive information of the process, such as:

>   Process identification
>   Process type (user/system)
>   Priority of process
>   State information
>   Resource requirements and state
>   Process size
>   Present memory location

This information is used by the operating system to determine what must be done to set the process into motion when its turn comes up and what is required of the operating system in terms of resources to be applied to or used by this process. Processes are either of the user-applications type or the systems type. The user-applications type is any process that a user supplies to the system for service. A system-type process is one that is supplied by the operational environment to aid in the controlled sharing of the computer resources.

2.3.1.1 Processor States

Processes exist in the system in many different levels of completion; these levels are called states. For example, when a user process has not even been brought into the system, it is in a dormant or dead state. Upon initiation, it is brought into the conscious world and put into one of three major states: ready, running, or waiting. Each of these is brought about as a result of the conditions a process has passed through during its execution (fig. 2.14).

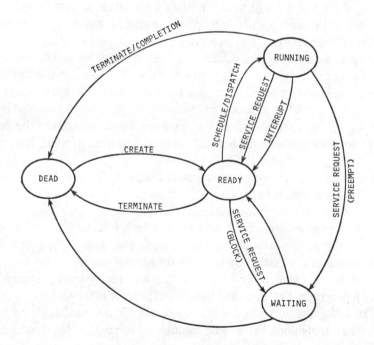

Figure 2.14 **Process State Transition System**

The dead, or initialization, state is the state from which all processes are created and into which they die or are terminated. This state represents the point at which a program is loaded into memory but has yet not been activated for service. Transitions from this state are caused by process creation (bringing any status up from loaded to ready to run), and process termination (bringing any status from any active ready state to a completed and inactive one).

The ready state refers to the state in which processes are prepared to execute if given control of the processor. This indicates a condition in which the process has all the necessary information within it to execute on the bare machine. Transitions from this state are: terminate a process (the result of a user command or a kill command caused by another process in execution); schedule a process (the result of a process, readied for execution, being inserted into the ready queue); dispatch a process (an activity caused by a switch in control in the CPU, which selects the next process in line on the ready queue for execution); and a service request (block) caused by a ready process losing some condition (for example, a resource) necessary to execute if selected. The waiting state for processes exists to hold processes that are active, yet not ready for service because of some condition. The condition causing the waiting could be the waiting for a block of data to be returned from the disk unit or an inability to acquire a necessary resource for execution. Transitions to this state are caused by requests for service of some type, such as a loss of necessary service, inability to get the maximum memory space required, waiting for service or a device, or waiting for another process to complete. Transitions out are caused by either satisfaction of the waiting condition, which will wake up the process and insert it back in the ready queue of waiting service processes, or termination of the process due to some condition, which would cause the process to transition into the dead state.

The final state in the state transition diagram (fig. 2.14) is the running state. This state refers to the condition in which a process has total use of the CPU and is executing instructions. Transitions to this state occur only through the interaction of the scheduler (which selects who will go next), and the dispatcher who takes this process and puts it into execution). Transitions out are caused by requests for service (for example, I/O), interrupts (external event driver or timer interrupt for operating system's entrance), or termination or completion of the process in the CPU.

The following sections describe some simple mechanisms used to provide these transitions, in a walk-through of a process from inception to death.

2.3.1.2 Process Creation

In order to provide for process management, we must have the ability to create or spawn new processes into the system. To do this requires a system process that builds the proper block of information for the user process to be recognized by the system and the created process. A process can be created by the system using its creation capabilities and priorities (this occurs when a user first logs onto a system or when a user process requests service from a system resource). A process can additionally be created by another user process (spawned) using a system call similar in structure to a system process initiation call. This creation of a process involves the construction of a process control block as previously described. The process for doing this is as follows:

> Create-Process (Process-Name)

This in turn will initiate the following sequence of events by the creation process:

> Acquire a process control block address. (This is acquired from the free pool of PCBs).
> Provide the PCB address as the process ID to the process. (This is used to uniquely define the process in the system.)
> Process location is provided as the location in physical memory where the process is located.
> The size of the process is recovered.
> The required storage for data storage is allocated.
> The required map for I/O resources is initialized with resource designations from the I/O resource pool.
> A priority is assigned to the process based on user and system supplied parameters.

Once the process control block is completed, the process is ready for upgrade into the ready state. At this point, it now possesses all the resources and conditions required to run.

To initialize or prepare the process to execute, the operating system must insert the newly completed process control block into the queue of ready-to-run processes. This queue represents all processes for this computer that are ready to execute. The processes in the system ready queue are linked together to form a chain of active ready processes (fig. 2.15).

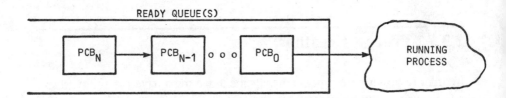

Figure 2.15 **Concept of Linked Ready Process**

The next phase in the life of a process is scheduling for service, which refers to the process of selecting a time in the future for initiating the execution of a process. The time can be selected as immediately or be based on an event or some predetermined time in the future. The process remains in the queue of ready processes but is not included in the determination of who gets control of the CPU until its time to run has come up (fig. 2.16). Scheduling has the overall function of selecting who goes next, that is, which of the active (not delayed or timed) processes will be selected for execution.

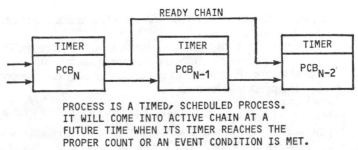

Figure 2.16 **Timed Processes**

Many schemes have been developed for scheduling processes, including:

```
FIFO        First In, First Out
LIFO        Last In, First Out
PRIORITY    Highest priority first
LTRF        Least Time, Remaining First
MTRF        Most Time Remaining First
DLSF        Dead Line Scheduled First
```

The goal is to select a process based on some criteria and bring it to active execution on the physical hardware.

For example, if we look at the FCFS queue implementation with quantum (time slices of the CPU) used, the scheduler will work as in fig. 2.17.

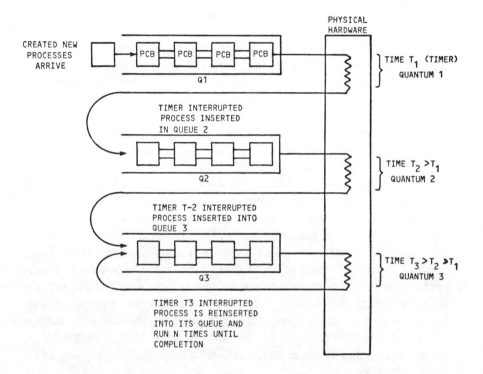

Figure 2.17 **Multi-level Time Slice**

The created processes enter the system in queue one (Q1). This queue has the highest priority for acquiring the CPU but also has the smallest quantum size. Processes that are small will therefore get instantaneous (perceptual sense) service and run quickly (for example, a terminal response). If a larger process is inserted into the system, it first executes a chunk of its code during the quantum it is given. It then is inserted into Q2, which has the next highest priority, and a larger quantum time than Q1. The process will use this time to execute a larger section of code. The majority of processes usually will be performed at this point; that is, most processes will require from

Q1 to Q2 time to execute. If a process does not complete during its time in execution in Q2, it is interrupted when the quantum is up, removed from active execution, and inserted into Q3. This queue has the lowest priority, but when it does get the CPU, it has a large quantum time. Processes continue to circle into active and ready states until they complete their processing; they then exit the system. This type of arrangement for scheduling is seen in many contemporary systems and is one used originally in the Multics operating system.

Another form of scheduling is real-time or event scheduling. These classes of schedulers operate on the premise of sharing the resources, based on the perceived real-time or event conditions that will drive the selection of the proper active ready process to execute.

In real-time scheduling, the scheduler responds to real-time stimuli. These stimuli will initiate an operating system process that interrupts the signal to determine which process to schedule. The scheduler may also be required to initiate a process, kick off a timer, and spawn or reinitiate the same or another process(es) based on the termination of the clock count. This is the concept of periodic processing. Such processing may be due to a condition that must be checked at a boundary time, or the processing of time-inputed data at particular intervals. Additionally, the scheduler may be asked, in such systems, to select a process to run based on its estimated "time to complete," which refers to the deadline upon which the particular process must complete its processing in order to meet some condition of the real-time system. For example, in order to insert a part into a moving assembly, a robotic arm (upon perceiving the assembly's presence) must acquire the CPU, process the perceptual information supplied (determining where to put the object), and insert the object before it passes the boundary area of the robot's operation.

Another form of scheduling deals with events. Events are activities that have a duration, an activity, and an output. The output is the event completion boundary and is used as input to drive the initiation of another. In operating systems, events are treated as time-scheduled activities. They arrive at the system and cause an interrupt to the operating system, which responds to the interrupt by effecting the proper sequence of subprocesses in response to the event driven stimuli.

Events can exist as one of two types, synchronous or nonsynchronous. Synchronous events must coordinate their actions among each other. In centralized systems, this coordination is done using semaphores. A semaphore is an indivisible constraint that allows processes to get at common shared information in a singular, noninterfering fashion. Synchronization can also be effected by message-passing or condition-setting services. Differences depend on how tightly coupled the processes are and how much they depend on each other for synchronicity. In general-purpose systems, a mailbox or simple communication facility will facilitate loosely coupled synchronization; conversely, in real-time systems, hardware signals or highly resilient semaphores are required to effect the proper speed, upon which the synchronization relies to perform system synchronization. Events can be other types of system processes, namely I/O. Events may be waiting for the signal of I/O completion to kick off some processing; at that time, the event is scheduled and proceeds to process the supplied information.

2.3.1.4 Dispatching

The big question is how a process that has been scheduled acquires access to and control of the CPU. This is accomplished through the use of the dispatcher module of the operating system. The dispatcher accepts the given PCB and loads the proper physical registers with its parameters to effect startup of the process. Once the operating system completes its task, the new program counter address is used as the start point of the user process. Once running, a process has many conditions or activities that can occur that will effect its operation. For example, if a process requires I/O, the operating system will be asked to respond to the I/O request. The operating system will initiate the I/O process to acquire the data and will put the requesting process in a blocked (waiting) state. The blocked process will be reinserted into the ready queue upon completion of the I/O. This is accomplished by the wakeup command, which selects the proper process from the waiting queue and inserts it in the ready queue.

Other possible actions that could effect a running or ready process include terminate, abort, priority deletion, and delay. All these affect the state of a process in the sense that they change the view the operating system takes of the process. Further details of these processes can be found in [PETE83] and [DEIT84].

2.3.2 Memory Management

A resource as critical as CPU time, if not more so, is main memory, a vital element in computer performance. It is of utmost importance that the operating system use this resource to optimal potential. Because memory is used to store data and programs in both the logical and physical forms, it is involved in every sequence of events in a CPU.

The problems associated with memory management concern how to allocate, deallocate, access, and control memory resources among many users that have widely varying storage requirements and uses for memory. From these problems five major functions for memory management are evident:

> Allocating physical memory
> Mapping of logical address to physical storage
> Sharing memory among users
> Extending memory (virtual storage)
> Protecting user information

2.3.2.1 Allocation

Memory allocation deals with the problem of how to assign blocks of physical storage to user processes and to additionally keep tabs on this allocation for future reference. In the simple case, the allocation is done statically, that is, at load time only. All required memory is allocated at the same time. A handler condition is allocation in a dynamic fashion. Dynamic allocation requires much more interaction with operating system mechanisms and on a much finer granularity, as will be seen later.

In order to allocate memory, the operating system must have a view of the present memory allocation (figure 2.18a).

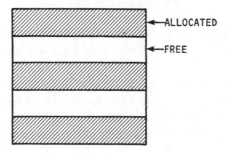

Figure 2.18a **Memory Allocation**

It must additionally have a list of free blocks of memory and their size (fig. 2.18b). Each block contains the starting location of the block, the size of the block, and a link to children of this block. With this information, the operating system can go about the task of allocating memory to requesting processes. The allocation of physical memory can be done based on many criteria. For example, do we look at a sequential allocation of memory and locate a load source in a physically sequential piece of memory (contiguous), or do we have memory linked into chains that are randomly selected (noncontiguous)?

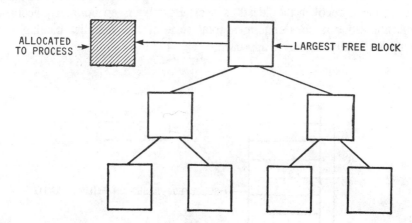

Figure 2.18b **Memory Free Block List**

To actually select blocks of memory, the allocation mechanism uses algorithms such as Best Fit, Worst Fit, and First Fit. Each has merits and benefits for memory usage.

In the Best Fit algorithm, the goal is to find a chunk of memory in the free list of such a size that it will waste the minimum amount of memory. It will examine all available pieces of free memory (fig. 2.19), looking for the one that leaves the minimum remaining if the allocation was performed as shown below:

> While there is an element of the free list not scanned.
>
> > do
> >
> > > Block selected = Min [block selected, mem[element] load size
> >
> > end while

This algorithm will take on the order of N comparisons to perform its function; that is, it must scan all items in the list at least once.

The algorithm will terminate when all free-list blocks have been examined. At this point, the block selected will contain the address of the free block of memory that will fit the item we wish to load with the least wasted space. Even with this criteria, some wasted space will exist. We will discuss later how to recover the "dead" spaces. Best Fit is an optimal placement algorithm, but it does require a total scan of the free list making it a computationally expensive approach.

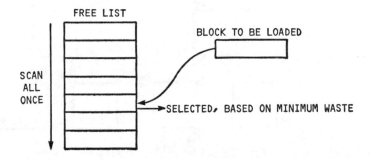

Figure 2.19 **Free List for Best Fit**

The Worst Fit algorithm uses an opposite criterion in selecting the memory for allocation. This mechanism will strive to select memory using a condition of finding the space that will waste the most memory. It requires the ability to reform the heap storage list on a load basis, recovering the wasted space into a new block on the list with its new smaller block size (original size - load size = new size). If we assume the free list is always ordered as a heap (largest element on top), the algorithm is done as follows:

```
Remove top element of heap
-block - selected = top [heap]
    compute the new remaining block size
- block - remain = (block-select)-(load-source)-(size)
    insert this into free list
- heapify (heap, block - remain)
return
```

This algorithm will allocate a block in time order 1 (reading heap top) and will require approximately $O(\log N)$ time to reform the heap with the new item. It terminates when it hits the first element of the free list. It will require a recovery algorithm to redefine and reorder the heap to recover the dead space on the fly. The improvement, however, is made by not requiring the algorithm to search all items in the list. The Best Fit algorithm could be improved by having the free list ordered as a binary tree. This would drop the search time for the Best Fit space to $O(\log N)$ as opposed to $O(N)$ time complexity to complete.

The third approach is the First Fit algorithm, which has a list of free blocks that are accessed in a serial fashion. The first one encountered that will fit the load source will be used. Ordering by an abstract data type will not increase the efficiency of this algorithm appreciably. The only mechanism that might improve its performance is forming it into a heap ordered by maximum size. This, however, makes the approach the same as the Worst Fit algorithm. In most implementations of this algorithm, an unordered free list is assumed; therefore no management is required to keep the list ordered. The algorithm works by sequencing through the list until a block is found that meets the criteria of fitting the source; it will then be allocated to the load source, with the dead space being returned to the tail of the free list. The algorithm in its best performance will find the First Fit on access to the first block of the free list. Conversely, the worst performance arises when the First Fit is found in the last block of the free list. Therefore, the range of performance is on the order ($O(1)$) to $O(N)$ with the average being $O(N/2)$.

The problem with any of these allocation algorithms is that they leave holes in physical memory (fig. 2.20).

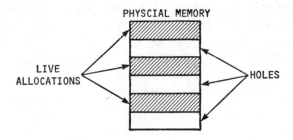

Figure 2.20 **Physical Allocation of Holes**

Holes represent either chunks of memory left over from an unused portion of allocation, or deallocated memory due to program termination or other factors.

The problem becomes how to recover these holes and bring them back into the fold of free-memory blocks available for future access. Periodically, due to dynamic allocation, deallocation, and the run-time dynamics of programs, the operating system must come in and "garbage collect" the memory space. Garbage collection, the process of recovering the lost memory blocks in physical storage, breaks down into two aspects; coalescence and compaction.

Coalescence recombines adjacent smaller holes into larger ones, creating larger segments of memory that can fit programs (fig. 2.21).

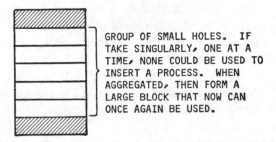

Figure 2.21 **Coalescing Holes**

Coalescing holes has the effect of dropping the number of entries in the free list and creating larger blocks for use. Ordinarily, in real systems, this feature has boundaries of operation; that is, it will not combine segments of a certain minimally sufficient size together, and it will not create new segments greater than a set limit. These boundaries keep the memory from being turned into one free block or from having only a few large blocks, in an attempt to optimize the size of the memory blocks based on the system's usage patterns.

Compaction is used to help make the memory system more efficient in storage and access, by separating memory into an active section and a free memory section (fig. 2.22).

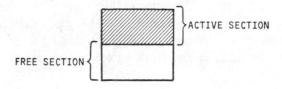

Figure 2.22 **Compaction**

Like a garbage truck, it likes to compress the contents into one end of the container, freeing the other end for more "garbage." The process of compaction is performed by taking the active program segments and reorganizing their access addresses and storage locations into one end of memory, thus freeing up the other end of memory for future allocation. This reformatting requires reinitialization of the free list.

2.3.2.2 Mapping Physical to Logical

The purpose of address mapping is to translate a program-supplied logical address to a physical-memory address. This translation can be done at various times in a program's life, namely:

> At compile time: Absolute translation fixes logical references to physical addresses
> At load time: Static when the program enters the operational system
> At run time: Dynamic on each reference to an item

Absolute translation, in assemblers, performs the task of setting the absolute address in memory that a program resides in and that its instructions will address for data. This scheme will do the translation only once. It usually assumes that we have a dedicated machine with no interference; otherwise the compiler needs much more data on which to perform its task. Static translation is usually performed at the load time of the program. The operating system looks at the available space that can fit this program; it then allocates this space, sets the locations in the program's symbol table to a fixed physical address (translation), and loads the program with its new physical access addresses into the proper place in memory. This type of allocation again is based on a runtime environment that will not change; that is, the memory addresses are fixed and cannot change once the program is inserted into physical memory.

The last method of memory mapping or translation, runtime mapping, is the most common scheme and is seen in most systems of appreciable size today. Dynamic memory mapping refers to the function of taking logical addresses (singular notion) and, on an instruction-by-instruction basis, converting memory access from the logical view to a physical one. This approach allows for very dynamic configurations and transformation of the contents and meanings of memory storage.

To perform memory translation at this level of granularity requires the combined use of hardware and software to effect the translation process. The scheme used for performing this is paging translation, at the low level, and combined paging and segmentation for program-level memory. The process has additionally been sped up through the use of associative cache memories at the lowest level (the small instruction block). This is made possible through the dynamics of programs in execution.

The process of translating and accessing memory in paging is explained in the following paragraphs.

In a paging-based system, the address as constructed at compile/load time is given as a page and displacement value within that page (fig. 2.23).

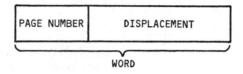

Figure 2.23 **Paging Address**

To translate this logical address, the paging hardware operates as follows: the logical address is fed to the paging hardware. This address is interpreted as a page number and displacement. The page number is extracted out of the logical address and is used to point to a location in the system page table. The contents of this location is used as the base address (physical) start location of the wanted page. This base address is concatenated with the second half of the logical address (the offset on the logical page), which then maps to the physical address of the item in memory. This scheme allows the memory manager to easily shift code and data as the operation requires, without disturbing the code that was generated by the compiler. The only thing that need change, if the location is changed, is the base start address in the page table of the code/data, not the internals of this code/data (fig. 2.24).

2.3.2.3 Sharing

The next step in this concept is to allow sharing of pages. This is desirable in order to allow processes that must communicate or synchronize to get at shared data or code (critical section, for example). To effect this, the operating system must allow the addresses (logical) generated by the compiler to reference the same page in memory. For this to happen, when code is generated that must share data, it must generate the same globally defined logical address. This address is then, at run time, translated to the same page address, thereby allowing this page of physical memory to be accessed. This does not apply the same page number, just the ultimate same physical address (fig. 2.25).

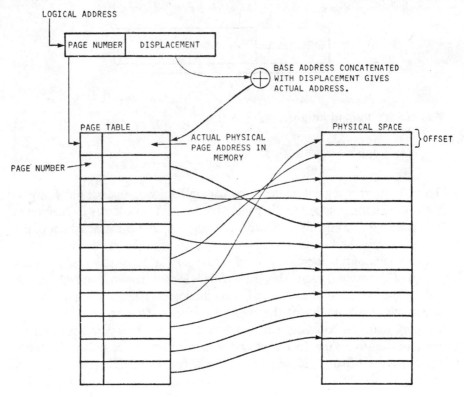

Figure 2.24 **Page Table Addressing**

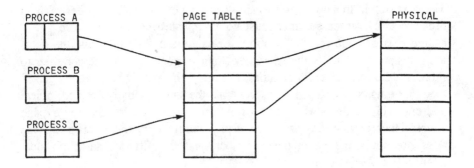

Figure 2.25 **Sharing in a Paging System**

2.3.2.4 Virtual Storage

The next evolution in memory management is to allow for a larger view (logical) of memory than is physically realizable in the primary memory. This refers to virtual addressing, which allows processes to be allocated to memory larger than the physical space. This is accomplished through a hierarchical segmentation of the logical space into blocks called segments, that in turn are broken up into pages. Segments can be of variable length and are comprised of a varying number of pages.

This scheme lengthened the sphere of interest and control in which the memory manager was responsible. The memory manager must now be cognizant of whether a page is a primary or secondary memory. To access a word in this scheme requires the programs to be compiled/loaded with virtual addresses inserted for the logical addresses (fig. 2.26).

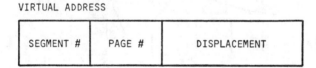

Figure 2.26 **Virtual Address Format**

To translate the virtual address to a physical one, the following must occur. The virtual address is supplied to the virtual memory translation hardware. This in turn extracts a segment number, a page number, and a displacement. The segment number points to a location in the segment table that has stored the segment number, the length of the segment, the residency of the segment (in or out of primary), and the base, starting physical address of the segment. Additionally, the segment location will also have a pointer to the page table for the segment. The segment information is used to get the next level of the access information. The segment number points to the page table, if the segment is in memory. The second component of the virtual address is the page number. We use this to access the proper page number in the pointed-to page table. The page address and displacement are then interpreted, as before, to supply the actual address of the item (fig. 2.27).

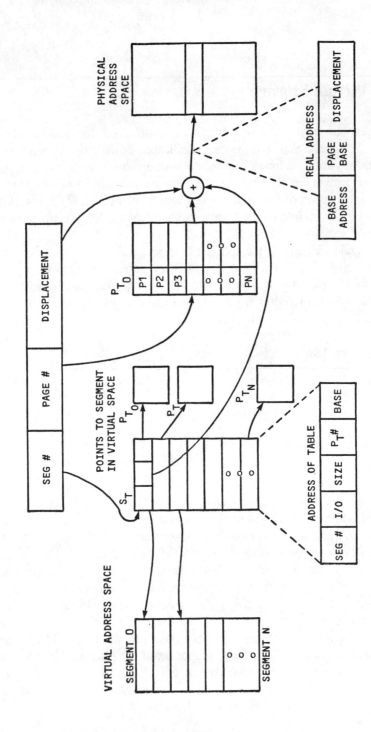

Figure 2.27 **Mapping of Virtual to Physical Space**

The memory manager must use information on active pages and sequence of processing to determine what virtual memory to load and keep in primary physical memory. The job of the memory manager at this point is to determine which to load and when, and which must be removed when this occurs.

To do the page management, the memory manager uses the notion of "working set," which describes the activity of active executing or accessed pages in memory over a set period of time. The working set is a sliding window that changes dynamically based on program dynamics.

The memory manager uses this data to determine which to remove when a page not presently in memory is accessed. Methods to determine which to remove include:

FIFO	First In, First Out
LIFO	Last In, First Out
MRU	Most Recently Used
LRU	Least Recently Used
NUR	Not Used Recently
RANDOM	Select Any

The goal in all of these is to examine the set of active pages in memory and to remove one based on its perceived value to future process. Intuitively, we can see that Least Recently Used has desirable characteristics that should enable it to select a good choice for memory; conversely Most Recently Used seems intuitively to be the worst possible. We would, in the first case, remove some item which is not likely to be used in the near future; by selecting the Most Recently Used, we might select the item to be next accessed. As an example: for the Least Recently Used option to perform its function, a tag must be kept on each page identifying when it was last referenced. The algorithm will then examine the list of all active pages (in primary memory) to determine which one was accessed the least recently over the period of interest. This page is removed to secondary memory (if it has updates) and is replaced by the new page. This action requires updating the page table entry for this page.

2.3.2.5 Protection

Protection, another important issue in memory management, deals with the problem of allowing only the proper, authorized user to acquire and use physical memory assets. This is an issue in hardware and software design and use, and is beyond the scope of this section. Some details on protection for distributed operating systems will be provided later, in Chapter 6.

2.3.3 I/O and Device Management

The thrust for development of I/O and device management services was to remove the user from dependencies on particular systems and their devices in order to provide a clean, clear, and transparent mechanism to facilitate I/O for the process being performed. I/O management allows a user to view I/O in the logical sense; that is, he views the data being used as input or output in his internal logical user data structure formats and leaves the details of formatting, translations, and access to the I/O device and device management systems.

This "device independence" provides the software developer with a powerful tool for increasing his effectiveness in developing and providing software-intensive systems. At a period in time when software costs are far outweighing hardware costs, this is a significant attribute to consider in operating system design and structuring. Additionally, by providing this hardware independence, the system has increased its ability to more fairly share the resources (I/O devices) among the many users. This is accomplished through the ability of the operating system I/O and device manager to view the requirements of the entire system for I/O, not just those of a particular user, as was the case in early systems.

2.3.3.1 Structure

The mechanisms to perform the I/O and device management are bound up in the I/O manger and device managers. The major mechanism or tool used by the I/O manager is to treat all I/O applications as file manipulations. Therefore users have a file-oriented view of the outside world. They may view it differently by opening an I/O file, which in essence is a terminal. The I/O system treats all devices as the same from the user's side. For example, if a user wishes to read from a file, he simply issues an open command on the file name; the operating system will look for the file, acquire it from the device, and store it in memory or open a channel to it. The device could be one disk unit out of 100, a tape being read in, or a card reader.

Opening a file links the user process to the device that the file is on. This is like a physical channel allocation to the device from the user process. The problem here is that the devices do not work in a pipelined, file-oriented view of the world. Devices work on physical blocks of storage. Tapes store files as sequential blocks of storage on the tape. Disks store files as records (blocks of storage) on the physical media.

The architecture for I/O and device management has five major components, or levels:

> File interface
> I/O control: channel, file, and buffer control
> Channels: access and control
> Buffers: management
> Device Control: access methods

The following paragraphs describe these levels and their interfaces among each other and the outside world.

File management provides the system its transparency. It is the interface between the user community and the I/O subsystem. The user's view of all I/O is based around this file concept; that is, a file is a bounded and named storage repository. The file system must support the ability to create or destroy files; to open a previously created file, to close this file, and to read or write from or to the file. Additionally, the file manager must provide security, integrity, and consistency of the files it controls. Security is provided traditionally by authentication of access rights for use of the file. Integrity and consistency are typically guaranteed through mechanisms seen in database systems, for serialization and atomic (singular) read/write access to the files. Details will be covered later in this chapter.

I/O control or management is concerned with the interface and control thereof between the logical file system and the generic device interfaces of channels and buffers. This I/O manager must be able to accept commands from the file system such as open, close, create, delete, find, read, and write, and must determine what the action must be to effect the proper sequence of operations to perform the wanted action. The I/O control function takes these file commands and performs their function through the proper use of the channel controller and buffer controller, in conjunction with the underlying device managers (see fig. 2.28).

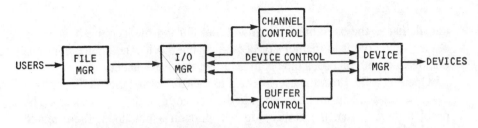

Figure 2.28 **I/O and Device Management**

A channel controller acts as the mechanism to link specific physical devices with logical devices. Logical devices are set by the I/O controller via open or create commands from the file manager. These commands map down to a logical number that is related to the number of channels the channel controller can have. These channels in return are mapped to the physical device that has the file to be opened resident on it or that tells where the new file to be created will reside. The mapping is performed by the I/O manager, which uses information on residency of files or devices (directory), and has the form of logical ID, logical channel number, or device designator. This is used from here on to transfer the control commands to the proper device. A channel has associated with it a physical device, physical buffers, and logical file designators.

To create the physical link and control, the I/O manager must additionally allocate physical buffer assets to the I/O channel to utilize in the computer to peripheral device I/O. The buffers are used as the intermediary between devices and CPU. They allow for the concurrent operation of I/O with processing in a system. For example, on a read (file X) the use of buffers allows the operating system to put the reading process into a wait state until the I/O completes. The CPU does not have to operate on the I/O request other than to initiate it. The I/O manager will control the actual data transfer by causing the device to put the required file into the allocated buffer, then once the file is resident in the buffer, will transfer it to the physical primary CPU memory via direct memory access mechanisms. When the transfer is complete, the I/O manager will signal the operating system via interrupt. This will awaken the process and allow it to acquire the data from the "file" memory.

The final piece of the cycle is the device manager, which effects the actual control and transfer of physical blocks of secondary storage from the devices to the control process unit. This is accomplished via a tight processing loop in the device manager with the device. This loop effects transfer of physical bits of data in a block frame, word, or other format, via a control loop that synchronizes the device hardware transfer with the buffer in the CPU environment. Details will follow.

2.3.3.2 Device Management

Device management must effect control and physical data transfer between the CPU and its peripheral devices. The major peripheral devices are terminals (interactive devices), disk drives, tape drives and printers. Physical details of these components have been widely published over the years in numerous texts [FLORE72], [SONE80], [BAER40] as well as in manufacturers' reference manuals and will not be covered here.

Device management is concerned with four major functions:

> Device allocation
> Device control
> Device access
> Device status

These four functions have similar requirements and characteristics for all devices. Device allocation is concerned with the issue of how to allocate a device to a user process. This is accomplished through the use of a systemwide, unique device identifier that will tell the device manager which device is being accessed. The allocated device is described through a device control block that provides information on the status of the device and requirements for using it.

The device control block has embedded in it an element that describes the present status of the device. For example, the device status word may have information on:

> Type of device
> Device availability
> Read protect
> Write protect
> Input buffer status
> Output buffer status
> Status conditions

The actual necessity for the information and its conditions will be different for various devices. To control devices, the CPU has various options. It can take control of the device itself (programmed input/output) or, if it has available an input/output controller, it can turn over control to this device to effect the control of peripheral devices.

In programmed I/O, the CPU must perform all the necessary tasks itself, such as setting and clearing all necessary device flags, initializing the device control register, interrogating and interpreting status registers, and transferring the data to and from a CPU register from or to the device data registers.

The actual steps the CPU must take to perform a block output to the device are as follows:

1. Place the start address of the block in a CPU register.
2. Place the count of words in the block to be transferred into another register.
3. Using the address supplied in 1, extract a word from the block to be transferred.
4. Place the word from memory in a CPU register (buffer).
5. Decrement the block count.
6. Increment the block memory pointer.
7. Test device busy flag.
8. If device busy then wait, go back to 7.
9. Transfer word from CPU buffer to device data buffer.
10. Issue command to insert word into device memory, etc. Start device insertion process.
11. If word count = 0, then exit.
12. Issue command to clear device status.

This sequence is more detailed if a word or block is to be written into an existing file. The sequence, after start, would also need to find the file on the device and add the inserted data to it. The biggest problem with this approach to management is that the CPU is required to perform all actions including busy-waits, which eat up precious CPU cycles. This leaves little time for other more useful work, such as processing user applications. The central problem is that the CPU must control and wait for the slow device to do its job.

The other method for device control and interface with the CPU is the interrupt-driven system. This class of system requires an intelligent device that can perform its own control. Interrupts can be based on many types of systems. In one case it could be simple. The interrupt signals the device that it is ready to send word; or in a DMA (direct memory address) environment, the device would dump the I/O into memory, then signal the CPU that it is done with an interrupt. The biggest difference between this and the other scheme of CPU control is that the CPU can continue doing useful work during an I/O operation.

Beyond interface to the CPU, each device has unique control requirements. Terminals look different than disks, tapes, or printers. The unique aspect of each will be covered in the following paragraphs.

Terminal management is concerned with how to manage the transfer of information in and out of a video display device. The terminal device is usually treated by the I/O system as two logical devices: an output display and an input keyboard. The input management process of the terminal manager operates as follows:

```
Do
        Ready the keyboard by clearing TTY-ready
        While ready = false do
                Test reads and wait until ready = true
        End while
        If data in buffer
        Place into CPU buffer
        and signal CPU (interrupt)
Until done = true
```

This routine will read one character at a time from the keyboard to a device buffer and into the CPU. This routine could easily be modified to send only one block at a time: for example, load the buffer until return key sensed. Output to the terminal is similar. The CPU places a character in the buffer, waits until the device is ready, and when the device is ready, extracts the character out of the CPU buffer and writes it to the proper display spot in device memory.

Another important peripheral device is the disk drive. In contemporary systems there are numerous disk units to use and control. This control is effected by the disk manager. The CPU places requests for service (I/O) on the disk queue. The disk manager sets up all the disks for use by the user processes. It then waits for calls for service. When calls enter, the disk manager initiates a read or write process based on the request. The read or write is a file-oriented request that the disk manager converts into a device number, cylinder, track, sector and block(s) which is its physical addresses. This in turn is used to transfer the requested file from the disk unit to the CPU memory. This is usually accomplished by writing the file from the physical disk into a buffer, then DMAing (direct memory access) this buffer to the location supplied in the physical CPU memory space.

The tape manager is concerned with how to access files stored on a sequential media for storage/retrieval by the system. Tapes are physically organized as sequential files separated by markers called gaps (figure 2.29).

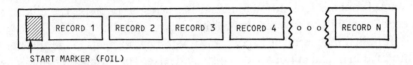

Figure 2.29 **Tape Storage Format**

Storage is organized into records, and files are comprised of one or more records. The record manager can do the following functions: rewind tape, skip tape files forward, skip tape files backward, erase tape, initialize tape, release tape, write a file marker, read a file, and write a file. To acquire a tape unit, the I/O controller will access the tape via an open command. This will associate a channel with a specific device. Once the device is allocated to a process, it can use it to read or write files from or to the tape as follows:

> Acquire control of device
> Read a record
> If end of media, then exit and release device
> Restore status
> Release device and adjust status

Writing is the same, but the tape manager must have buffers reversed and must write to buffers instead of reading from buffers.

The final device to be covered is the printer. To print a file (logical I/O record), the printer manager is supplied a start address and a count of what is to be outputted. It then must acquire access to the device via a busy-wait mechanism until free. Once free, it locks the device and begins its print sequence. Printers are sequential machines and must be dedicated to the print task until completed. To print, the process occurs as follows:

> Acquire access (line printer)
> Request user file space
> Request start address
> Request size of file
> Move file to printer buffer
> One character at a time move characters to printer output

When done, exit
Restore line printer to initial status
Return to manager

2.3.3.3 Channels

A channel represents a pipeline from a device to a program. It allows the user process to talk to a device without reacquiring the device. Channels have associated with them a channel control block, which describes the characteristics of the channel, such as access mode, file and device linkage, associated buffers, and device status information.

Upon linking a program, a user declares the number of files, and therefore channels, his program will require. The channel manager's job is to determine how many channels to associate and where. The tradeoff is efficiency against time and cost. Channels in essence represent the logical allocation of physical buffers to user processes in their I/O operations.

2.3.3.2.2 Buffers

From the previous discussions we can easily ascertain the necessity and reason for requiring buffers. Buffers are the intermediary element or mechanism between the physical and logical world. The buffer is simultaneously a physical and a logical repository of data. It represents a means to solve the speed differential problem between the CPU and the devices it requires for storage. The issue with buffer management is how to allocate this limited resource and maintain a high level of throughput among the processes and devices.

Buffers are allocated to devices and I/O channels from a buffer pool (an area that contains a sequence of free unallocated memory used for I/O only). Mechanisms for allocating buffers include circular, ping pong, FIFO, and others.

In a circular buffering scheme, the available buffer space is allocated in a circular queue method. When full, the buffer can take no more.

In ping pong, one buffer is allocated for input and the other for output. The CPU loads the output while the device loads the input. Then the CPU extracts data out while the device inserts data in. This is fairly efficient for I/O systems with low activity (terminals).

Typically, buffers are allocated in a fashion to allow the input and output device to operate at their optimal speeds based on loading. Dual port buffers allow a unit to input to one, while extracting from the other, buffer, at optimal speeds. The references will lead interested readers to additional details of these systems and mechanisms.

2.3.4 File Management

This is the view of the system closest to the user. Files represent a collection of related information that has a structure created and imposed by its creator, the user. Files are managed and known by their logical name. Files come in many flavors: source files, list files, object files of programs, load modules, and data files. These files are abstract representations of the real world entities that they model or represent.

Files represent a convenient way to view programs and data from a logical user view, as well as from a physical storage view.

The file manager can be a simple or very complex entity within the system. It can be a simple translator from the logical user view, and a manipulator of files from the physical system view. Or it can be a complex data base management system, allowing powerful query and read manipulation constructs.

From a simplistic view, the file management system must provide users the capability to create, delete, and change their files. It must allow the users of files to share files, to control their access, to structure files to best meet algorithm operations, to name or rename files; to split up or append files to each other, to create copies, and to manipulate these files in a straightforward logical fashion.

Control, management, and use of files are the three major functions for this portion of the operating system. The file manager must keep track of what belongs to which files and where they are stored. This is accomplished through the use of a file directory (fig. 2.30).

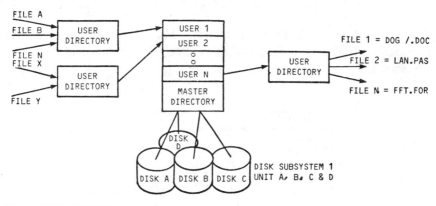

Figure 2.30 **File Directory System**

The file directory system keeps track of who has files on the system, where their files are stored, and access mechanisms. To access a file, the file manager takes the supplied user file name, the user number, the disk subsystem number, and finally the disk designation to get a unique system address for the file (fig. 2.31).

DS1:DA:UN:FFT.FOR

Figure 2.31 **Unique System Path Address for User N File FFT.FOR**

Files have unique meanings to system services based on the qualifier supplied. For example, a FORTRAN file has a different meaning to the system than a document, Pascal, ADA, or list file, and must be categorized appropriately. A FORTRAN file is designated as .FOR; a Pascal file is designated with .PAS; and an ADA file is designated with .ADA.

File organization in the system is dependent on one of the following structural schemes: linked, segmented, contiguous, serial, directory, or a combination of these. With these structuring schemes, files can be organized in many ways.

Each file has associated with it information necessary in the control process. This information is stored in the directory in the form of a file control block. This block has the form shown in fig. 2.32. This block allows the file manager to acquire the necessary data to effect the proper use of the file by system users.

```
FILE NAME
FILE TYPE
FILE ATTRIBUTES
    WRITE PROTECT FLAG
    READ PROTECT FLAG
    PERMANENT FILE FLAG
    LOCK CONTROL FLAG
    OUTPUT BUFFER ASSOCIATION
    INPUT BUFFER ASSOCIATION
    CHANNEL FLAG (OPEN, LOCK)
    DEVICE FLAG
LINKAGE INFORMATION
FILE START ADDRESS (PHYSICAL DEVICE)
SIZE OF FILE
CREATION DATE
CREATION TIME
OWNER
OUTSIDE USERS (SHARING LIST)
MODIFICATION ATTRIBUTES
ACCESS PROTECTION
```

Figure 2.32 **Some Attributes In a File Control Block**

The access protection component provides the ability for the user or system to specify what type of access is allowed on the file. For example, the creator can specify if read, write, update, delete, change, or execute access is allowed. Additional information can be included in the file control block if the file is part of a data-base system. This would allow for an even more abstract view of the information stored. Files can be viewed as collections of similar data, with files related to each other by either entries in each one's file or links (pointers) from one file to another. By organizing and linking files in such a way, data bases supply many users with controlled shared data. More details of all these features of operating systems can be found in [DEIT84], [PETE83], [FORT86], and [STON72].

2.4 Summary

This chapter introduced the computer as a collection of hardware (CPU, memory, and peripheral devices). These were discussed in terms of their components, structure, and operations. Following this, concepts of traditional operating system structures were introduced at a review level to aid in the discussions to follow. We covered process management (characteristics and operations) and memory management (including paging and segmentation) in normal memory systems, and concluded with I/O and device management, and file management.

3. Distributed Computing

3.1 Introduction

Distributed computer systems represent an evolutionary path from early computer systems. This path led from single user standalone environments, through multiuser mainframe systems, and ultimately to resource netsworks. Resource networks such as arpanet represented the first phase of distributed computing. These early systems were constructed in order to provide a tool to investigate and study a wide range of new topics in computer science: the overall challenge was how to control the sharing of resources not under the control of a single computer operating system. Arpanet provided the early vehicle for the study of various methods of communications control, such as routing, flow control, addressing, line-level protocol, security, and remote job access and control.

These early studies led to the development of mechanisms to operate and control the movement of data, programs, and control information though a network, and allowed other concepts to be spawned. The problem with the early networks was that they were built for users who were widely dispersed geographically. The goal of the system was not to control the operation of the other sites in the system; it was to share resources, but on a loose basis. These systems could be allowed to share a high-speed printer or a supercomputer, but only as a batch-type job; that is, users of remote resources would download their programs and data to the remote site, kick off execution, and wait for the result. They could not, for example, interactively be involved with their process on the other machine. This, however, was an improvement over the earlier days: previously one could not get at additional

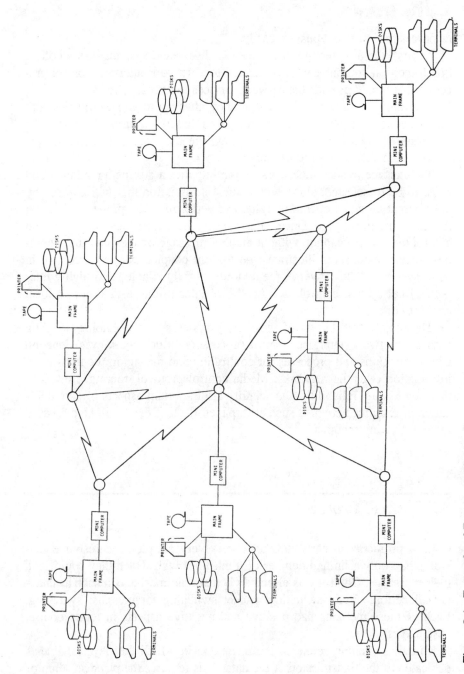

Figure 3.1 Example of Resource Network

resources that were not busy so easily.

At first, the architecture of these early distributed systems was a collection of central computer sites connected to a network interface control processor that would provide the network services to the user (fig. 3.1).

The mainframes would operate as they always did and would link into the network to send or receive messages based on user demand. The transmission lines were leased lines of high speed and were controlled by the network interface control processors.

To interface to such a network, a user supplies a destination address and a file to be transferred, along with control information that will be used by the destination site's operating system in performing the proper actions on the file being transferred. Once the user sends his file or message, he has no control over it. He cannot, without another message, request that the operation be canceled. This illustrates the loosely coupled nature of control in these systems. (The converse, the notion of tightly coupled and highly integrated total system control, will be shown later in the discussions of local area networks.

The major contribution of these early systems was technology dealing with the network interface control processors. Much work was done on communications and processes for controlling and managing the transfer of information over the networks. Media control protocol, routing, flow control, addressing, reliability, and security are important aspects of communication in resource networks such as Arpanet. Each of these will be discussed in the following sections.

3.2 Control Protocols

Control protocols in early networks were very simple. The resource networks had only a limited number of trunk lines with which they could send their messages. Control was effected via a simple mechanism such as channel allocation, circuit switching, packet switching, or message switching. Each of these methods had positive and negative aspects in terms of use, cost, and efficiency.

Circuit switching refers to the technique in which the physical line is dedicated to the transmission of the data. This requires the physical setup of the physical lines linking sender to receiver before the transmission begins. This mechanism is like a dedicated point-to-point link.

Channel allocation is a similar mechanism. In this technique, a logical virtual circuit is set up between the sender and receiver. Channel allocation differs from circuit switching in that it may not utilize a point-to-point circuit, but a linked set of lines that are allocated and/or deallocated based on need.

A different class of network is the message or packet-switched type. In this class, a packet (part of a total message) or a message is sent into the network and works its way through the network, using buffering to store the packet or message in transit and routing with flow control to determine how to work toward its destination. This type of network requires dynamic mechanisms to move the packets in a store-and-forward fashion. This latter mechanism is used in many systems today.

3.3 Routing

Because of the irregular or mesh structure of the early networks (fig. 3.1), a form of setting up the links was required. This linking of source to destination is referred to as routing. Routing in circuit or channel switching is done by searching out the links in the circuit that, when allocated in a chain, form a point-to-point physical link from source to destination.

In packet-switched networks, routing refers to the method used in finding and assigning to each entering packet a switching node or output link that will send the packet out toward its destination node in a store-and-forward fashion. Routing algorithms have been classified as one of two types: adaptive and nonadaptive. Nonadaptive, or static, routing methods do not react to traffic changes. These methods are statically defined and do not change with time. Methods that fall into this category are random, flooding, and fixed (single or multiple) route methods.

Random routing is a simple mechanism that will access its outgoing links randomly. The random choice can be made based on equal or weighted probabilities thereby providing for some measure of tuning for some networks. If an algorithm operates in a perfect form (that is, it always picks the right, minimum-cost route) that algorithm is optimal. On the other hand, if it always picks wrong, it will be an endless running algorithm that may never get the message transferred. Most algorithms operate somewhere in the middle, giving the best choice once in a while, the worst choice at other times, and more often than not something in between. One optimization for algorithms is to weight forward-moving paths with higher probabilities and backward ones with lower probabilities. This would tend to keep packets moving in the proper direction. The problem is that we must possess a global map of all messages and their sources and sinks beforehand to make such optimizations. This clearly is impossible for large networks such as Arpanet.

Another static routing scheme is flooding, which is a very simple algorithm that places all incoming packets out onto all the links it has, except for the incoming line on which the packet was received. This method requires each node to have information only on each of its I/O links. The problem with flooding is saturation of the network. If the network has many loops and interconnects, the transmission and retransmission of packets could escalate to the point that no data is able to be sent because of saturation of all the links by duplicates of messages. To alleviate this, the algorithm must be adjusted to remove duplicates when it receives them. This can be done by tagging messages with a unique token that can be recognized if the message or packet returns. When it returns, the duplicate is discarded. The unique identifiers can be a sequence count or source, destination, count triplet, etc. Flooding will find the optimum path for the message, but at an exorbitant cost in transmission traffic and overhead. Other optimizations include sending only in the direction (east to west, for example) of the destination.

The last nonadaptive method we will address is fixed routing. Fixed routing refers to techniques where one, two, or N (N being a small number) of paths for output message routes are defined a priori. This form of routing requires the nodes to keep road maps of, say, how to get from node X to node Y. A road map is usually stored as an array with N entries for 1 of N possible destination nodes and up to N entries for paths that will lead to the destination site being addressed, depending on the level of redundancy wanted. If messages must get there, all possible routes may be enumerated. It is important to note that each site keeps track only of the nearest neighbors that will ultimately get the packet to site N. If there is not a critical requirement, only one will be stored. This would equate to an array of dimension N as opposed to a multidimensional array of 2 up to N. In selecting which entry to use, we could operate in many ways. For example, if we receive a packet destined for site 23, we could look at our table in array dimension (23,X), where X is the choice factor.

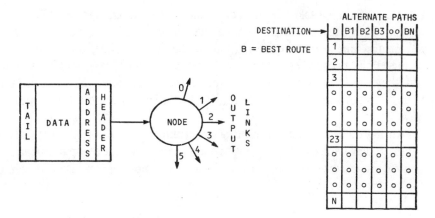

Figure 3.2 **Routing: Static by Table**

If we assume that the best route, the next best route, and so on have been computed a priori, the table can be organized as 1=best, 2=next best, etc. with N being worst or none. Then the simple selection case to use is to choose first X in the order that is available. This makes for a simple run-time algorithm but is expensive in apriori setup time.

Static routing is viable if we have a good knowledge of the traffic loading in volume and source/destination pairs beforehand. If this is not available, the method is impossible to make work properly. If loading and source/destinations and links change, many fewer links may be defined.

An alternative to static or nonadaptive routing is adaptive routing, which allows the paths to be redefined during operations based on status. Adaptive algorithms that have this quality include: centralized, HOTPOTATO, delta, and distributed routing.

Centralized routing techniques are characterized by the existence of a central hub routing controller. This center performs the calculations for updating of the remote routing tables. All the remote sites send link status information into the center. The center in turn recalculates the routing tables for the sites and transmits them back to the remote sites. This simplifies the remote sites, requiring them to have little intelligence; in essence, they are equivalent to the static fixed-path method previously described. The problem with this approach is that the information received from the remote sites may ne inaccurate, because of changes in link status since the last update. Additionally, the time it takes for the central hub to recompute the link tables and to ship them back out to the remote sites is sprinkled with many delays. If the central site reroutes information to the remote sites, telling them to change links because of saturation or failure of other links, and if the new link they are to use goes down or itself becomes saturated, the sites will not be able to perform their intended tasks. For a large network, this option is unworkable.

An alternative adaptable routing algorithm is the HOTPOTATO algorithm, which works as follows: When a packet arrives at a communications control processor, it tries to get rid of it as fast as possible by inserting it into the output queue with the least amount of waiting packets. This algorithm makes no attempt to determine the right path on which to send the packet to minimize its total transmission. It merely places the packet in an output state as soon as it can (greedy algorithm style) without regard to the global consequences of the action. This algorithm adjusts its outputs based on the dynamic loading of the links. It is similar to the random centralized case but will more evenly balance the load on the links.

Another adaptive routing mechanism, delta routing, is adaptive in relation to the cost (queue delays, bandwidth utilization, etc.) of each link at the remote sites, which will send their change status to the central router periodically. This site then computes the optimal path from all nodes I to all other nodes K and distributes this to the remotes to be used for their routing paths.

The last method of routing to be discussed is distributed routing. This family of algorithms represents the more dynamic mechanisms. They do not act on known global data but on best guesses or estimates of the best global environment. Most algorithms of this class gather information about their outside environment by either inquiring from nearest neighbors or taking data supplied by passers-by. The information supplied deals with the best path to use to get to node N and the approximate expense to get there. With each adjacent node transferring its known status information to the others around it, ultimately each node will have a reasonable estimate of how to transmit a packet from one node to another. This status information can be propagated from the closest node only or from some number of adjacent interested nodes. This class of algorithm is much more robust than any of the others in its capacity to adjust its operation based on system loading and degradation.

3.4 Flow Control

The previous section described methods of routing packets or messages in store-and-forward networks such as Arpanet. These methods were either adaptive or nonadaptive, with the consistent goal of attempting to route a message from source to destination as rapidly as the mechanisms allow. Not addressed in the previous section is a problem that packets may encounter during their travels: congestion of links. Congestion may be due to normal operations during peaks or high points of the averages used to calculate the routes. It can result from changes in traffic due to a link failure or transition to new route tables or even from a receiver's inability to accept any new packets due to saturation of its input buffers.

Methods developed to guard against or inhibit these situations fall into two categories: congestion control and flow control. One set of methods strives to avoid congestion at any site, whereas the other tries to keep the level of flow at a specified level over all the links. Methods of congestion control include preallocation of buffers, packet discarding, and isarithmic congestion control.

Preallocation of buffers is a congestion avoidance method that works as follows: The sender ships requests to the destination and its intermediaries to reserve storage buffer space for the message to follow. This, in essence, preallocates a route for the message to transverse and reserves intermediary and destination storage space for the message. The reserved space may be only a single buffer or the entire size of a message, depending on the available buffers and the speed at which buffers can be emptied at the destination and its intermedaries. The problem is that this control information will, in itself, increase the volume of traffic over the network while decreasing overuse of node assets; additionally, idle buffers cannot be used until deallocated by the sender.

An alternative scheme for congestion control is referred to as packet discarding. This scheme controls congestion at each site by discarding new arrivals if there is no storage buffer space in which to place them. This scheme will cause a greater level of retransmission of packets within the network, thereby increasing the communication link utilization levels. It is, however, a very simple scheme and requires no additional control information except for negative acknowledgement to be transferred to senders.

The method known as isarithmic congestion control manages congestion by striving to limit the total number of packets floating around in the network. To do this, the network maintains a pool of permits, which represent the number of packets that can be in the system. To transfer a packet, a sender must acquire a permit, after which the sender can transmit its packet onto the network. When the receiver receives the packet, it creates a new permit to replace the one used by the sending process. This algorithm sounds nice, but the problems are how to distribute the permits to requestors and how to control the movement, consumption, and creation of these permits. Permits could be equally distributed to all sites when the network comes up and allowed to distribute themselves out based on source/destinations pairs. This mechanism will work only if there is a balance of traffic among sites; if there is not, some sites may concentrate permits while others have none. Another option is to have the permits localized to some number of sites in the network. The selection of a cluster site should be based on proximity to large concentrations of sites. In this scheme, the permits are requested from the cluster site, and the cluster site determines who gets them. Upon message termination, the permit is returned to the cluster site for reissuance to other requestors.

The other type of network control is flow control, in which there are two major mechanisms: choke packets, and stop-and-wait. The first mechanism accomplishes its job by monitoring the volume of traffic flowing over its links. If the volume exceeds a certain level, it sends choke messages to the senders, telling them to slow down their rate of transfer. The sender in turn will slow down until it receives no more choke packets; it will then increase its output until it is again told to slow down.

Another scheme is to require all senders to perform end-to-end packet or message transfers and to not allow them to transfer any other information until they receive a positive acknowledgment from the receiver. This will limit the total volume of traffic any site can insert into the network and therefore what the network will see.

3.5 Addressing

For these networks to operate, the sites need to determine how to uniquely define the senders and receivers of packets in the networks. This addressing is required because the sites are not directly attached to each other. Addressing is related to network topology architecture and geographic location of the sites. Addresses are typically constructed as hierarchies from highest logical user to host machine to net machine to cluster and to network (Arpanet, Milnet, Tymnet, etc.).

This physical hierarchy of addresses can be hidden from the user process or be forced on him. The optimal method is to supply a mapping service that provides network-wide logical names for processes in the system. In large networks, this is usually impossible, and we must settle for something less. Typically, we are forced to access another system via a connect to its network (for example, Arpanet to csnet), then to a particular logical node name and a logical user name, and ultimately to a process name. The method is at least devoid of physical addresses, leaving the user to remember logical, instead of physical, designations. The network mapping function will take the logical names and, using a directory, look up the physical designations. This process may be done for each level of the network. For example:

TEST.FORTIER.ADA.U-L.ARPA.USA

To send a message to a node in the system, one would first see if one is on the same network. If not, one would then pack the designator (TEST.FORTIER.ADA.U-L.ARPA) into an address format and ship this from the network server to one on Arpanet. This new server on Arpanet would strip out the address, remove the ARPA designation, and form a packet to be sent to location U-L (physical address). After this packet was received at the U-L site, it would strip out the information that indicates which host computer on one's site to send this to (ADA). It would form a packet and send this to the proper physical host. When the packet was received at the host, it would form a message to user FORTIER and to his process test. This translation of logical to physical locations is totally hidden from the users. This is for the point-to-point case. If addresses are global (that is, they must be sent to all), the system must possess some global repositories that will have the same logical designation. The mapper must determine that it is a broadcast-type message and form the proper sequence of control characters to ensure recognition of it by all sites. The address could be interpreted to mean "copy this message and send out to all adjacent sites," or it could indicate that all sites have a logical port (buffer) from which they will recognize this message. The network will have to ensure that the message is sent from site to site in some fashion.

3.6 Reliability

An issue of extreme importance is how the network ensures the reliable transfer of information; that is, what measures are in place to ensure that messages ultimately get through in the face of link failures, control processor failures, or just intermittent noise? In the case of link failure, ensuring reliability of transfers usually requires alternative paths by which to approach the receiver site. If the network control processor has more than one link to other sites, it can utilize the additional links to get to the receiver. The process required to do this is simply a change in the link status table (routing table) to indicate a failed link; the original algorithm will then select an alternative.

Additionally, the network control processor must have the intelligence to retransmit packets that were in transit on the link that just failed. This is accomplished either through a negative acknowledgment, indicating a bad reception, or a timeout, indicating that a packet did not arrive within its allocated time period.

Another condition to which the network must be able to respond, if it is to be reliable, is node failure. Failures can be of many types and durations. A failed network control processor brings down the node unless a redundant copy of it exists. A host processor failure additionally renders a site inactive, at least in relation to the processes and users on that host. To keep the network active, messages addressed to down sites must be either returned to sender for future retransmission or held at intermediary sites for transfer when the failed site is returned to the network. More common conditions are network errors of the intermittent type. This type error, referred to as a burst error, is typically random in nature and occurs over short periods of time. It causes the loss of some number of bits in a transmitted word. Other errors, such as simple transmission or reception errors, could cause the loss of single or multiple bits in a message. The latter errors are more random, and techniques for detecting and correcting them have been developed.

Techniques such as parity checks and cyclic redundancy checks have been developed to detect if an error exists. Coding methods, which parity special patterns with data, have been developed to help in correcting errors in messages. Codes, such as binary and cyclic coding methods, have been developed for this purpose, along with hardware to implement the coding and decoding of the messages [PETE61].

3.7 Security

In all networks, some level of security is necessary. Security can be as simple as a user name and password pair or as complicated as intricate encryption/decryption systems. In early systems, security was simple. All the organization needed to do was to provide for physical security around the system; that is, encase the system in a room and control access to the room. As more users were added to early systems and these users interfaced via video display terminals (possibly in their offices rather than in the computer room), the need for security grew, and security became more of a system issue. The computer system needed built-in mechanisms to ensure that allowed only proper access to the machine. This was accomplished in early systems by authorization codes (passwords). With the advent of networks, the need for security increased drastically. One could no longer provide security by ensuring that only authorized people had access to the system's CPUs. Unwanted access on any system could happen through another system that is listening. To alleviate this problem, network transmissions were scrambled when sent and descrambled when received, leading to the development of encryption and decryption algorithms. The main similarity among the many techniques that have been developed is the need to use a key (for example, some known value) to encode the message, using the encryption algorithm; on the other end, the receiver needs to use the same key in deciphering the message. The problem is one of how to distribute these keys to the nodes without compromising their meaning.

3.8 Resource Sharing and Distributed Processing

The early systems, such as Arpanet, were mainly concerned with resource sharing, not distributed processing. Resource sharing deals primarily with how to share resources among users that are geographically distributed. The main use of resource sharing was to allow users to transfer files from one site to another, or to log onto one site from another. Typically, files transferred are mail files or batch-processing job files. Users log onto other systems to set up execution of program files that they have sent previously. The reason for doing this is to acquire use of devices that are better designed and set up to perform the wanted task. For example, if a user has a large simulation program to run, he may wish to find a large unused mainframe somewhere, say on the West Coast if he is located on the East Coast. He would then download his simulation program with its data to the mainframe in order to set up his program to run. Then he would initiate processing and ask to be notified by network mail when it is completed. By doing this, the user can execute his job much more quickly on a more powerful and less loaded machine. Additionally, since he is on another machine, he can do other work while his job is being done elsewhere, thereby increasing his efficiency. The main benefits of resource sharing are to provide communications between widely distributed users (mail system) and to provide access to specialized processing and peripheral devices (array processors, data flow processors, mainframes, high-speed printers, massive data-storage banks, specialized graphics equipment and plotters, and dedicated special-purpose hardware).

There was a limit, though, on the level of distribution of processing that could be performed on these early networks. For example, one could not distribute portions of a single job that needed synchronization over a wide area, mainly because of the excessive communications delays that exist in these networks. The processes could not do the job and at the same time maintain an adequate throughput. If they tried to do this, the time spent on communications waiting could exceed the time spent on performing useful work. This and other issues led researchers to begin work on more high-speed, localized collections of computers networked into local area networks. This class of computer network began to allow more real-time distributed computing.

Distributed computing is a term used to describe the notion of a job (process) being performed at multiple sites in parallel. The connotation is of a single job broken up into multiple tasks that run concurrently, not multiple, separate, unrelated jobs running in parallel on separate machines. The important point is the job is unified, with a singular goal being executed at multiple sites. This point allows for a wide range of interpretation. The user is supplied a high-speed interconnection environment with a unified operating system, providing the user with the capability to distribute a job based on its structure, in order to realize a higher level of performance than would be possible on a uniprocessor system.

This concept of distributed processing or computing relies on a tightly coupled environment. The computers must be able to talk to each other with data, control, and programs at high speed and with high reliability to provide a true distributed computing environment. Additionally, if we wish to make the environment more transparent to users, the level of distribution and the physics of it must be hidden from the users unless they specifically require a partition to perform a function. This is the notion of implicit and explicit use of distribution of functions. To effect this, the distributed computing facility will require computers for languages that compile programs looking for implicit structures (hidden concurrences) that lend themselves to distributed processing and, additionally, accept and process explicit user-supplied directives for distribution, such as collateral statements in Algol, fork, and join, or enter and accept constructs in ADA. The system must supply these capabilities to fully utilize and realize the merits of distribution. Distributed processing supplies to the users the power (capability) of the full suite of computing resources encased in a view that is based on the singular model of a computer.

3.9 Models of Computation

Many models of distributed computation have been developed and more are sure to follow. Presently, the main models of computation in use in distributed systems are the hierarchical model, the federated model, the resource-sharing model, the homogeneous model, and the data flow model. Each of these will be discussed in detail in the following sections.

3.9.1 Hierarchical Model

The hierarchical model (fig. 3.3), seen in many real-time control environments today, represents a logical view of the flow of information and control within distributed processing systems. It can be physically implemented on a centralized, federated, or distributed system, and on any number of computers and topologies.

The model operates as follows: The lowest elements are used to effect real-time data collection and control of physical systems. For example, these low-level devices may be used to monitor the operations of robotic arms and feeders in a fully automated automobile factory. These devices interrogate components coming in, determine what they are and where they go, and ef-

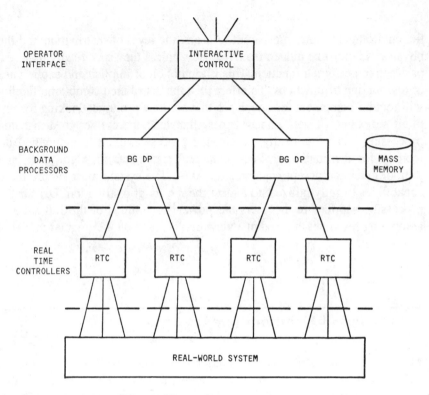

Figure 3.3 **Real-Time System Hierarchy**

fect the control of the robotic arm in acquiring a component, inserting it into the moving assembly, and completing the integration of this part in the assembly before it passes by. Above this level are data collections and analyses. These devices extract status data and operational data from the low-level controllers and analyze it for conformity to its model of what the total subsystem (collection of low-level controllers) is designed to do. If it finds a problem with the health status or operational status of any control device, it may institute a reconfiguration or adjustment of the control element to maintain operations. Additionally, these midline logical devices collect data to provide operational total assembly-line status to the coordinating control center. This element is typically the point at which human controllers or monitors come into play. Monitoring, for example, total system status and loading, or reinitializing the system for operations on a new set of parts to be assembled. They use data tied up and condensed from the other subsystems to ascertain total system state and operations. This level performs system-level control; that is, it works on total system's goals and objectives as a unit subset. It is concerned with checking tolerance and quality of the operation, as well as providing the knowledge to adjust operations to unforeseen conditions.

3.9.2 Federated Model

The federated model of distributed computing is based on a centralized macroprocess level and many distributed miniprocess levels. It is best viewed as a type of master/slave processing. This model will perform processing at the local site of inception until it exceeds some boundary capacity level. At this point the additional processing will be off-loaded to other sites for processing. The model attempts to use the notion of localization of processing based on demand. An improvement would be to centralize the control of the job at one site while shipping off as many processes as possible to slaves to process in a quicker fashion. The results of the processing will be directed back to the central originator for recombination and total job completion. The feature here is that many "central" sites can exist in parallel, each striving to maximize their processing through the master/slave relationship. Again, this represents a logical view of the processing. It could be physically realized in many topologies, with each topology having aspects that either aid in or hinder this type of processing.

3.9.3 Resource-sharing Model

The resource-sharing model makes the assumption that all resources (CPU, disks, tapes, graphics systems, plotters, printers, etc.) are singularly available for users to acquire and use in performing their tasks. Additionally, generic software functions are viewed as shareable resources with fixed interfaces. In this view, users perform their jobs on the system by setting up a sequence of functions to be performed that meet their requirements. If the functions are generically available and do not require serial synchronization, the option would be to execute them in parallel. Additionally, if the job has aspects requiring specialized processing or resources, the mode would be to acquire the specialized resource(s) and load the software to utilize it. This method of distributed computation becomes feasible only if we have a unified global operating system that can control the sharing of diverse elements distributed over some topology. Additionally, we require a high-speed environment to ensure timely distribution of control, data, and programs. This method lends itself to the notions of object management and object programming, which will be addressed in Chapters 6 and 8.

3.9.4 Homogeneous Model

The homogeneous model of distributed processing assumes a collection of computers of the same relative capacity and resources. The goal is to distribute the processing of jobs to as many processors as possible; maximal distribution is sought. Jobs are broken up into their lowest distributable elements, and these elements are distributed using a scheduling algorithm that seeks to minimize or maximize some system heuristic, such as degree of parallelism, speed of total computation, equal load on all processors, minimum load on all processes, or maximum load on a cluster. This model is among those being intensively investigated in the search for techniques for process distribution and scheduling.

3.9.5 Data-flow Model

In the data-flow model, processing is performed in waves. The data arrives at the input and is processed through special-purpose devices that perform a particular function. The output is then delivered to the next device waiting for the data; that device processes the data, and so on until a result is fed out of the device. This type of distributed computation requires extremely tailored languages. Problems solvable by such machines have special properties. The processing can be done by special hardware or by specially programmed general processors. The major feature of this model is that control is effected by the flow of data items in the network. No processing ensues without the availability of all data items for the process. Data-flow processing can be performed on special-purpose machines such as the MIT Data Flow machine, or on a collection of processing engines connected via a communications network.

3.10 Local Area Networks

The outgrowth of early networking studies was the concept of local area networks. Researchers saw a need to augment wide area networks such as Arpanet with connected subnetworks by means of high-speed communications networks, in order to provide local users with quick access to each other's information. This concept is based on the localization principle: Users in a local geographic area need better access to each other's data and programs than those of geographically remote area networks.

The local network approach was envisioned to provide local users with reduced response times to network requests, increased processing capacity, increased throughput, improved resource sharing at a finer granularity, improved reliability and availability through redundancy, components of higher reliability, graceful degradation and/or growth, as well as ease of change. Local networks represented the evolutionary step beyond geographical networks.

Local networks come in many configurations and cover a wide spectrum of capabilities and power. A local network can be comprised of N microprocessors connected together via Ethernet links, forming a moderately priced and powered network capable of many processing jobs, or it can be comprised of a collection of minicomputers or mainframe computers with very-high-speed data paths, forming a high-powered local network. Additionally, it can be comprised of some combination of microprocessors and computers.

All local networks have a common component: they combine computers and resources to supply network and extended services to users. Variations among networks typically involve varying topology (connectivity), protocol (communications control scheme), processing devices, and operating environment. The sections that follow will acquaint the reader with the diversity that exists for each of these components.

3.10.1 Topology

Topology refers to the connectivity within the network. The connectivity in local networks is very rich, and many variations exist between the bounds of each major category. The major categories of network topologies are the ring, bus, star, and irregular connectivity schemes. The basic ring topology (fig. 3.4) is comprised of network interface units, with processors interconnected neighbor-to-neighbor, ending with the first unit connected to the last.

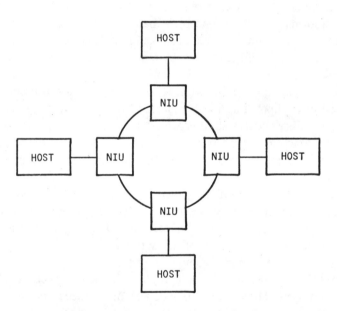

Figure 3.4 **Basic Ring Topology**

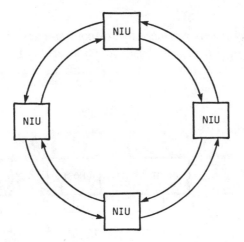

Figure 3.5 **DDLCN**

The basic mode of communications in this type of topology is circulating messages that are intercepted and interpreted as they transverse the circular ring communications media. Noteworthy variations on this basic topology are the double-loop computer network (fig. 3.5) and multirings bridged together (fig. 3.6).

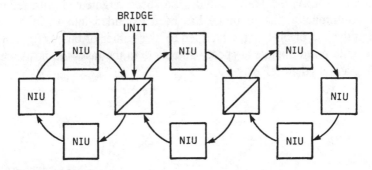

Figure 3.6 **Multiloop**

The bus topology covers a wide range of configurations and control protocols, as will be seen later. The basic structure of this topology is a global shared communications medium (fig. 3.7) with all NIU (network interface unit) and host pairs strung off it.

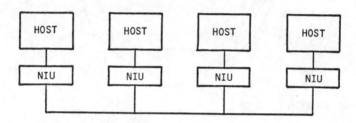

Figure 3.7 **Basic Bus Topology**

Basic communications are carried out by the devices acquiring the shared media, then transmitting their message. Many varied protocols have been devised for this topology, as well as many topological variations; for example, for reliability, the basic topology has been augmented with redundant links. Additionally, the topology has been extended into various hybrids through the use of bridging, which led to hierarchies of buses (fig. 3.8) that can be tailored to operate at speeds amenable to the tasks the hosts are performing among themselves.

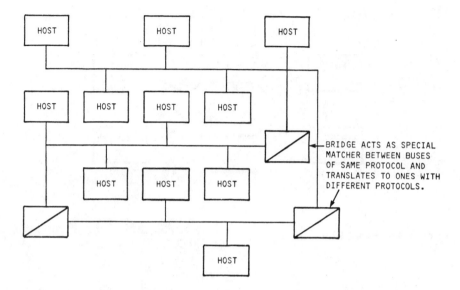

Figure 3.8 **Hybrid Bus Tiered Topology**

The next class of local area network interconnection scheme is the star, or centralized, topology. The star topology consists of a central hub, that acts as the switching center for all communications among the network processors. This hub is an active device that performs the routing function between the connected devices (fig. 3.9). The control of this topology is based on selection schemes implemented on the hub, such as polling, random, prioritized, etc. Variations of this topology have been devised and are mainly of the class of star-to-star or combinations of this topology with the previous two.

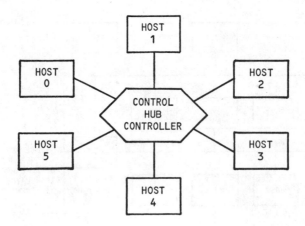

Figure 3.9 **Basic Star Topology**

Irregular, or graph, topology consists of a set of hosts and NIU pairs that are interconnected in some irregular style. This can be viewed as a localized copy of an Arpanet-like system (fig. 3.10). Because of its irregular structure, this type of topology has the same requirements and problems as the large Arpanet systems; that is, it requires routing algorithms, flow control, etc.

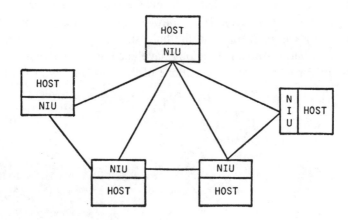

Figure 3.10 **Irregular, or Graph, Topology**

A final class of topology is termed hybrid, and is a combination of the previous four. Such a configuration may be devised to utilize some of the best features of all the above to meet specific system communications requirements.

3.10.2 Protocols

As indicated above, just as there are many varied ways to interconnect a set of computer resources into a local area network, there also exist a myriad of methods to control communications in these networks. The major classes of protocols can be categorized follows:

>Daisy-chaining
>Polling
>Independent request

The basic daisy-chaining protocol operates as follows: The control of the communications medium is given in a first come, first served fashion. In the centralized controller scheme of daisy-chaining, the devices that want service (access to the network) send a request for service to the controller. The controller then initiates the process by propagating control from the closest device to the furthest. This, in essence, prioritizes control based on proximity to the controller. The decentralized version of this protocol is implemented as a rotating token on a ring architecture. (Details of algorithms for this are found in [FORT84]. The daisy-chaining algorithm for control is typically implemented on ring architectures.

In polling, the process of control is either to have a central site initiate a poll (random or organized) of the devices to determine which gets control, or to have distributed sites that have a unique count, that, when received, indicates that the unit has control. This type of control has been implemented on star and bus topologies.

The last major category of protocol is independent request, the collection of the most varied set of protocols in use in local area networks today. The basic mode of operation for this class of protocols is as follows: The users who wish to communicate "contend" for use of the media. The "winner" of the contention acquires the communications media and transfers its data. The others wait until he is finished and try again. Schemes of this type have been widely implemented on global bus topologies.

3.10.2.1 Examples of Protocols

Daisy-chaining, which is based on a physical sequencing of devices, is mainly seen on ring topologies. The major style of protocol seen in this topology is the rotating token or regenerated token. The basic token ring operates as follows: The token rotates around the ring, contacting each network interface unit in physical order. The network interface units receive the token. If they have a message to send, they append it to the back of the token and send it on to the next NIU. This technique provides for the transfer of variable-size messages but restricts this transfer to a fixed physical sequence.

Examples of polling include the HXDP bus or the Hughes IR&D bus architectures. The HXDP performs a global poll by sending an update counter signal through the network. Each device on the bus increments its internal counter when the signal is detected. It then compares its sequence number to the global counter. If they match, this unit wins use of the bus. If not, it waits until the next count to try again. The winner uses the bus and when done sends out the update counter signal. This performs a logical poll of the devices having the proper sequence numbers. Such a protocol allows the designers to assign more than one entry to devices, thereby allowing for tuning of network use.

The Hughes IR&D bus operates by logically polling devices in sequence. A logical/monotonically growing poll sequence is computed at each device. The devices have a code stored and use this to determine if they have control. If the global code that is sent out is the same as mine, I get control; otherwise, I wait for the next poll. The winner uses the bus, then computes a new poll code and sends this out.

The last category of protocols is the independent request (request/grant). Protocols that meet this criterion include the carrier-sense multiple-access scheme and the distributed system data bus [FORT84]. Local area networks of the carrier-sense multiple-access scheme, such as Ethernet, operate as follows: If a unit wishes to communicate to another on the network, it listens to the communications line. If it is not busy, it transfers its data. If it is busy, it either continues to listen until the line is not busy or delays to some random time and tries again. If two units sense the line is not busy and transmit at the same time, a collision occurs. Once the units sense the collision, they will both randomize some number of time slots (packet-size) and retry later. More details of this and other contention schemes can be found in [FORT85].

The other contention scheme is one described in [FORT84]. It utilizes a technique that operates as follows: Units that wish to communicate over the media contend by sending their message priority and device priority in bit-sequential order. The bits from all the devices are ORd together, one at a time, with the following consequence. All devices send out their first bit and listen to see what happens on the media. If it is not what they sent, they drop out of the contention until the next frame (bus contention cycle). If they do hear what they sent, they continue until they get past all bits (in which case they have control); otherwise they lose and wait until the next cycle. More information on this protocol and others can be found in [FORT85].

3.10.3 Processing Devices

Just as there is a wide range of topologies and protocols for local area networks, so is there a myriad number and variety of processing and peripheral devices. Local area networks have been built to share a wide range of devices. Manufacturer's nets, such as Decnet, Primenet, and Wangnet, have been developed to link a wide range of vendor's products. Networks of this type have been developed mainly for the office environment, and consist of collections of personal computers, word processors, minicomputers, database machines, mainframe computers, and a wide range of the vendor's peripherals. Beyond vendor networks, there are many special-purpose networks built for real-time process control. These networks are usually typified by real-time control equipment (devices such as sensors, relays, control devices) connected with high-speed local area networks.

3.11 Operating Systems

Early computer networks were typified by loosely connected collections of computer systems. Each computer system possessed its own local operating-system environment and utilized the network through an operating-system extension called a network service. This piece of software provided the necessary features that allowed these early resource networks to share the resources as specified. As these early networks evolved into local area networks, the need for tighter synchronization also increased. The first efforts attempted to better utilize the increased capacity of the media. Beyond this, researchers began to look at these local area networks more as integrated systems, and as such, they wished to view the distributed environment in the same fashion as they did the centralized uniprocessor environment. The first efforts tried to extend the local computer's operating system with services required for the extended capabilities. Scheduling of processing, data-base management, resource management, and network control were some primary areas of work. This style of operating system is referred to as a network operating system. The basic notion is to integrate a group of centralized computer systems with their operating systems and, by adding software on top and around the central operating systems, to provide the synchronization of the local sites in order to integrate them into a cooperating set of units. These operating system were the predecessors of fully distributed operating systems, in which there is only one operating system, which controls and manages all resources, dispersed through the network. Chapters 5, 6, 7, and 8 will look more deeply into this type of operating system.

3.12 Services

Networks of computers require differing levels of system support based on their coupling. If the collection of computers is loosely coupled, the need for high-powered system services may not exist. On the other hand, if the system requires tight synchronization, there exists a great need for a unified and tightly controlled operating system.

In loosely coupled systems, the operating system is mainly the local one, located at each individual site; it controls the central resources augmented with a network server process. This network server is the only aspect of the early, loosely coupled networks that was different from their centralized predecessors. The network server process is utilized by a call to the process, which then performs the routing, flow control, packetizing and depacketizing, and transmission of the user data over the network.

As these systems progressed, there continued to be a growth in the type of services wanted. A need evolved for information management across the networks, increased protection for user processes, more transparent use of the network, resource balancing, and event management. This growth was typically added by extensions to the local operating systems. The distributed components were scheduled and controlled as regular user applications. This was the network operating system method of operating system design for local area networks. Problems arose as users acquired more experience at using the networks and began to demand much richer services for their expanding applications. They wanted languages for aiding in developing distributed algorithms, system support for data migration and control, process scheduling and management, more clean and consistent interfaces to the system, transparent use of resources and processes, reliable communications and process support, and distributed file systems.

3.13 Languages

Present languages for distributed computing generally are based on message-based mechanisms for process communication and synchronization. Others are striving toward shared variables (objects) as well as remote procedure invocation as the synchronization mechanisms. Table 3.1 lists some languages that fall into these categories. The interested reader is directed to these for further details.

Table 3.1 Programming Languages for Distributed Computing

Concurrent Programming Languages

Concurrent Pascal
ModulA
MesA

Message Passing Languages

CSP
PLITS
GYPSY
SmallTalk

Guardian-Extended CLU

Remote Procedure Language

Distributed Processes
Argus
ADA

Hybrid Languages

*Mod
SR

The use of these languages in distributed systems requires the availability of system services to provide process location, interprocess communications, the information migration, and the synchronization of remote processes.

Services for process location include mechanisms to perform logical to physical address translation (to keep the transparency requirement to users), and routing, if necessary, in the topology.

Services for process communications include mechanisms for packetizing and depacketizing messages, control of buffers for data reception or transmission, low-level communications media, access protocols, and communications protocol management, as well as mechanisms for reliable transmission (such as CRC checks, parity, coding schemes, retransmission schemes).

Information migration and control are services that are related to database systems. The distributed collection of data that is required for use by all the sites has the following requirements:

> The data is located closest to the site of use.
> It must be available to any site.
> Data may be factored, partially distributed, or replicated through the network.
> It must be kept consistent and correct.
> Use of the data must be controlled to guarantee proper correct use.

These requirements have driven distributed data-base research into areas dealing with:

> Transaction management (encapsulation of database manipulation commands)
> Varying data models (view of the stored data)
> Synchronization issues (concurring control)

Data replication and location issues
Distributed dictionary/directory management and use
Deadlock detection and resolution
Query processing
Recovery

Details of these data base issues can be found in [FORT85] and [DATE83].

3.14 Synchronization

Synchronization of remote processes is an issue that arose as users required more controlled use of the distributed resources and as they determined how to use the resources in concurrent yet coupled ways. Synchronization is accomplished through the use of either synchronous or nonsynchronous mechanisms. In one case, processes synchronize by coming together at some point at the same time. This usually causes one process to wait for the other to arrive. In nonsynchronous synchronization, one process arrives at the rendezvous point first; it places a message for the other process to acquire for synchronization, and then continues to do its processing. In this scheme, one process does not wait for the other. It merely signals the other that it reached its point and has gone on. This method allows for more concurrency but may introduce errors into the processing sequence if not properly controlled.

Finally, as systems grew in complexity, researchers and developers realized that the use of augmented central operating systems was not providing the services wanted. They determined that to provide optimally tight synchronization and coupling, these areas required integrated operating systems that provided total system control. These new operating systems, referred to in the literature as fully distributed processing systems, distributed operating systems, or distributed processing operating systems, must provide global, logically singular, operating environments in order to realize the potential of true distributed computing and the power of such systems. To do this requires the development of new philosophies on a systemwide basis for:

Process Management
Device Management
Memory Management
I/O Management
Communications Management

These issues will be covered in further detail in the coming sections.

3.15 Summary

This chapter introduced the reader to the concepts encompassed in distributed computer systems. Addressed were concepts of resource management, communications protocols, routing, flow control, and services required of wide area networks. This was followed by discussions of local area networks, with an emphasis on topology, protocols, and services associated with local area networks, followed by an introduction to concepts of operating systems for distributed computer systems.

4. Introduction to Distributed Operating Systems

4.1 Introduction

A number of well-designed operating systems have been built for distributed computers. They fall either in the NOS (network operating system) characterization (fig. 4.1) or into the DOS (distributed operating system) characterization (fig. 4.2). The first builds on what exists and extends it to make it provide adequate response; the second builds an entire environment from scratch to optimize operations for the network as opposed to the local sites. In either case, the goal is to provide services to the applications for process management, communications management, device management, memory management, and file management. Each of these in turn is driven by systems requirements for security, reliability, simplicity, flexibility, and power. The major difference found between the two techniques is in how the

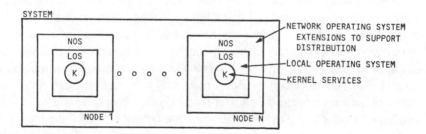

Figure 4.1 **Representation of NOS**

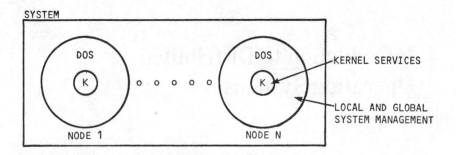

Figure 4.2 **DOS View**

local/global resources are viewed and managed. The NOS model views the resources as locally owned by the nodes and available by request to the local site with the intervention of the network control and management component. The DOS model, on the other hand, views the resources as globally owned and manages them as such. Access is performed via global mechanisms rather than local mechanisms. The system controls and manages based on a single-system policy.

In the NOS case, if a user wishes to schedule a process to run elsewhere because of the beneficial aspects of the remote site, the user must know he is going into a network, that is, he must log onto the network, associate any process with the remote process (this may require the source site to migrate the process or data from any site to the remote site), and request the remote site to schedule any process on its site. The remote node will, in turn, view the process as a newly created process within any local operating system's environment. In turn, this local operating system will manage (schedule, dispatch, block, unblock, acquire resources, etc.) this process in the same fashion as described in Chapter 2; that is, this processor acts now as if it were in isolation. It acts as a uniprocessor with no outside intervention. It makes all control decisions based on its local "mind set" to process the given task. If synchronization with remote sites is required, the process would have embedded in it calls to the network service code (added on top of the local operating system), which would provide the communications between the two processes on the different devices. This implies that the job of synchronization is left up to the user and is only partially supported by the system.

The distributed operating system deals differently with this problem. If any site has a process it wishes to spawn, it provides this to the operating system as a regular process. The operating system will examine the process control block to determine the specific requirements for this process. It then, utilizing its scheduler, determines how to best execute this process based on this site's best guess or knowledge of the state of the total system. The scheduler then takes this process, along with all the other processes ready to run in the network, and recomputes the order of execution on the nodes in order to optimize global run time and prioritize the collection of global processes. Emphasis is on the global nature of operating system functionality and goals. The operating system acts for the good of the total system as opposed to the local sites.

This discussion implies that a distributed operating system is viewed logically as only one native operating system that exists for all the distributed components. A distributed operating system tries to manage the entire suite of resources within the network in a global fashion. Many mechanisms to perform this management have been postulated and built but most represent prototypes and engineering research vehicles. This author feels that in the near future many manufacturers of computers and local area networks will construct and provide networks and operating systems with this quality, in response to the demand. This class of system is categorized by decentralization of the control in the network; that is, the operating system functionality is not dependent on the knowledge or state of one site or process. Typically a distributed operating system is comprised of a replicated kernel operating system (low-level hardware-control software, or firmware) with a set of system-level software for resource management. These software components may be singular, factored, federated, or replicated in the system. The reason for their existence is to allocate and manage the aggregate of global system resources so that system policies, as opposed to local policies, are maximized; that is, there is no exclusive, local administrative control nor any requirement for users to know whether they are on the network. This implies a transparency construct that hides the network and its intricacies from users. Users view the system as a logical single system, not as a collection of autonomous cooperating devices. Distributed operating systems built to date have been striving for these goals and cover a wide spectrum of implementation uniqueness.

To reiterate an important point, distributed operating systems are developed, designed, and implemented with the total distributed system requirements in mind from the start, in contrast to the previously discussed network operating system, in which the system (distributed network case) goals and requirements are typically afterthoughts. With distributed operating systems, the emphasis is on distributed or decentralized computers, which consist of multiple physically dispersed computing sites. These, nonetheless, possess a functionally singular, native, systemwide concept called an operating system, which is the same concept as that for centralized systems. Control in this type of system is derived via consensus, negotiation, and compromise among the peer sites in the distributed system. As in central systems there are bounds on what class of systems fit within this category. A distributed operating system could strive for total minuscule control of all aspects of all the computers in the system, or it could span a subset, such as process management only. With this in mind, the following discussion will deal with the first case; that is, it will look at what such an architecture does if it controls all aspects of a computer. The latter subsetted scheme will be seen when the reader looks at present systems. Technology is not quite able yet to realize a totally distributed environment without any centralized control component.

The major goal of any operating system is to control and manage the use of resources in the system by the consumers of the system. The operating system therefore must manage the processing cycles, the memory allocation and operations, the devices under its sphere of control, the input and output paths, and the communications among all these. These are the same for all centralized or distributed systems. The difference is that in one case, in order to make its management decisions, the controlling operating system has total knowledge of all aspects of the environment available to it at all times. In the latter type of system, the controlling operating system does not have an up-to-date, consistent view of the total knowledge about all aspects of the environment. Therefore, the distributed operating system will be required to make its management decisions based on some "best guess" of the total state or some past notion of total state or some combination thereof.

How does such an operating system do this? Before this question is answered, we must address some conditions upon which the management decisions are predicated, namely: for each major management function (process, memory, I/O, device, communications management), the percentage of the total resources of the system involved in the management aspect; the percentage of the decision makers (peers) that participate; the extent to which these decision makers need to be involved; and the level or degree to which a decision maker's opinion is utilized in the process. These conditions influence the level of coupling possessed by the distributed operating system.

The management functions previously described must be supported by the DOS. It must have mechanisms to support user processes over the wide range of devices and sites, without the user being required to know which specific device or site he is utilizing. Additionally, to be able to manage and control processes, the system requires processes to carry state information as to its criticality, value (how long and to what extent are the results of the processing useful), and timing and synchronization requirements in relation to others in the system. (This data could ultimately be defined by a compiler or system architecture engineering function).

The distributed operating system will perform the management function through the use of peers (equally weighted components in the network) that use some decision-support algorithm to determine how to perform the management. Techniques applied strive to guarantee the proper consistent use of distributed resources and include such methods as:

> Data-base concurring control algorithms
> transaction management
> serializable processing
> time-dependent processing
> sequence-dependent processing

Partial solutions include:

> Game theory/team theory
> Random graphs
> Decision theory
> Stochastic learning automata
> Divide and conquer
> Best effort
> Bay scan theory

All of these methods look at the management problem across many sites based on some level of knowledge. Additionally, these models each provide for some level of global control over the local resources. The global control mechanisms provide the synchronization among the peer sites that effectively perform the actual management. The management includes cognizance and control of processes and their resources.

4.2 Process Management

The goal of global process management is to provide policies and mechanisms to create, delete, abort, name or rename, find, schedule, block, run, and synchronize processes; to provide real-time priority execution, if required; and to manage the states of execution. To do this, each computational device in the network will be required to have a run-time kernel that manages the lowest-level operation on the physical device (fig. 4.3).

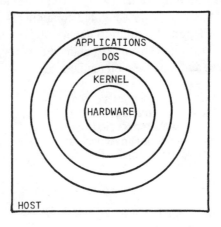

Figure 4.3 **Kernel Placement on Device**

The kernel effects the actual control and operation of the devices (CPU). It manages the queues used for states of execution (ready, running, waiting), although the mechanism in ordering how process control blocks are stored in the queues or how they are selected to run is driven by upper-level system policies, not at the kernel. This implies that the kernel is a fairly simple piece of hardware/software that aids in the effective run-time realization of the system's operational goals.

The kernel's states, in turn, are dependent on the external global system's scheduler and dispatcher. These in effect organize the queues within the local CPU and indicate what running policy to utilize in executing the processes on their queues. The scheduling function in the system is comprised generically of three parts:

> A decision mode
> A priority function
> An arbitration role

The decision component determines when to perform a rescheduling of the resource; that is, this component is the policy that indicates a method of scheduling, such as quantum, round robin, preemptive, or nonpreemptive.

The priority function component is used to describe the policy for assigning order to the execution cycle. The priority can be derived via a calculation based on event occurrence, task periodicity, loading levels, runtime (most time remaining, least time remaining, etc.). The priority function is required to provide the proper order to the scheduling policy (algorithm) being utilized.

Finally, the arbitration rule is a policy used to resolve conflicts between jobs of equal priority. This role would be typically structured as an order to execute these same priority jobs, for example, LIFO, FIFO, round robin, etc.

The policies derived in the three parts named above would need to be re alized via mechanisms that implement the decision mode, along with the proper priority, function, and that dispatch the selected job based on the outcome of these implementations.

Most work to date on job scheduling in distributed systems has been wrapped around either graph theory or heuristic solutions. Examples of scheduling techniques include:

Bidding
Queueing theory
Estimation theory
Statistical decision theory

Bidding refers to techniques by which jobs are matched to processes to be run, based on current availability of the processors to do the work. The process occurs by devices making bids for jobs and acquiring the jobs to execute. An example of estimation theory is a scheduler based on process priorities and periods. This method will schedule processes to run in chunks, based on their priorities and periods. It uses the latter to compute and schedule the optimal interleaving of process chunks, in order to maximize the systems throughput.

A last word on scheduling: recent work has indicated that a big win in distributed scheduling is to migrate the scheduling function and policies to all aspects of the system, including I/O, devices, processes, and communications.

Synchronization of processes in distributed operating systems is effected typically via message passing or remote procedure calls. The creation of a process in a distributed system involves creation of a process control block with information similar to that discussed in Chapter 2. The extensions to this deal with location in the distributed system. To delete or abort a process, the process control block must be found and authority to access it obtained; it is then deleted. To find a process requires use of a system directory or process that searches kernel queue spaces. All of the above assume support for interprocess communications, which leads us to the topic of communications management.

4.3 Communications Management

The job of communications management, as part of a distributed operating system, is to provide policies and mechanisms to effect intra- and intersite communications among consenting processes. Typically, this requires that the communications manager possess functions to register (give an identifier to) processes within the network, open or close logical paths from processes to other processes (one to one, one to a few, one to many, one to all, and vice versa), and manipulate these paths in dynamic fashion. In the case of a limited resource, paths must be allocated and deallocated to effectively share the resource. The communications manager must be able to perform routing of messages through the network, find processes in the network, keep tabs on media utilization, provide for reliable transfer (through, for example, coding and decoding of messages, retransmission of errors, parity, CRC, redundant links, and messages and replies, if necessary). Additionally, the communications manager may be required, in a real-time network, to provide guarantees as to the ability to successfully and within time transmit messages requiring real-time service.

Registering a process in the network typically entails providing it a unique physical designator that can now be distributed out to the other sites, thereby logging this process with all sites in the network. To effect the ability for processes (or objects) to converse with each other, the communications manager must posses a means to link the processes together. Typically, this is accomplished through the concept of a port. A port is a logical door (fig. 4.4) on one process that can be linked with the port on another process, establishing a logical path for communications between the devices.

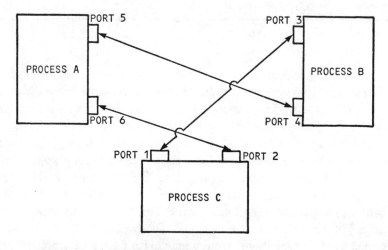

Figure 4.4 **Example of Ports and Processes**

Ports typically are associated with physical buffers (I/O channels) and therefore represent a utilization of physical assets. These ports can be assigned to one process or to many thereby providing the proper association of process to process, etc. The concept of a port additionally maps down to other functions of the communications manager. Because of the underlying topology and process locations, routing at some level is required. It could be as simple as a process-device pair address that associates a logical process with a physical site, or could be comprised of many levels traversing multiple links in either direct (N, tuple) form or in a hop count form. Another major job of the communications manager is to maintain statistics on use of the network for use in message scheduling, fault localizations, rerouting, etc. Finally, a very important function of communications management is to provide to the system mechanisms to aid in process time synchronization. This typically is referred to as a system wide clock. This allows the distributed operating system components in the various sites to compensate for variations in time that are due to delays caused by distributed communications.

4.4 Device Management

In a distributed system, as in a centralized one, devices must be managed. At the lowest level (physical device) the actions are the same in the distributed system as was described for the centralized system. Devices must be opened, closed, read, written, status bits must be set or cleared, and the device specific parameters must be initialized. These can be done on a global basis, a cluster basis, or a localized one. From a distributed operating system sense, we wish to have devices requested by name, file, and have the DOS determine which device within the named devices is file xon and how to set it up. If a user needs specific control or a device, then the user can name a device by name. For example disk 0 or tape 1, 2. The control of the device will be performed by the DOS. It will acquire the device for the user process on an open command, examine the device's status, reinitialize it and set the status if necessary. The DOS device manager will have components specialized for each device as well as generic ones. Specialized portions deal with device specifics such as serial use of printers, serial read/write nature of tapes, the random access and addressing schemes on disks. The DOS must keep a global accounting of devices and their availability. This information may be distributed over all sites, partially distributed (names/locations only) or centrally located to the devices being controlled. The DOS maintains the device status records and control blocks. The DOS device manager must select which device to allocate to a user process upon an open command. The DOS may allocate a device amongst many processes in a shared mode. For example, a disk drive may be allocated to many devices as well as a printer. Though control must exist at the site to force serial use of the devices (perhaps the concepts used in data base transaction management could be applied here). Once the DOS device manager has allocated a device and successfully completed initialization, it supplies back to the requesting process a name to address the device by (unique) ID. The device is available with the proper controls to the user device to now use to read or write to. Once completed, a user process will release a device by sending a close command. The DOS will reset the device's state information and return its device control block to the ready queue of devices for use. Underlying this is the physical device driver. This supplies a stored file view to the DOS environment.

An example of use of a DOS device manager for a printer spooler might be: A user desiring to print a file, executes a "print" file "X" command which places a copy of the file in the DOS spooler directory. The spooler process selects the file from the spooler directory, at which time it initiates an open request to the system file manager. Once it receives "open OK" it initiates another open request to the DOS line printer device manager. Once the line printer is ready, the spooler sends the file to be printed from the system file repository to the printer input buffer. This could be accomplished through a direct message transfer of the file or a packetized transfer. Once the printing is done, the copy of the file is deleted from the spooler and the device is reset. The DOS then closes the device. Pictorially (fig. 4.5) the DOS device manager is a collection of remote device drivers connected and associated with the devices, but controlled via status data from the DOS.

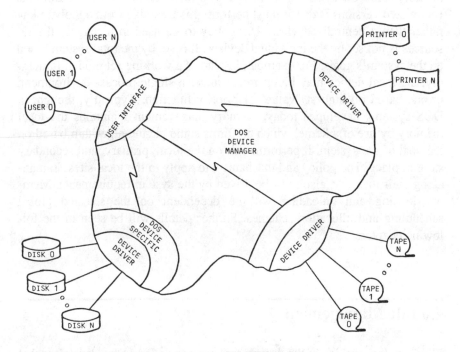

Figure 4.5 **Example of DOS Device Manager**

Additionally, the DOS has a device dependent portion that may or may not be distributed. This portion carries specifics requisite for a class of controlled devices (disk, tapes, printers, terminals, etc.). Finally, the DOS device manager will have a user interface which is the view the user sees of devices, namely an open, close, read, write, set, or unset device command. More specifics of this portion of a DOS will be seen in the example systems of chapters 7 and 8.

4.5 Memory Management

As in a centralized system, a distributed one requires the management of the memory resources available for its use. The variation or divergence from the centralized versions is that it must perform this task also from a global view rather than a centralized view. The policy to be used in managing the resources is not set by the individual devices. It is set by the total system based on the system's goals. For example, instead of a working set model of memory, the local device may be operating under a single process environment, or one based on highest "value" or priority function. Typically, though, in DOS systems developed today, memory management maintains the local memory by use of a kernel which performs some paging algorithm based on the goal of the system. It performs this on the local, primary, and secondary store in place. The policy and mechanism to apply to the local sites, in managing their memory, also must be driven by the system requirements. Memory loading and unloading will be dependent on the selected global scheduling and allocation schemes. Further details will be seen in the following chapters.

4.6 File Management

Files are data entities in the system that exist for a long time. It is clear that such long term storage needs a method for control and management at the systems level. The goal of Distributed File Management is to give users the illusion of a single, logical file system implemented on a collection of devices and computers spread over the network. The main functions of a DOS file manger is to provide transparent mechanisms to open, close, read, write, copy, create, delete, and find files in the network. To open a file, a DOS must first find the file in the system. This requires some means of storage allocated at the sites that has information about stored files. This is referred to as a dictionary and/or directory. The DOS must examine the contents of this list, determine where the file is located, and issue the request to open (acquire use of) the file. To close a file, the DOS sends a command to the remote device server to release the lock on the particular file being accessed. This is typically accomplished by changing the information in the dictionary at the file's storage site. To read a file, it must first be opened; then the DOS sets up a channel to the file and using simple file access schemes, as previously described, accesses the data. The read requires that no one is presently writing to the file for it to succeed. To write to a file a process must have exclusive use of the writing process and file. This is accomplished by requesting that the file be locked. Locking refers to a technique frequently used in data-base systems. A lock table is kept that indicates which records (files) are not accessible at this time due to usage. Creating files requires the acquisition of a unique file designation in the network and space on some device. Deletion is the opposite. File management systems are a subset of data-base managers. Data-base managers supply much more capability to user processes than a file system does. More importantly contemporary local area networks, as a majority, are implementing distributed data-base management systems as part of the total system. Therefore, our model of jobs required to be performed by a DOS also include those generically found in a distributed data-base environment. A data base provides a data model to the users. This is a mechanism that provides the users a way of organizing and thinking about their data.

A data-base system provides the mechanisms necessary to provide consistent, synchronized, and reliable management of system and user information assets. Distributed data bases involve a myriad variety of controls and mechanisms in performing their function; namely:

>The transaction model (serial, nested, compound)
>Concurrency control mechanisms
>Data redundancy and location transparency
>Update synchronization
>Distributed directory/dictionary
>Deadlock resolution/recovery
>Query processing

The transaction model provides a vehicle for users to group a sequence of data-base actions into a logical execution unit.

When executed on a data base and controlled properly, the transaction migrates the data base from one consistent state to another. The main feature supplied by the transaction component is the atomic processing of the transactions in the system. This is accomplished via the concurrency control mechanisms. Concurrency control is the mechanism that provides the logical serialization of actions on the data bases of the system. It provides the mechanisms to guard against simultaneous and/or erroneous operations on the data-base items. This supplies the characteristic of being correct in relationship to all others; that is, it supplies the effect of transactions being executed in isolation. The concurrency-control techniques provide for the proper execution of the transactions to allow concurrent reads and writes as long as they are noninterfering, thereby providing the "serial execution view" on the data base. Details of techniques can be found in [FORT85].

Data transparency is related to replication and partitioning in the system. Data transparency is provided via mechanisms that map data logical items to physical locations. The mechanisms usually utilize information about data that is stored at all sites. This information is in the form of directories or dictionaries. Data redundancy, or partitioning, is an issue related to availability and reliability. It has positive effects on access to data in the read cycle, by allowing the closest copy to be read. Also, it has beneficial aspects from a recovery viewpoint. If a site fails, the process can be reinitiated on another site that has the same information. Additionally, the failed site can be recovered to a consistent state by copying all updates done since the failure. The problem with redundant data is one of updating. When writes occur, they must be directed to all the sites and must be performed based on system-oriented reliability goals.

Updates can be required to be performed at all sites before any reads occur to a master site or to a majority of sites, based on the algorithm used and the method of recovery. Typically, update algorithms are one of the following five types:

1. Unanimous agreement (all sites must accept in order to have the update done--an all-or-nothing case.)
2. Primary copy (all updates are done to primary other sites that are updated later, based on the system policy in place.)
3. Moving primary (the update is done on a "primary" that can migrate during execution, with another node always required to stay consistent for recovery reasons.)
4. Majority vote (a majority of the sites in the network must accept the update for it to be successful.)
5. Majority read (the update is done at the initiator and sent to all sites; the problem is that reading an item requires collecting data from N sites, with the concurrence of the majority of read data for the item to be used.)

A dictionary and/or directory manages transparency of data location and also enhances recovery of data for users. The dictionary/directory contains definitions dealing with the physical and logical structure for the stored data as well as the policies and mechanisms for mapping between the two. The directory additionally contains the systemwide names of all resources (files, relations, programs, nodes, devices, etc.) and the addressing mechanisms for locating and accessing them. This mechanism of the data-base manager provides the means to define, name, and locate objects in the system's data bases.

Deadlock detection and resolution are critical issues in distributed systems. The problem also extends into process management. The major issue is to detect and recover from the circular wait-for condition, which occurs when one device requests the use of one resource (file, disk, etc.) and also has exclusive use of another, while a second device requests use of any held resource and also holds the same resource under exclusive use (fig. 4.6).

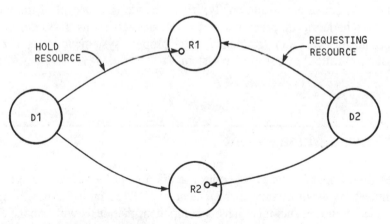

Figure 4.6 **Deadlock Condition**

The problem is that neither device can continue its processing without the resource; therefore, they are both helplessly suspended in a state of limbo. To address this, researchers have looked at multiple schemes; namely, detection and correction, prevention, and avoidance. Detection strives to recognize the condition (usually accomplished through the construction of transaction wait-for graphs and detection of cycles in them). Prevention tries to prevent a transaction from executing unless it has all it needs. Avoidance tries to allow execution only when a state that can complete is found. Good examples of techniques for these are the wait/die protocol and the banker's algorithm [FORT85].

Recovery from deadlock is typically done by selecting a victim (a transaction that when killed will provide others the opportunity to complete), removing its held resources, and allowing others to acquire them. Recovery also deals with system-level failures and the mechanisms to recover from these to known system state.

Query processing deals with the method by which actions on the data base are organized; that is, it looks at how to best process a request for information that minimizes a value function. The techniques applied deal with maximizing the effectiveness of global query execution sequence, local site processing sequence, and device processing sequence. These all relate back to the global process scheduling problem. If the query processing strategy is integral to the processing scheduling strategy the entire system scheduling scheme is consistent. Additionally, if we include the concept of transaction in the scheduling of processes and data-base actions as a system control mechanism, we can guarantee the proper systemwide serialization (synchronization) of tasks in the system.

4.7 Event Management

The final important aspect of control in distributed local area network environments is event or time management. Any DOS built for use in tightly coupled environments must have a component that deals with events. Event management refers to a system's capability to detect, process, and respond to an external event within the time allowed to drive the external event's actions. The goal in a distributed system is to detect all actions and sequence their processing and actions so that those of the highest priority or value are processed first. This is analogous to the scheduling and is internally related. If we allow the actions of the system to be driven by random events, priority inversion could occur; that is, if low-level processes are allowed to interrupt possibly higher-priority processes and get service as a result of event-handling routines, priority inversion could occur. This implies that a distributed operating system must have the capacity to review events and determine if they should preempt a running process or not. Systems covered later on in Chapters 5, 6, 7, and 8 address this issue in greater detail.

The previous discussions dealt with the question of what a distributed operating system must do. The next issue is how these capabilities are realized in a distributed system. The next section introduces the mechanisms for this.

4.8 Models of DOS Design

Most operating systems for distributed computer systems developed to date can be placed into one of two major categories, based on the mechanism by which they implement the notions of functional entity and synchronization: process-oriented systems and object-oriented systems. Systems within each category closely resemble each other in terms of functionality; that is, they use similar structuring mechanisms, similar synchronization mechanisms, and similar operations.

The process-oriented system model is characterized by a collection of processes that provide services to the system. Typically, these are large processes, and the DOS consists of a relatively few number of them. These processes perform all the DOS functions in the system. Synchronization and control of user processes and system state are performed via the passage of messages. The object-oriented system model is characterized by a collection of objects that provide operations to the system. Typically, this class of system is comprised of a large number of objects, each doing a small number of operations in its local object environment. Synchronization and control is effected via the management and allocation of capabilities. These provide the authorization and access for applications on other system objects to perform operations on the accessed object. In principle, each of these models does the same job; they control and manage resources and states within the system. Differences lie in the mechanisms they use in performing this system management function.

4.8.1 The Process-oriented Model

As stated previously, at the level of policy the two models are equivalent; that is, they are each other's duals. Logically each model has equivalent components; therefore, processes in this model can be mapped into objects in the other. It is at the level of mechanisms that they differ. At this level, the process-oriented model is characterized by facilities or mechanisms for passing messages easily, effectively, and efficiently among processes. Another important feature of this type of method is its mechanism for queuing up messages at the service processes and destination processes until they can be acted on. Some architectures developed for this model use scientific scheduling principles to handle queues of messages, while others act on them in order. Processes in this type of model contain primitive operations to send messages, wait for messages, wait for specific messages or classes of messages, and examine the state of message queue facilities. Preemption typically occurs when messages arrive for processes of higher priority than the running process. Processes in this style of architecture control all activities in the system. Some high-level similarities between systems exist Most distributed operating systems of the process class utilize specific communication paths between each other, such as ports, channels, links, sockets, or other mechanisms for linking processes. These mechanisms are utilized to allow the establishment of specific forms of communication between synchronous or nonsynchronous processes in the system. The binding of process to port, for example, typically lasts the duration of the life of the process, or the duration of a major system activity (for example, the loading of a process, its running, and death). During these phases, the required ports are acquired, linked, and used for the process involved and relinquished only when the process is complete and is deleted. The number of processes in this style of operating system tend to be static as all processes required to control the system are created at load time. This is done in response to the difficulty in creating and deleting processes in the system, situations in which links made to others can be lost, causing those attached processes to fail. Messages queued for processes cannot be easily deleted because of response requirements. Another important feature exhibited by this type of DOS design is the tight coupling of DOS processes with system resources. Control of the resource is effected by the encoding of control signals into a message, the sending of the message to the device, and its acceptance of the message (via an acknowledging message back to the sending process). The device processes the provided information and sends back the wanted response through yet another message.

The synchronization of processes is effected through their transferring of messages among each other. Many schemes for scheduling and synchronization have been devised using this message-passing scheme. Some depend on the queue management scheme's ability to distinguish priorities, etc. Others look at synchronizing via time stamps, clocks, or locks passed by messages. Details will be demonstrated in Chapter 7. To manipulate data required by more than one process, the data is either shared via message passing (implying serial uses) or is stored in data bases (possibly redundant, allowing parallel reads and controlled writes). Typically, in process-based systems, priorities tend to be statically assigned to the DOS components at the time of design. These priorities are usually tied to the timing requirements of the processes and the resources they control. Processes operate on a limited number of messages at a time and usually complete one computation sequence before another is begun.

To summarize, the process model requires mechanisms to provide for messages and message identifiers. It must possess mechanisms for defining channels and message ports, which define routes and buffers for the messages to utilize. Ports can be shared, thereby providing for various communication combinations, such as one-to-many, one-to-one, one-to-a-few, and broadcast. Processes in this model are comprised of long strings of code with much functionality. There must exist the capability to create processes, delete processes, and associate processes. The most important aspect is that the primary mechanism is the message, which provides control and data messages to processes that use them to ascertain system state and the actions to be performed in their spheres of interest.

4.8.2 The Object-oriented Model

The object-oriented model of distributed operating system exhibits the same type of policies controlling resources; that is, resources are managed from a global view and with similar goals and restraints in place. Again, the major difference between this model and the process-oriented model is in mechanisms used to realize these policies. The main entity in the first case was the process, message pair. In this case, it is the object and its capabilities. The capabilities ticket, or access rights, control the protection, addressing and access to the system control elements, the objects, represented by global and local parts. The local part is known only to the object and represents its sphere of control. The global part contains the data structures visible to the outside world. Control and cooperation among objects is achieved through the acquisition of capabilities, through locks, semaphores, monitors, or other abstract synchronizing data structures. The variation here is that queue for access to "critical code" is now accomplished at the capability list, not at the individual process or object. This mechanism is similar to the lock manager in data-base systems. The object is viewed as an engine that can do only a limited amount of work. It has very specific interfaces. These interfaces provide the remote requestor with operations that can be performed on the object or that the object can perform. This implies the encapsulation of all data and instructions into these protection spheres. These mechanisms facilitate the protection and efficient access of data used on the system. Objects can be easy to create and delete because they have no hard links to others. Known access to any object is done only through the operations that are allowed on the object. Objects typically have only a small number of operations performed on them, but there typically are many objects, and they can be combined in many ways to provide the wanted effect. Control of resources in the system is effected by acquiring the capability for the object from its manager (a particular resource or resources). The object then will perform the operation requested without user intervention. Once completed, the user would be notified through some status fields and would release the capability (lock) on the object so others could also use the object and its controlled resource. This concept is very analogous to the data-base one of transactions looking to perform actions on a data base. The actions can be performed only if there is no conflict and, once they are accepted, no others can use the data until the transaction has completed and released the resource. Because of the structuring and control environment, the distributed operating system's resources and mechanisms are encoded into globally known encapsulated data structures (fig. 4.7). These data structures provide the global view of the managed resource. A major concept of this architecture is that encapsulated in it is all the information it requires to perform its task. The only exterior interface it may require is operations on global data objects or resources, but these are encapsulated in some other objects. By including all the state data with the object, efficient task switching can be performed. Control and interaction in the system is totally based on operations on objects. The operations requests steer the system through the proper sequence of actions with each object synchronized, as in the data-base world, into some "serializable" (that is, consistent, correct) state, based on the proper controlled actions of the operations on the system objects. Chapter 6 describes additional details of the concept.

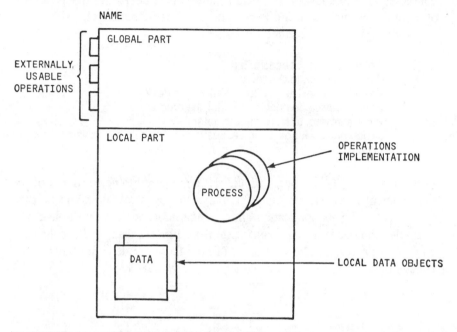

Figure 4.7 **Example of Object Structure**

The goal in any contemporary system design is to provide users with the maximum flexibility and performance in performing their applications on the computer. To provide this flexibility, the distributed operating system designer must strive to keep the intricacies of the network and its synchronization hidden from the users during their sessions. The users must know about resources and other users of interest; for example, if a user process A has the necessity by design to converse with user processes B and C, it must know of the existence of these processes and their logical names. They should not be required to know each other's location or status on the system. Additionally, if the user process A requires system assets such as disk drives or tapes to store or retrieve raw data being extracted from a sensor, the user process must know about the existence of devices and their usefulness in certain situations; for example, if the user is streaming in raw data for later use, the process must know of the existence of the inputting device and a storage device capable of serial access and allocation. The process should not be required to know the physical location of the devices or the intricacies of setting them up and using them. The user should have a clear interface; for example, it may be required to:

> Open a device, to acquire it
> Close a device, to deallocate it
> Associate a device, to allow sharing of a device
> Read a device, to acquire data for the program
> Write a device, to store data for later use
> Synchronize with other processes (a send or call mechanism)
> Initiate other processes (create, run, spawn, etc.)

In other words, a user process should not be required to perform any of the management functions associated with system resources. It should be concerned only with its application and its requirements for doing a task. For example, one needs to read data, write data, process data, and synchronize with other processes. The intricacies of how these are done are transparent. Greater details on actual views taken will be given in Chapters 7 and 8.

4.9 Summary

This chapter introduced the reader to the concept of a distributed operating system. It described what it is, what it must do for the system, and models of how this is accomplished. This was followed by comments on how the users of such systems should view them and utilize them.

5. The Process Model

5.1 Introduction

As the earlier chapters described, there exist multiple methods upon which to describe and build operating systems for distributed computing systems. If one takes a hard and analytical look at the diversity of distributed operating systems in existence or postulated today, many similarities in their basic structure and services are apparent. It can be seen that today's distributed operating systems possess the same capabilities that their early predecessors had; that is, a distributed operating system must still possess the capability to create, synchronize, identify, destroy, interrupt, and associate processes. It must be able to manage its memory and I/O devices. To do these things, the distributed operating system must have all the same mechanisms that exist in uniprocessor operating systems. The major difference is that these mechanisms will be extended and augmented to provide the multiple processor control and synchronization required to make the distributed system work as a unified system providing systemwide cohesion. This extension and augmentation of the operating system provides users with a system that behaves for them as a single abstract machine; in reality, the distributed operating system does much more to provide the same user-viewed capability.

The process model of distributed operating systems represents an evolution from the early multiprocessors into the arena of local area network operating systems. This means that the process model of distributed operating systems is comprised of the same set of mechanisms and is operated in much the same way as that of the early operating systems. The major difference is that it is not based on a single computer but multiple ones.

In a uniprocessor, the operating system enters and examines the state of the computer at some predefined time (typically established via a hardware timer device that sends an interrupt to the computer on its set boundary). This time period gives the operating system process control of the computer and allows, for example, the scanning of the state of peripheral devices and job queues, and rearrangement or reallocation of memory, based on the condition in effect at the time of the scan. As an example of what could transpire on this time boundary and during the processing of the operating system, fig. 5.1 is presented. A uniprocessor has some number (N) of processes presently active (that is, in the ready, running, or suspended states).

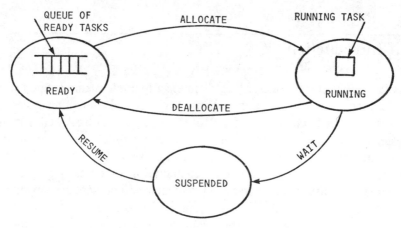

Figure 5.1 **Status of Active Processes**

The hardware within the system is set up to provide an interrupt to the running process at a predetermined period. At this time it places the running process back in the ready queue, if necessary, and initiates the operating system process when the timer boundary condition is met. The interrupt signal, derived via the timer, sends a signal to the CPU's control unit to insert a jump opcode with instruction to jump to a particular place in low memory, which in turn holds the address that the operating system's interrupt server is held. The operating system process once loaded into the computer or restarted, will begin its task of seeing what has transpired since the last entrance. The main operating system process typically does this by running through various subprocesses that examine the state of the system's processes, the applications or user processes, device drivers, I/O drivers, and memory status. Each one of these activities have specific jobs or functions that they must perform; for example, the process that checks the status of the system and user processes performs this by checking the queue of active system processes to see which one should run next, based on the state of operations. It also examines the queue of user processes to determine which one should be inserted into the dispatcher queue to be executed next during the user quantum (time slice). This is done through the use of a scheduler that implements some form of precedence relationship on the processes, based on some chosen system parameters such as place in entry queue, time remaining to process job, I/O required, value function associated with process, time to complete, or event conditions. This sets up the next user process to run in the system. Other operating system jobs include memory management, device management, I/O management, and synchronization between processes. To perform process synchronization, the operating system provides mechanisms such as semaphores (a synchronization mechanism) [DIJK65]. These allow processes to synchronize using the P and V or busy and signal operations.

The operating system provides to the user the ability to define a semaphore and manipulate it using a P(X) or V(X) system call. The V(X) operator will clear the synchronizer variable thereby signaling to the other processes examining it that the critical item being synchronized on is ready. Conversely, they could use the P(X) operator to perform a busy wait on the variable in order to acquire the critical item.

Using the operators, two or more processes can synchronize with one another. They can rendezvous on the variable and set up an operational relationship. A classic example of the use of semaphore is the producer/consumer relationship. To clarify the use of semaphores in this example, we will first look at the semaphore in more detail. As described by Dijkstra, semaphores exist in one of two states, true or false. No other state is valid in a semaphore. Additionally, Dijkstra devised operations that can be performed on a semaphore and defined the conditions that must exist to make the operation valid. As indicated previously, the operations are the P(X), which is a request to acquire the semaphore or V(X), a release of the semaphore. Analogous to semaphores are lock and unlock actions.

To illustrate the semaphore, the following action is defined:

P(X)   If X = O then X:=1 else enqueue;
        which deciphers to this:
        If the semaphore is not set, then I will set it.
        If it is set, then I will wait until it is cleared.

V(X) X:=O;
        If queue <> null then dequeue;
        which deciphers to the following:
        Clear the semaphore (reset it to available for use)
        If there is a process waiting to use the semaphore,
        then recover it else release it for others to use.

The above semaphore will allow one process at a time to acquire the semaphore, while all others are forced to wait. This is sufficient for most simple forms of synchronization, such as a read/write variable. But if an item is read only, this form of semaphore is very inefficient. A more general form for the semaphore has been devised; it is referred to as a counting semaphore or a general semaphore. The general semaphore differs from its simple cousin in one way: it replaces the true-or-false-only condition of the singular semaphore variable with maximum count or null conditions. The operations are illustrated below:

P(X)
        If X < max, then X=X+1; else enqueue;
        If the number of entries on the semaphore is less
        than the maximum allowable, then allocate a
        resource else wait until one is available.

V(X)
        X:=X-1; if queue < > null then dequeue.

When this operation is encountered, release a semaphore-controlled item, and check to see if any items (requests for the semaphore) are pending in the waiting line. If someone is waiting, wake them up to use the item controlled by the semaphore.

Now that the conditions and operations on a semaphore have been described, we can put them to work in an example of synchronization. The producer/consumer relationship is intended to control the production of an item into a second area and the consumption of items from the area. Pictorially, this is shown in fig. 5.2.

The Process Model [123]

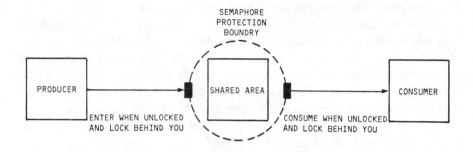

Figure 5.2 **Producer/Consumer With Semaphores**

The pseudocode for this relationship is shown below:

    Producer process

    begin
        P(S)
            Produce item into buffer
            Buffer = buffer + 1;
            Release the buffer for consumption
        V(S1)

    Consumer process

    begin
        P(S1)
            Consume item from the buffer
            buffer = buffer - 1;
            release the buffer for production
        V(S)

To work properly the start condition must be set as follows:

    S = 0 and S1 = 1

This example demonstrates the usefulness of semaphore operations in controlling the sharing of resources among processes. The operating system, by providing the capability to create and use these, has provided users with a powerful means to organize and synchronize the operations of the processes.

The other functions also must have their processes examined and operated on in some predefined order. Again, this order is based on the policies in place within the operating system. Before the operating system relinquishes control back to user tasks, it will service some of its other system tasks that are pending. Memory management may operate to reorganize the free blocks of memory in the system, the device manager could be run to extract and format the inputted information of user processes, the present configuration of input/output channels to users could be adjusted by the running of the input/output manager. In short, the local operating system must support the noninterfering sharing of the resources available to it and under its control, among a diverse and possibly conflicting set of loading requirements. To do this, it uses all its available processing cycles to assess the system state, to determine the next most appropriate set of steps to perform, and to initiate as well as manage the operation of the determined sequence of operations. This is all done in support of the multiple user processes sharing the system and its resources.

The difference in the requirement of the operating system in a distributed system at its boundary time (entrance period), as opposed to that of its local kin, is mainly in its requirement to synchronize the same activities (process synchronization, process scheduling, process dispatching, device management, memory management, I/O management, etc.) over many sites with many more resources. However, this synchronization and control of the system must be accomplished with a handicap. In contrast to its local dual, the distributed operating system must perform its synchronization and control function based on partial, incomplete, and inaccurate status information; that is, the local operating system, in doing its job, could use a complete and accurate picture of the computer system resources and state, whereas in the distributed system, a complete picture can be had only if all activity is shut down and state information is collected from all and updated at all sites. This would provide to the distributed operating system processes a complete and accurate snapshot of the present system state. The problem is that we cannot stop a system for the time it would take to provide such a consistent systemwide view. We must instead find new control paradigms to perform the same tasks of control and synchronization, using this incomplete and possibly inaccurate system information.

5.2 History and Motivation

Before delving into the structure of distributed operating systems and the process model in particular, we will give a presentation of how technology progressed from the single local computer to collections of highly integrated distributed local area and wide area networks.

In early systems, each of the computers had a local operating system that controlled the local environment. For one computer to converse with the other (that is, to exchange programs and data), the users of one system had to physically store the message (information to be transferred) on some removable media, remove this media from one machine, load it into another, and retrieve the transmission by copying it from the media onto its logical system store. Once this was done, it could use this transferred information in doing its processing. Examples of such a system might be a manufacturing plant's inventory computer and sales computer. The sales computer would gather information about the sales of items and other salesman-related tasks. To process orders for merchandise with regard to their ability to be filled from the inventory at hand, information from the sales computer about the item ordered (such as its name and description, and the quantity ordered) would be loaded onto a tape; the tape would be physically removed from the sales computer and installed on the inventory computer. The inventory machine would then process the order and indicate whether it could be filled. The early machines involved much more interaction with operators, whereas a totally distributed system would need fewer operations to do the same task.

Computer researchers knew that there had to be a better way. The next phase in the evolution was to link machines to each other's I/O channels and rewrite the driver software to make them think they were each talking to a secondary storage device (fig. 5.3). To converse, computer A would send a signal to ready its attached device (computer B); once device B was readied, the initiator would write a file to its output file (computer B's file server), while in reality it was writing into the computer B's setup input file. This form of communications required an augmentation of the user's application code to provide the mechanism to write a file out on demand or upon seeing some condition set. It also required an augmentation of the input/output controller's code and operations to allow them to talk to each other as attached devices. Although this scheme worked, it was less than ideal; however, it did mark the beginning of networking.

[126] Design of Distributed Operating Systems

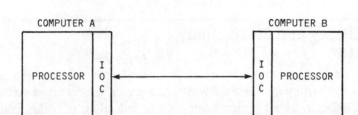

Figure 5.3 **An Early Network (Master/Slave)**

The next step in the evolution was a large one, in that it represented the phase in which much informative groundwork for networks was performed. This phase, represented mainly by the work done on Arpanet is typified by a separation of hardware for communications over the network from user applications hardware. Also typical of this networking and operating system phase was the use of point-to-point trunk transmission lines for communications from site to site. Operating systems for these early networks were built on top of the existing local operating systems and were referred to as NOS, or network operating system. A network operating system connected many sites over a widely dispersed area (fig. 5.4). Because of the dispersion and the characteristic of not being connected point-to-point to all nodes, this network required new techniques for sending and receiving information, beyond those used in the earlier master/slave systems.

The network operating system in Arpanet is broken up into layers: the local network, the network server, and the communications component. Each has a different function to perform. Keeping in mind that Arpanet has for the most part been developed for file transfers, we can see that the local operating system is the same as any central computer's operating system. The extensions to it are in the network server. This component accepts requests from users to transfer information from one site to another in the network. The network server component must format the message with information required for the transfer such as source/destination address, packaging information. One important aspect is the packetizing or breaking up of messages into equal chunks called packets, which allow multiple messages to be interleaved across the transfer media.

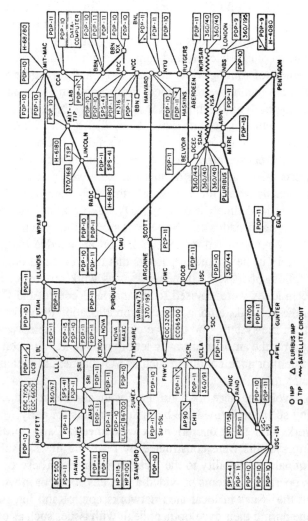

Figure 5.4 Logical Net of Arpanet (April 1976)

The last component, communications, which controls the transfer of information over the trunk lines, entails many functions. Due to the mesh style of the topology, the communications component must possess mechanisms for determining the destination of a packet/message, and for determining a route and a way to forward it. It must have mechanisms to send and control the flow over its lines in a way that does not cause congestion; to recover from errors; and to store incoming packets and ship them out in some reasonable fashion. The functions of routing, flow control, store-and-forward protocol, and error detection/correction were studied from many angles, and much was learned about methods and techniques for performing these tasks.

Numerous techniques for routing have been developed, among them flooding, which takes every incoming packet and sends it out on every line other than the line the packet arrived on. Another routing technique, directory routing, utilizes tables of source/destination pairs with path definitions to perform its route allocation for a message; this technique can be static (tables set up only at load time) or dynamic. Dynamic routing requires information on loadings and path status to be sent around the system. The tables can be centrally recalculated or done based on knowledge that a user site has collected from its neighbors or packets that have come through. Another important fallout of these early networks was work on congestion or flow control. Techniques were devised to balance and control the flow of messages within the network, among them the preallocation of buffers, limitation of packets in the system, and the use of processes in the network interface units that limit the amount of traffic let out of a node, based on some predetermined system or node condition such as I/O channel utilization level or network channel utilization.

The work on developing network control software and network operating system interfacing software formed the basis and impetus for early work on local area networks and their operational environments. Early local area network operating systems were constructed by rewriting the I/O software and adding additional functionality to the local environment. These early local area network operating systems provided a rich environment in which to learn more about the issues in local area networks control and integration. The research done during their development dealt with issues such as control protocols for control of the network transfer media, process synchronization and communications, resource sharing and control, accessing and addressing of processes in the system, protection and security of system processes and resources, and task or process device and channel scheduling.

Control protocols dealt with the issue of how to best allocate and utilize the communications media in the network. Three basic methods have evolved to address this issue: request/grant, polling and daisy chaining, with variants for the centralized or decentralized cases. These methods have been extensively used in network communications media control and are further described in [FORT85]. Of greater interest to this text are the overlying methods for addressing, process synchronization, and communications.

The addressing issue in distributed computer systems has many facets. Names are used for all areas of operational control in local area networks. They are used for recognizing and accessing a process in the system, and for scheduling processes, devices, and I/O. Names are used to allocate or deallocate devices, to or from a named process. They are used to allocate network links and to associate these links to logical processes in the system. Names in distributed systems are used in error control or for process and information reallocation during failure modes. The names, or logical addresses, are used to associate a physical processing resource in the same number of logical processing devices and users. Addressing is also used for synchronization of processes and sharing of resources in distributed networks. What this represents is a breadth of coverage. Logical names are used extensively in systems to remove the users and processes from needing to have explicit knowledge of the physics of a system in order to use it. Names in reality are a logical means to identify physical addresses. Making the connection requires a mechanism to map the logical name to a physical address or designator. Addressing in distributed system can be static, that is, one-to-one for the duration of the transaction. When a link is formed that links a physical to a logical entity, it holds for the duration of the entity's life in the system, and all know the entity by this name. The other side of the coin is dynamic addressing, in which a single logical entity (say a port) can have many processes and physical entities linked to it during its lifetime.

Another important issue is process synchronization. Early computer networks brought into operation mechanisms that were extensions of early centralized schemes. The two basic modes were message passing and remote-procedure calls. These two mechanisms were used extensively in early systems for synchronization and are still the stalwart operators for synchronization today. Another aspect of synchronization is control. Control of a distributed system is effected by the cooperative interaction of the sites in the system. The cooperation can be loose, thereby exhibiting a more autonomous view of each site, or it can be tight, providing for highly interactive distributed processing. The lion's share of work being performed on decentralized control concepts is based on extensions of the earlier solutions of centralized computer systems for decentralized control, especially if real time deadlines are added as a constraint. Protection and security are other interesting areas that arose during these early studies in distributed local area networks. The goal of protection and security is to protect the system from unauthorized use and to ensure that those using the system are authorized and authenticated. In one form of authorization, only a user who had access and who could acquire the proper semaphore could enter the protection sphere; once in, however, he could do as he pleased. Other systems were much more rigorous and had protection wrapped around fine granularities of objects. The problem with these techniques is the additional storage and processing overhead they forced onto the system in order to ensure security.

Before local area network researchers could look at such problems of total system control such as I/O, memory, and device management, they needed to address the issue of process scheduling and management on a global level. Early machines performed all decisions based on maximizing their local operations, not on the aggregate of the global systems. As time went on it became apparent that in order to make these systems more usable, flexible, and reliable, decisions needed to be made on a more global level. This need arose as a result of the shrinking cost and size of computers and the insatiable need for more processing cycles to handle more difficult problems. Scheduling can be done statically or dynamically. If we have sufficient computer power and prior knowledge of loading and reliability requirements, we can set up some number of scheduling load sequences to ensure proper operations. The processors will be loaded and run with a known load and with known interaction requirements, therefore allowing designers to set up the proper temporal sequence of actions to perform. This scheme is fine for static environments, but in more general-purpose dynamic environments, it scheme will not work. Research performed in this area has looked at ways to schedule processes based on system load factors such as available memory or processor utilization level. These schemes assumed that there was little, if any, interaction between jobs. If processes required much interaction, these schemes could turn out to be much less than optimal in performance. To provide adequate service to the user processes in scheduling and synchronizing their processes, the system must possess a greater quantity of knowledge dealing with the interaction of the processes. This extended knowledge has components dealing with processing time requirements; memory utilization requirements; dependency relationships on memory, data, and resources; precedence relationships on concurrently active processes; some notion of value associated with the proper and timely execution of a process; and interprocess communications requirements, to name a few. Much work has been done in this area and some will be discussed later in this text.

5.3 Process Model

Any operating system for a distributed computer system consists of elements to manage network communications, process operations, connected devices (disks, tapes, sensors, terminals, work stations, etc.) memory usage, and I/O channels (fig. 5.5). As a minimum, an operating system for a collection of computers must posses extensions to existing software to handle communications. The process model of distributed operating system design is no different. It, too, must possess the above entities and must provide for their efficient and fair use.

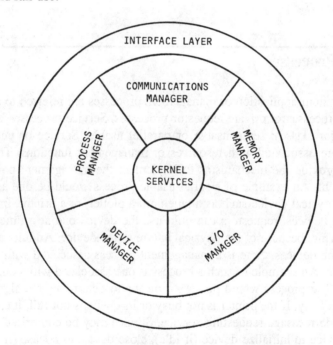

Figure 5.5 **Basic Functions of a Distributed Operating System**

The process model of distributed operating system design is comprised of elements, referred to as processes, that are used to control and manage the resources of the network. A process is comprised of a collection of code and data in a known system state, for example, ready, running, waiting. These processes are used in combination with user applications processes to construct an operational system. The operating-system-related processes are used to implement mechanisms in support of operating system policies to control and manage the system's resources and their interaction. A process is associated with each resource that must be managed; for example, there will be a memory management process; a process management process; a device management process for tapes, disks, floppies, I/O channels, serial ports, sensors, etc.; and a network management process, as a minimum. Each user application will be brought into the system as a process that uses the operating system service processes in performing its function.

5.3.1 Processes

These system application or management processes are referred to as public server processes or private/requestor processes. Service processes can be of two major classes: serial usable or parallel usable. Service or public processes are associated with resources or management functions. These processes provide the mechanisms to implement the management policies for the system. An example of a serial usable process would be one associated with a physical device such as a tape unit, a plotter, or a printer. In the case of these devices, requestors can only use the device one at a time with no interleaving, because of the physical nature of the device. Additionally, with these type devices, there is a management process associated with this type of device. An example of such a process is one associated with controlling a printer. The process would possess a means to determine and signal if the printer is busy. If the printer is not busy or its queue is not full, it can accept an outside message requesting service. Service may be comprised of either open device to initialize device (if idle), close device to release (if the last), or print file to output the file to a physical device based on conditions. This is shown pictorially in fig. 5.6.

```
PROCESS PRINT SERVER
┌─────────────────────────────────────┐
│  SPECIFICATION PART                 │
│                                     │
│    PARAMETERS                       │
├─────────────────────────────────────┤
│ BEGIN                               │
│   PRINTING:=FALSE                   │
│ LOOP                                │
│   ACCEPT (MSG)                      │
│   CASE MSG. SERVICE OF              │
│   OPEN:                             │
│     SET UP DEVICE                   │
│   CLOSE                             │
│     DEALLOCATE DEVICE               │
│     RESET PARAMETERS                │
│   PRINT                             │
│     OUTPUT MSG. FILE TO MEDIA       │
│   END                               │
│ END                                 │
└─────────────────────────────────────┘
```

Figure 5.6 **Print Server Process Shell**

Parallel usable servers or public processes can best be described as the control processes that manage disk units, mass memory, central processing units, etc. These processes perform control and management of their resources in a much more parallel fashion. The resource is time-sliced or multiply-accessed in an interleaved fashion. If more than one device is available, the management process will control the allocation and deallocation of private or requestor processes to the server processes devices.

For these requestor and server processes to perform the proper task for control, they must be able to transmit information as to what needs to be done in effecting the control management operation. The mechanism for this is the communication of messages between the processes. Messages constitute the method by which the processes are linked together and operate in harmony to perform the management tasks. Messages provide the means to send status, control, or information among the cooperating processes. They provide the mechanism that allows for the cooperation of the processes. Therefore, messages represent requests or responses for service in the system. All actions are controlled via this message-passing scheme.

The two major facets that distinguish the process model from the object model are the concepts of process as 1. the mechanism that implements the control and management policies and 2. the message that provides the cooperation and synchronization between them (fig. 5.7).

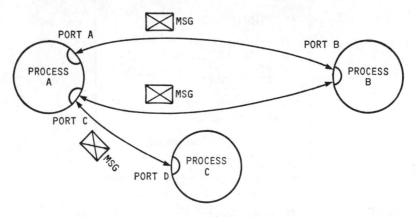

Figure 5.7 **Basic Elements of the Process Model**

5.3.2 Ports

These concepts, in conjunction with the proper process implementations, provide all the capabilities necessary to manage the system's resources. These alone, though, will not ensure the proper associations of processes or ensure synchronization. Another important aspect is how the loose collection of linked processes forms a correct architecture for a distributed operating system and how such connections or associations are managed. The crux of this issue is how the processes communicate their need for services on their actions or resources. Process models of distributed operating system designs have provided various techniques for process interconnection. These concepts in turn can be easily linked to physical realizations through a mapping process. The major means for providing this logical/physical interprocess linking has been through the techniques of ports, channels, and links, or pipes, as they have become known.

The function of these ports is to provide to processes a mechanism that allows them to logically link up to one another, based on their communications and synchronization needs. Before getting into further details of process synchronization, operation, and control, an in-depth presentation of ports and their uses is provided for clarity.

When a process is created, the operating system, through the use of a registration process, typically acquires a port name for the process. This acquisition may include the creation of a new port, because of a lack of available existing ports or an incompatibility with ports already in use. It also involves the connection of the process to the port that associates with this port, the creating process name, identifier, port designation, role (requestor or server or both), synchronization type (periodic, aperiodic, broadcast, etc.), and flow of information (input, output, or both); and the association of this logical port to the logical processes with which this new process needs to communicate. The process name is examined during this cycle to verify the uniqueness of the process' name, which will aid in the security of the system. To determine where other processes of interest lie and the ports with which they are associated, a process location function must exist. The role of such a function would be to search the known network sites and determine where the given process is, if it exists. Additionally, a process must exist whose function it is to determine what ports are associated with a process and if the status, type, and users of the port match the requestor's needs; for example, in order to have a broadcast mode, all processes must be associated with a port, pipe, etc. that is used as the destination of all broadcast messages. This port identifier is a logical entity. The physical realization may be a buffer at each site's interface unit that is loaded by the hardware with incoming data when a particular identifier (header address in message) is detected. This mechanism will allow for the easy detection and operation of a broadcast port. To use the broadcast mode, a process would send a message to the broadcast port designator. This would allow all of the connected nodes to copy a message into their broadcast buffers. This simple example assumes that all the sites can simultaneously hear the message and copy it. Ports can be static or dynamic in nature. What this means, for example, is that if a pair of processes wish to communicate with each other over their entire life, they would create source/destination ports (fig. 5.8) that associate the source port of one process to the destination port of the other and vice versa. The ports would be set up and maintained over the entire lifetime of the processes. This form of creation, association, and use is static; that is, it does not change over time. This type of association of ports is matched clearly to processes that are created as coroutines (fig. 5.9), tightly coupled multiprocesses, or distributed processes that require sharing of control and computation information with some level of synchronization.

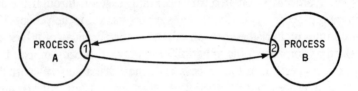

Figure 5.8 **Process Ports and Associations**

Conversely, in the dynamic case, ports are created, associated, utilized, and disconnected in real time; that is, the ports being used must perform all the tasks of finding the process, linking to the process, setting up the proper linkage to the process, and sending and/or receiving messages to or from the

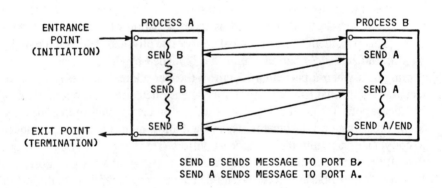

Figure 5.9 **Coroutines**

process as the activities deem fit. An example of such a dynamic usage of ports is for a specialized device. The device control process is viewed as a server process to the system; therefore, it is available to all and any who need its service, if they possess the proper credentials. The device's input/output port is kept active; when users wish to use this port (in order to access and use the underlying resource) they create or use an active port, associate (connect) their port to the server's (specialized device control process) port, set up the proper status, control, and parameter information, then use the resource via message passing across the ports. Once completed, the private or requestor process returns the device-control process back to its quiescent state, and releases the sender and receiver ports; then both go about their business, oblivious of each other until they need each other again.

From this cursory coverage, one can see that the port (conduit, link, channel, etc.) is the mechanism that can be used for process synchronization, control, and associations.

For processes to communicate and control each other's actions, the proper associations must exist between and amongst them. The associations between the processes in the system must have meaning and purpose; that is, to be useful process A associated to process B must be necessary for some predefined reason. A good reason for associations to exist is to provide the mechanisms (collection of processes) that implement the policies of an operating system's designers. What this means is that through the proper linkage of processes, we can implement a wide range of synchronization and data exchange associations that can provide a wide range of service and cooperation in the network. For example, to allow requestors to acquire processing resources, I/O resources, and synchronization among each other, the associations of requestor process to scheduler process to device manager process to other requestor (private) processes must exist (fig. 5.10). These associations are formed via the port creation and association actions.

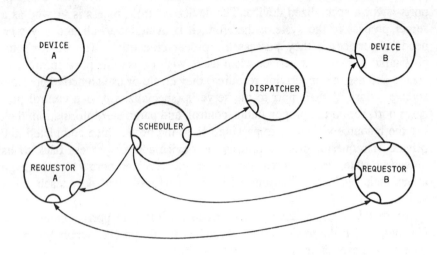

Figure 5.10 **Associations**

Following is an example of associations and their criticality to operations. Five private (requestor) processes exist. Their functions are to perform:

        Payroll management, which controls and manages employees'
            time schedules, project work bound to, and salary.
        Accounting (inventory), which maintains the status of all
            product items for sale. It computes available inventory
            based on production output, sales binding of items,
            and actual shipments.
        Ordering (sales), which provides a means for the sales
            organization to determine if items are available and to
            lock and account items as sold if they are, and otherwise
            to signal accounting that more of a particular item
            must be built.
        Shipping, which has the job of preparing orders for
            physical shipment from the plant. It bundles items
            into packages and once all physical items are collected
            and shipped, it informs accounting of the items
            shipped and their quantities so that an accurate
            inventory can be maintained.
        Plant scheduling, which has the job of sensing when
            inventory on items is below some safe level and

initiating the process of setting up the plant's operations to produce the items whose inventory has been depleted.

These functions are performed in conjunction with a data-base management process that controls and manages the reads and writes to the underlying data repositories and device manager process that controls the input and output of physical data on the attached device. If we assume that the system these processes reside on is spread throughout the physical plant on separate computing sites, the performance of these tasks of information management requires that the processes and their immediate data be located at the site of need, with possibly the data-base primary storage (secondary device) on one site (fig. 5.11).

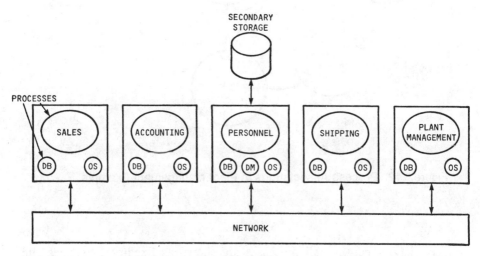

Figure 5.11 **Possible Configuration for LAN in Example**

With this distributed system in mind, the issue becomes how to provide the association or logical linkage between these singular processes to provide the entire plant management function that is wanted. The answer is to provide ports (channels) between the processes that must communicate with each other, with proper associations provided, such as input, output, and class type. Port linkages and associations for the aforementioned example are seen in fig. 5.12.

[140] Design of Distributed Operating Systems

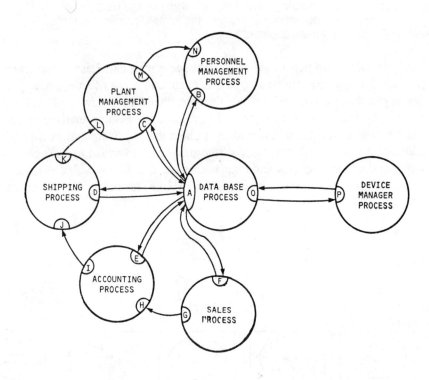

Figure 5.12 **Process Associations in Plant Management Example**

Associations between all processes are shown as fixed-port linkages and paths. In reality, some of the associations will be dynamic; that is, a port will be created and the processes set up (associated) to enable them to communicate needed information. The linkages (port associations) with the data-base process would be set up and used on an as-needed basis, based on the usage requirements of the data base and its attached device. When a unit needs a file, it will request it from the local copy of the data-base manager. If it is not there, it will query the site that has the secondary storage. To do this its local data manager process must acquire the port for the data manager on the site with its secondary storage linkup, then communicate the query to the storage site. In reality, these port associations may be set up at initiation time, but they are in a dormant state until needed. The other processes (the requestors or private processes) have links (ports and associations) that provide synchronization and control among the processes. The associations are fixed and in one direction. They aid the processes in knowing the state of the other processes and at the correct point in time (at the end of its operations). More will be said on synchronization in this model of distributed operating systems design.

5.3.3 Messages

The passing of messages between and among the processes in the system provides the mechanism for process synchronization and information exchange. Messages and the means by which they are used provide the synchronization for the system. Messages can be passed from process A to process B via a mailbox-type system mechanism or via semaphore-like mechanisms, or they can be passed directly to processes that use embedded synchronization primitives (send/receive). The messages can be of the blocking or nonblocking class. In the blocking class, the sending process is typically blocked until it receives an acknowledgment indicating success. Similarly, the receiving process, once it encounters a receive primitive, will block until the message is received. These mechanisms supply the wanted level of synchronization in the system. To make this mechanism flexible, a nonblocking receive is necessary. This is used to accept a message that does not require synchronization. For example, if data is being sent from one site to another and the data is noncritical, the receiver may wish to log it into memory, indicate it is there, and continue on. It may have higher priority processing to perform. It would go back to the message and extract the data for use when time permits.

The primitives just defined are similar to those used in the ADA programming languages. In ADA, the accept statement acts like the receive described above. It blocks until it receives the PUT command, which sends the piece of information to the receiver. This mechanism is referred to as the rendezvous and allows multiple concurrent processes to synchronize at various points in time. Other message-passing schemes, such as the mailbox, are nonblocking; that is, the mechanism does not require the sender and receiver to block in order to achieve the synchronization. The problem with this mechanism is that it does not allow tight synchronization. Messages are passed from mailbox to mailbox; the associated processes in turn, when they have time, are signaled that something has arrived; they examine the mailbox, extract what is addressed to them, and act on the message. This mechanism is widely used in systems that do not require tight synchronization. It provides for loosely coupled systems that occasionally must acquire information from other processes to perform their tasks. This mechanism, though, if used properly and religiously, can be used to provide tighter synchronization, as will be seen later.

As can be seen from the above discussion, messages form the basis upon which processes communicate their needs, desires, actions, and information to one another. To rely on this mechanism for control and information, the network must provide to the processes a message-passing scheme that is both robust and reliable. The message-passing scheme must provide processes with a scheme that signals to them when messages are sent, received, or lost. This helps the synchronization mechanisms and policies to operate properly. The efficient transfer of data to processes must be provided; that is, the message-passing scheme and mechanisms must provide for the detection, classification, and resolution of errors in transfer. This implies that the network must provide a means to either correct the errors or retransmit erroneous messages; additionally there must be some form of built in error detection mechanism, such as CRC, parity checks, etc. Finally, the message-passing scheme must provide for the control of messages flowing in the network. This must be done to assure the timely and effective transfer of the messages between processes.

5.3.4 Synchronization

Synchronization of processes (requestor and servers) is accomplished through the use of the basic communications services (port setup, message transfer, fixed or dynamic associations), based on a given operating system policy for synchronization, which must be enforced by the communications subsystem. Policies deal with the mode or class of synchronization and how to accomplish it. Policies can require loose synchronization, tight synchronization, or a combination of these. A policy for loose synchronization would specify that the cooperating processes involved in any synchronization do not need to come together at one time in unison in order to perform their computations. The processes may need to provide each other status and data at some point in time but they need not suspend and wait for each other to respond to the given information. They have interaction but of a noncritical form; that is, if one does not get the message to the other in time, they will not fail. They can still run and continue their processing. Processes of this type tend to be autonomous, with little effect on the resources they control due to a loss of messages from related processes. Tight synchronization refers to a condition in which the operation of one process is dependent on that of another. For one computation to continue, the related one must first complete. This is like a coroutine in contemporary systems. One process computes to some point and signals the other; the caller blocks itself; the other caller processes to some point, signals the caller, and blocks itself, and the process is repeated until the processing in each is complete. Another form of tight synchronization is semaphore operation. It provides a means for the processes to guarantee that they meet each other at some point, if necessary. This is done by having the first process block until the other reaches the synchronization point. At that time, both are released to continue processing. The last form of synchronization policy utilizes a combination of the two; that is, it has needs for tightly coupled processes and for loosely coupled processes. Most systems have needs for some amount of both types of synchronization.

The process model provides these synchronization policies through the use of messages and their semantics. For example, if loose synchronization is all that is necessary, a simple mailbox scheme may suffice. This scheme has mailboxes designated to a process or a group of processes. If one process wishes to communicate to another, it sends the message to the mailbox that has the attached process. The mailbox process signals by raising a flag that it has a message for the process. When the process is not busy or has time, it will go out, scan the mailbox for messages, extract what is intended for it, and act on the message(s) according to its established sequences of control. Conversely, if tight synchronization is what is wanted, the same mechanism can be used, but with different constraints. The processes that are tightly bound will synchronize on some boundary condition. The receiver will encounter a point in its processing at which it must stop at and wait for the sending process to signal it has arrived. The receiver will then read the message and act accordingly. while there are many other mechanisms to achieve these forms of loose and tight synchronization, the policy they enforce is the same. Such mechanisms are semaphores, ports, rendezvous mechanisms, the transaction, and the request/server process. Some of these will be discussed in Chapter 7, when example implementations are discussed.

5.4 Process Management

As in any contemporary operating system, the process model must also possess mechanisms and policies for process management. In any system implementation, the policies and mechanisms that actually implement the concept will vary, but the major concept will stay the same. The process model will provide for process management through the use of requestor/server processes synchronized and linked together via messages and ports (or channels, pipes, mailboxes, etc.). The major emphasis is on processes and messages and how they are used to provide the basic features essential to process management. These basic features or capabilities are listed in table 5.1.

Table 5.1 Typical Process Management Tasks

Process creation
Process destruction
Process scheduling
Process dispatching
Process blocking
Process suspension
Process wakeup
Process resume
Process adjustment
Process communication
Process identification

A distributed computer system that utilizes the process model for its operating system must still provide these services. The issue is how to provide them. The processes can be managed from a single copy of the operating system or from multiple cooperating peers or from some combination of the two. Operating systems for distributed computers typically are configured as a kernel on each site; all other services, dependent on particular devices, are resident on the sites where the device is located, though this need not be the case. The payment for allowing any arbitrary location of management processes to sites is extra communicated messages for synchronization. As users enter the system, they are provided with a process identifier that is unique in the system. They are then acted on by the scheduling process to determine a site to which to allocate the process. Scheduling of processes in distributed operating systems is similar to that in centralized systems, at least from the view of assignment of a task, job, etc. to a device for execution. The difference in a distributed system is the level of cooperation and sharing of actions and data possessed by the system sites in determining what process should be loaded and where it should be run. The process model does this through the exchange of messages between site operating systems. Scheduler processes use some scheme of weighing (voting, bidding, procedures relationships, etc.) to determine what needs to be run next and where. (Details of actual schemes will be addressed in Chapter 7, in which specific systems implementations are described.) Once a process has been scheduled for service, it must be initiated at the site derived. To do this requires a dispatcher. The dispatcher's job is to take the recommendation of the operating system's scheduler, allocate the device to the process, and initiate its execution. This process may require the movement of a process from one site to another site's memory, reorganization of a site's memory allocation, reorganization of a site's ready, running, and waiting queues, and initiation of the scheduled process. Scheduling and dispatching in the process model is done at the process level. The system recognizes only processes and their demands for service, and responds to them based on the policy for scheduling in place. The policy determines what must be done to manage the processes, not how to perform them. Policies for scheduling in distributed systems deal with issues such as load balancing, communications minimization effect, memory loading minimization, FCFS, LCFS, least-time-remaining, and precedence relationships with value functions.

Another important issue in process management is synchronization. In distributed as well as centralized systems processes must coordinate their activities. To do this, the process model provides message passing. Message passing provides a means for processes to implement many means of synchronization, from loose to tight coupling, as was previously shown. Processes pass synchronization parameters from port to port using primitives such as "send and receive," or "accept and put," to implement within the processes the proper semantics for synchronization. Processes, through the use of these primitives, can construct a myriad of synchronization capabilities. For example, if we had a distributed system with two processes running on separate machines that needed to synchronize on a particular event such as a sensor reading, process A would read the sensor and process B would act on the event reading. To synchronize on the event of "sensor-reading > max," the following conditions must exist: process A must have a port to communicate to process B, and process B must have a port to A to indicate success and provide feedback to A (fig. 5.13).

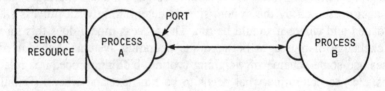

Figure 5.13 **Synchronization in a Distributed System**

The processes send information back and forth via messages and synchronize using send/receive primitives. The pseudocode follows:

```
PROCESS A
Loop
Read value of sensor
If value > max then
        send overvalue message to B
else
        continue processing
end loop


PROCESS B
Read value and process
Loop
        Receive A
        If value > max then
                Perform necessary corrective action
                Reply A (signal A that message received)
End loop
```

Process A, a continuous loop, reads the value of the sensor output. If the value of the output exceeds some maximum allowable value, it will force A to send a message to B, which is a server process. B will accept the message, act on the value, and reply back to A (fig. 5.14) The major emphasis is on the message-passing action and the processes' use of the messages to perform the synchronization.

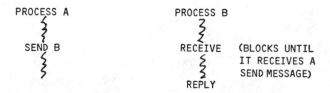

Figure 5.14 **Communications and Synchronization Actions**

Other functions that must be performed by the process model within each node include process blocking, suspension, wakeup, and resume. These also will be performed using message passing between the processes as the controlling activity. When a process reaches a point at which it needs service from an external source, it will send a message searching for the service (I/O, for example); during the time it is waiting, it is put in a wait state by the processor server process. Another condition that will cause a processor to change hands is an interrupt, which, again, is represented as a message. The message will be sent to the proper process for service. An interrupt may cause the active process to be blocked (to cease active execution) and removed into a wait state. The completion of the service for the interrupting requestor will cause the processor server to unblock and restore the process to a ready to process state. In any case, the active mechanism for performance of these tasks is the passage of messages from one process to another.

5.5 Device Management

All resources in the system are controlled via a server process called a guardian, proprietor, or administrator. The job of these processes is to accept requests for service on their resource, to process their requests along with others, to provide service to the requestor, and to return to serve others. A simple server process is shown in fig. 5.15, which shows a server process along with a resource under its control. Requestors send requests for service and receive replies with status.

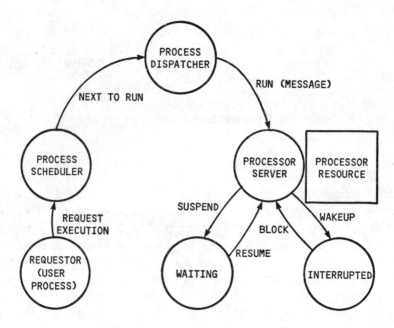

Figure 5.15 **Process Server Interactions**

But not all resources are simple. Systems have banks of disk units, printers, and tape drives, usually located in clusters around the system. To control these, most process-model-based systems are configured around compound server processes. These processes have the job of managing multiple resources or subservient processes. For example, if we had a bank of disk units, the server process could be configured as in fig. 5.16. The server process would be configured as a monitor process, taking in the N requests for service and processing them to return the wanted responses. Another form of multiple server process is shown in fig. 5.17. This type of server process takes in requests for service from the requestors and divides up the work to the subservient worker processes. Representative of such a setup would be the scheduling process and the underlying node on-site dispatchers that would actually implement the schedules for requestor (private process) execution. The subservient worker processes do not have to be associated with a resource. They could be processing endpoints that perform a function, such as data reduction or formatting, to be used by some other process in its computations. The controlling process that serves to control the resources is configured as a device manager in contemporary centralized systems.

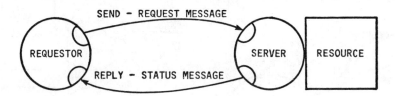

Figure 5.16 **Simple Resource Server Process**

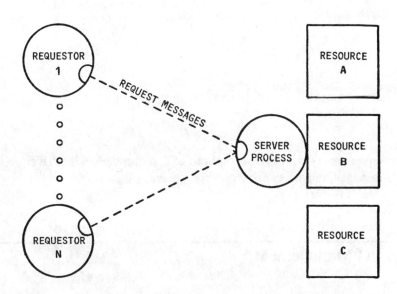

Figure 5.17 **Multiple Resource Server Process**

It is comprised of software to take local and remote requests for service (messages) and decipher the meaning of the requests and act on them (fig. 5.18).

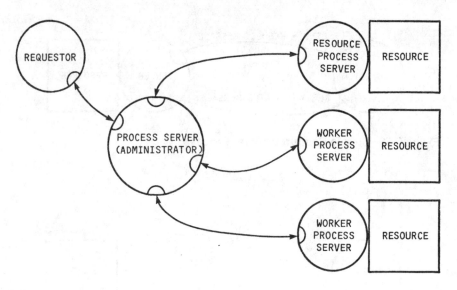

Figure 5.18 **Multiple Process Server**

The server process would be comprised of one or more device drivers, a device manager, and a network server component.

5.6 I/O Management

I/O management in the process model of distributed operating systems is handled by an I/O process manager. This process provides the interface between the I/O and the requestors and servers. Again, all activities must be handled by the use of processes and messages; messages effect the operation of the processes in the system. I/O management in most distributed operating systems of this type is mainly concerned with management of the ports in the system. Ports represent the only element that links processes to processes. They provide the naming and, mechanisms to effectively communicate with each other's attached processes. Ports act on this model as I/O channels do in contemporary systems. They provide a means to communicate information in a controlled fashion among the processes in the system

5.7 Memory Management

As in their centralized counterparts, distributed operating systems require the virtual memory space to be controlled and managed. From a distributed viewpoint, memory management is concerned mainly with providing storage to allow for process and data migration and initialization. To provide this, the process model must possess a component process that takes in requests for loading new processes, determines where to put them, and allocates the memory for that computer for the new process. This process must help in providing to the user processes a ready pool of available memory that can be used on demand. The memory manager receives requests from the processor manager and process management processes to allocate and deallocate memory based on usage patterns and demand. The memory manager process, on a local level, receives messages to allocate pages passed on the policy in place on the machine, and, form a global level, it receives requests from the process management process to provide memory to new or expanding private or server processes. The mechanism within the memory management process can be similar to its contemporary predecessor, but it must be extended to take as its input messages (requests for memory) from local or global sources. The emphasis again is on having a process whose job it is to provide the service to users based on their message flow to the server process.

5.8 Network Management

A final and major piece of the process model is the network manager process (fig. 5.19). Its job is to provide the interprocess communications in a transparent fashion to the users (requestors and server process(es) of the network.

[152] Design of Distributed Operating Systems

This process has the function of controlling the allocation of network ports to processes, of naming the processes in the network, of controlling the flow of messages in the network, and of guaranteeing the transmission and acceptance of the messages without errors. Typically, in systems developed to date, this component acts as the interfacing process for the processes in the system. It provides the basics of send and receive; that is, this component provides the message transfer mechanisms thereby

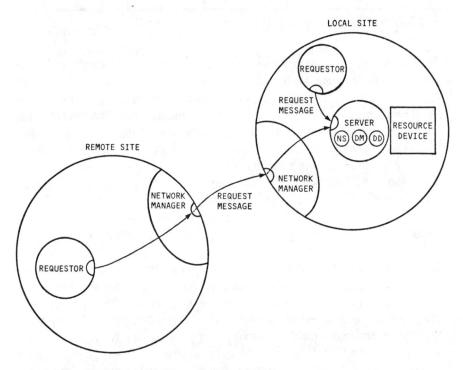

Figure 5.19 **The Network Manager Process**

alleviating the users from having to know where processes physically reside in the network. It accepts the processes' send/receive commands and interprets them, and transforms them into low-level actions that perform the actual transmission of the messages over the links. More specifics of these mechanisms will be seen in the coming chapters and examples.

5.9 Summary

This chapter has discussed the process model of distributed operating systems design, which links processes together by message passing and associations. These associations form processing hierarchies or dependencies that provide a road map to the flow of processing in the system. The emphasis within this model is that operating system processes are the same as others. They all perform a function, and use message passing as the link between them.

6. The Object Model

6.1 Introduction

We can take a different view of a computer system from that presented in the previous chapter. Instead of a computer system being comprised of resources and processes, it can be viewed as a collection of "objects." The term object is meant to represent both hardware objects (such as CPUs, memory, printers, card readers, tape drives, and disks) and software objects (such as files, programs, semaphores, and data). Associated with each object in the system is a unique name or identifier that differentiates it from all other objects in the system. Objects represent passive components; that is, they are viewed as abstract data types (physical or logical) that can go through a state change (change of context or view), act according to set patterns, be manipulated, or exist in relation to other objects in a manner appropriate to the object's semantics in the system. This means is that objects are defined and characterized by a set of invariant properties that define an object and its behavior within the context of its defined parameters. A queue, for example, is characterized by invariant properties that include the following: it can only be added to on one end and removed from on the other (fig. 6.1); you cannot insert and extract concurrently; its maximum capacity measured in number of items stored in the queue cannot be exceeded, nor can its minimum likewise be violated. Likewise, a stack (fig. 6.2), also has invariant properties that include the following: items can be pushed onto or popped from only the top of the stack; push and pop cannot take place concurrently; and its-bottom-of-stack and full-stack measures cannot be compromised.

The Object Model [155]

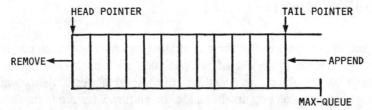

1. WHEN TAIL POINTER = HEAD POINTER THEN QUEUE IS EMPTY = TRUE
2. WHEN TAIL POINTER = MAX-QUEUE THEN QUEUE IS FULL = TRUE

Figure 6.1 **A Queue**

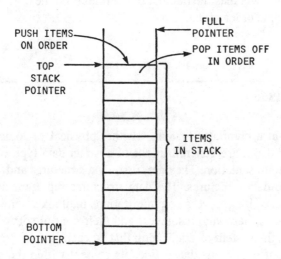

Figure 6.2 **A Stack**

If we use these simple laws or rules in constructing a simulation of a queue or stack, accurate representation of, and experimentation with, it is possible.

6.2 Object Model

An object model requires that these invariant properties be preserved. This is accomplished through the use of encapsulation and appropriate operations. To manipulate an object, an operation is invoked that performs the wanted task, such as push or pop in the stack, or enqueue (append) or dequeue (remove) for the queue data structures. This implies that in order to effect the state or even determine the state of an object, one must perform an appropriate operation on it. The identity of objects is derived from the set of operations for an object. When taken together, these define its behavior to the outside world. The combination of the operations with their internally defined data structures and computations represents an object's instantiation. In present systems utilizing this concept, the number of objects found in a system is large, whereas the number of operations on the objects is relatively small, say on the order of one to ten.

6.2.1 Objects

The objects in a computer system, whether physical or logical (hardware, programs, or data), are generalizations of abstract data types. This refers to the objects' representation. They are, first, data structures and, second, operations on the data structures. The data structures represent data files, executable modules, interprocess communications mailboxes, directories, applications modules, hardware resources, and their control software, which are all viewed in the system as equivalent; that is, each is an object with a fixed invariant set of operations that defines its context within the system. These operations represent how the data structures can be changed during operations.

The objects are referenced (addressed) as singular entities not by their constituent subparts (this is the concept of information hiding and encapsulation). Associated with objects are type designations or specifications that indicate the classification of an object as passive or active (along with subclassifications that delineate the object's view to the system; for example, process object, data object, resource object, communication object). Additionally, the object contains identifiers and information on associations and past history (state). This information is not available to the outside community but is needed mainly by the object manager for housekeeping purposes.

6.2.2 Operations

Objects in such a system are viewed strictly as data structures with external views that can be accessed and changed only by the use of the externally viewed allowable operations (fig. 6.3). The structure of objects differs slightly from system to system, but they all exhibit the same basic components; namely, an external part and an internal part. The external part provides the users' view of the object; namely, the operations allowable and the definition of the externally viewed data types. The internal part is comprised of the internal specification (data types, etc.), data, programs, resources, etc., that is, the actual object being manipulated, its implementation and representation.

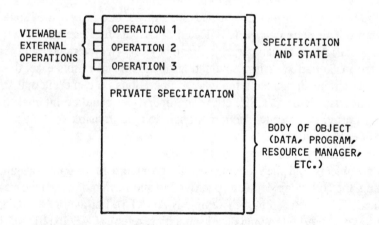

Figure 6.3 **Abstraction of an Object**

Another way of thinking about an object, from an electrical engineering viewpoint, is as a circuit with switches (fig. 6.4).

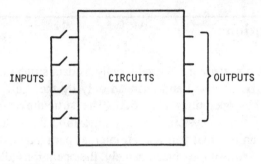

Figure 6.4 **Another View of an Object**

The operations one is allowed to do are represented solely by the setting and unsetting of the switches of the inputs (operations on objects). These are the only things one can affect. When one set's these, one affects the "state" of the circuit. This state change is reflected in outputs that one can view (like public specification or data structure in an object). The internal circuit represents the instantiation or implementation of the object, in this case, the circuit. This circuit implements the wanted operations on some internal structures (circuits, memory, CPU, etc.). The operations required internal to the circuit to provide the wanted external operation are invisible to the user as a result of encapsulation.

The discussion above represents another more abstract view of how to envision objects and their operations. To provide a more complete understanding, the following detailed specification and design of a queue object is provided. The code used in the example is ADATM. For a more detailed explanation of ADA code, syntax, and semantics, refer to [WEGN80].

One of the most common data structures is the queue. It is used in all facets of computer and algorithm design. As described earlier, the behavior of any queue (for example, FIFO) could be defined using four operations. The first one would be used only once, to create or initialize a queue, initializing its state; for example, the create operator would fix the relevant parameters of the queue, such as the number of elements in the queue, start point, and name. Once a queue has been created, the other three operations, append, remove, and destroy, can be invoked by the creators who wish to utilize this data structure. In the following example, only the procedures implementing the four operations would be able to alter the state of the queue. Synchronization of actions necessary to preserve queue invariants will be found in the code bodies of the procedures implementing the append and remove operations.

The general package queue shown in fig. 6.5 provides a finite queue object for use by requesting objects. Each instantiation of the package requires a type parameter that specifies the type of the queued elements. After instantiation, any number of queues may be declared by using the type queue.

To create a queue, Q, the invocation INIT-QUEUE must be made once. This invocation must precede any use of the active operators append and remove. Additionally, to make this a useful construct for applications development, we must have additional operators to check the state of the data structure. These are "is-empty" and "is-full." These operators will provide the capability to determine if there is something in the queue or if it is full. Finally, once a queue is no longer needed, DESTROY-Q should be performed to restore the memory to the system's memory pool. Additionally, for a queue to have usefulness to designers, it must have boundaries; it must have dimension to be realistic. Therefore, a discriminant called "max- Q-elements" is used to specify a minimum requirement on queue size in terms of number of items.

Semantics of append and remove operations must also be included for the handling of conditions in which, if the specified queue is empty and a call to remove is made, an exception must be raised signaling an invalid use of the data structure. If, conversely, the queue is full and a call to append is made, an exception also must be raised signaling an invalid use of the data structure.

```
Generic

    Type eltype is private;

Package queue-P is

    Type queue (MaxQElements:Natural) is limited private;

    Procedure append(Q:in out queue;E:in elttype);
    Procedure remove(Q:in out queue;E:out elttype);
```

```
Function is-empty(Q:in queue) return boolean;
Function is-full(Q:in queue) return boolean;
Procedure init-queue(Q:in out queue);
Procedure destroy-Q(Q:in out queue);

Full Q, Empty-Q ; exception;

Pragma inline (is-empty, is-full, init-queue, destroy-Q).

Private

    Subtype non-negative is integer range O..integer: last;

    type queue (max Q elts:natural) is
        Record

                First-Elt, Last-Elt:Non-Negative:=0;
                Cur-Size:Non-Negative:=0
                Elements: Array (0..Max-Q-Elts) of Elttype;
        End Record;
End Queue-P;

Package Body Queue-P is

    Pragma Inline(Is-Empty, Is-Full, Init-Queue, Destroy-Q);
    Procedure Append (Q: in out queue; E:in Elttype) is
    Begin
            If Q.Cursize=Q.MaxQElts then
                    Raise Full-Queue
            Else
                    Q.Cursize:=Q.Cursize + 1;
                    Q.Lastelt:=Q.Lastelt + 1) Mod Q.Max Q Ects;
                    Q.Elements (Q.Lastelt):=E;
            End if;
    End append;

    Procedure remove (Q: in out queue; E:out Elttype) is
    Begin
            If Q:Cursize=0 then
                    Raise empty-Queue;
                    Else
                    Q.CURSIZE:=Q.CURSIZE-1;
                    Q.FIRSTELT;=(Q.FIRSTELT+1) MOD Q.MAXQELTS;
                    E:=Q.ELEMENTS (Q.FIRSTELT);
                    END IF;
```

END REMOVE;

```
FUNCTION IS-EMPTY (Q;IN QUEUE) RETURN BOOLEAN IS
BEGIN
        RETURN Q.CURSIZE=0;
END IS-EMPTY;

FUNCTION IS-FULL (Q:IN QUEUE) RETURN BOOLEAN IS
BEGIN
        RETURN Q.CURSIZE=Q.MAX-Q-ELTS;
END IS-FULL

PROCEDURE INIT-QUEUE (Q:IN OUT QUEUE) IS
BEGIN
        NULL;
END INIT-QUEUE;

PROCEDURE DESTROY-Q (Q:IN OUT QUEUE) IS
BEGIN
        NULL;
END DESTROY-QUEUE;
END QUEUE-P;
```

Figure 6.5 **Queue Object Example**

What this example shows is a simple nonprotected instantiation of an object, a queue. The object has a data structure that can change only in specific ways; that is, it can be added to or removed from either into the end or from the head of the data structure. The object has provided state information (the is-empty or is-full operator) and manipulation operators (append, remove, init-, destroy). These provide the external view that any user function has of this object (fig. 6.6).

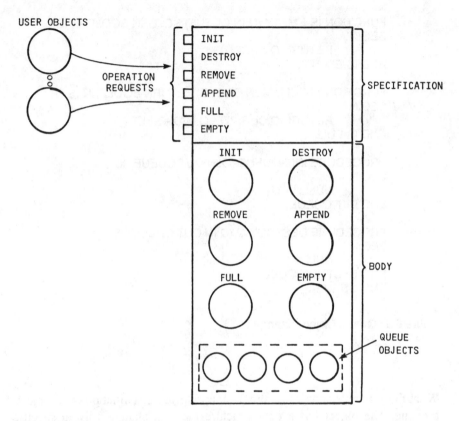

Figure 6.6 **Queue Object Representation**

The object encapsulates (protects) the actual manipulation code and data structure within its body. The body has an internal form comprised of private, protected code and data. These in themselves can also be objects.

This generalized queue object provides to requestors a means to create N queue objects that all have the same qualities, structure, interface, and operations, while still providing for a variety of simple data structures to be stored in the queue (integer, real, character, abstract, etc.).

What the above description provides is a basic view of what constitutes a single object. To build anything truly useful in order to do an end processing job requires the use of many simple objects. Even within an object, other simpler objects may be utilized or may be part of the object in order to provide the requisite service. As a result, the object model provides generic components that can be combined in various fashions to provide the service necessary. This implies that the object model represents a way of building systems that is much different from that shown in the process model. The process model uses large processes, albeit a few, to construct a system, whereas the object model uses numerous simple structures linked together to provide the requisite services. The object model services are more generic and simple, while the process models are specialized and complex.

But building a system using the object model requires the linkage of numerous objects. The object model is a structuring tool; it provides easy mechanisms and policies for linking objects. It does not imply any particular design technique; that is, it can easily be used with top down or bottom up design techniques. In top down, the designer defines high-level system operations on abstract components and iteratively defines the lower-level structures as necessary. In bottom up, the system designer defines the lowest-level constructs, such as queues, lists, trees, data manipulators, etc., and using these, continues to "build up" to a full system. These concepts describe design philosophies that provide to the designers only what they need at a particular time and that allow them to ignore unnecessary details. The designer focuses on the specifications (operations) and implementations (data structures) of the objects with their interactions, devoid of any other implementations.

For example, to build a scheduler the designer may deem it necessary to use top down development. He defines a scheduler object that examines three levels of queues containing ready-to-execute objects. The scheduler then selects one of the entries from the tree, extracts it, and inserts it in the dispatcher queue. The dispatcher, in turn, removes items from its queue, in the order in which it was designed, and places them in the running state, that is, on the physical hardware. Pictorially, this is shown in fig. 6.7.

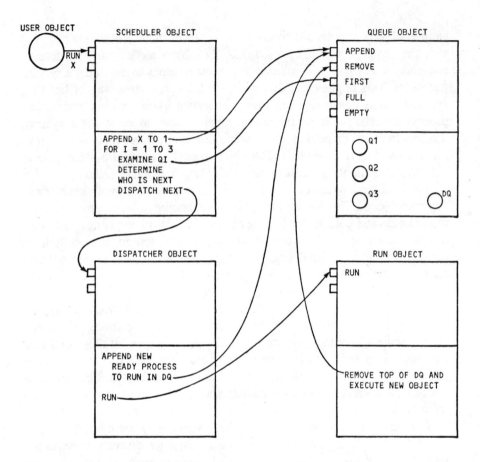

Figure 6.7 **Cooperating Objects**

This is a high-level example, but it does show how, through the combination of disjointed objects, each with their own unique function, operating systems can be built. In more general terms objects interact through requests for service and responses to service. Objects can be nested within objects. As examples: 1. an object could be comprised of a single process (fig. 6.8); 2. an object could be comprised of multiple processes (fig. 6.9); 3. an object could be comprised of multiple processes and shared objects (fig. 6.10); and 4. an object could be composed of multiple processes, shared objects, and nested objects (fig. 6.11).

The Object Model [165]

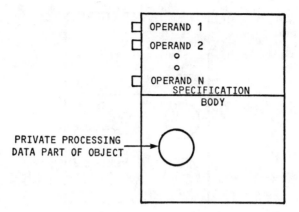

Figure 6.8 **Simple Object**

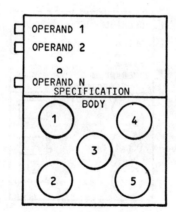

Figure 6.9 **Complex Object**

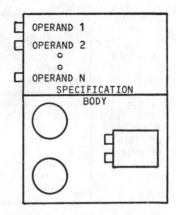

Figure 6.10 **Complex Object with Shared Data Object**

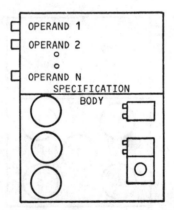

Figure 6.11 **Complex Object with Shared Data and Nested Objects**

Constructing useful systems entails the selection and binding of the objects together, using the requestor server capacity of the objects. The problem with this simplistic view is that it does not take into account conflicts for the objects' use. In order to operate properly, actions on objects must happen completely and accurately or not at all. This implies that objects support failure atomicity. This term, like its use in data-base systems implies, the serialized, nonconflicting, operation of the objects' operations among each other in the system; that is, actions on objects will occur in a given order that provides a proper and correct sequence of state changes on the underlying objects.

6.2.3 Capabilities

To provide this type of service, the object model requires mechanisms that control the interaction and access to the objects comprising the system. The scheme for providing this is composed of the capability and its semantic use. The concepts involved deal with protection, authorization, and precedence. Controlled use of resources (objects) is essential in order to provide logical, efficient, and accurate use of the computer system. For example, certain actions are permissible on physical/logical resources such as CPUs, memories, and peripherals. CPUs can only be executed on; memories can be read or written; disks can be read/written; tapes can be read/written or rewound; programs can be read, written, or executed; data files can be opened, closed, read, written, created, or deleted.

To guarantee the proper use of these objects in the system, they must be controlled to allow them access only to those server objects they have been authorized to access. Additionally, at any point in its execution, an object should be able to access only those resources that it currently requires to complete its execution. This requirement levied on systems is typically referred to as the need-to-know principle. This principle is necessary to limit the amount of mischief a damaged or faulty object can cause to the system. The object model, through its structure, provides some of this protection.

The specification part is the only part known and accessible to the outside world; while the internal part or body is the protected part; that is, the body part is inaccessible by outside forces. Users can request services but cannot actively process the objects' internals. Structure alone, however, will not guarantee the integrity of an object; it cannot guarantee that unwanted users will not access it. Any object could request any other object.

To correct this lack of control, a concept referred to as a "protection domain" is introduced. A process (the active portion within an object) operates within a protection domain or environment, which specifies what resources and rights to it a process may access. Each domain defines a set of objects and the operations that can be invoked on the object by another in the domain. The rights associated with an object provide its protection from unwanted users. These rights, referred to as access rights, provide to a domain the class of services encased within it. All objects operating within that domain have the rights to objects controlled by it (fig. 6.12).

OBJECT \ DOMAIN	FILE 1	FILE 2	TAPE 1	PORT 1	DISK
D1	READ	EXECUTE	—	READ	READ/WRITE
D2	—	—	READ/WRITE	—	—
D3	—	READ	—	WRITE	READ/WRITE
D4	WRITE	—	—	READ	—
DN	WRITE	—	READ	—	READ

Figure 6.12 **Access Matrix**

Typically in systems we would not use an access matrix, since it is usually sparsely populated. Instead we would use an access list. The access list is ordered as a list of pairs of domain and rights associated with each object (fig. 6.13). By doing this, the empty locations can be discarded, thereby more efficiently utilizing the storage available.

```
File/list;
         Domain 1, Read,
         Domain N, write,
End list;
```

Figure 6.13 **Access List**

To access an object On by domain x with operation OP1, we first access the access list for object On. We then scan down the entries, using whatever efficient scheme is in place (hashing, binary search, etc.), looking for Dx "rights." If OP1 is part of the "rights" associated with domain x, the operation is allowed, otherwise it is denied.

Access lists deal more directly with users' needs. Users create objects, and they specify which domains can access the object and what operations can be performed. Access lists are used to provide access, and as such, each access to an object by anybody must be checked. This can get quite expensive in a large system with long lists.

An alternative is used quite often in object-based systems design. Instead of associating the columns of the access matrix (fig. 6.12) with the objects as an access list, we can associate each row with its domain. This provides to the domain the list of objects it can access and the operations it can perform on them. This new association is called a capability list. An object in contemporary systems is represented by a physical address called the capability. To access an object, On and execute operation OP1, the caller specifies the capability for object On as a parameter. The caller, through his possession of the capability, implies access is allowed.

This early discussion does not deal with protection of capabilities. The user must acquire the capability in order to use it. In centralized systems, the capability list is associated with a domain (processes, etc.) but is never directly accessible to any processes executing within it. The list of capabilities is itself protected. It is controlled by an operating system primitive and accessed only indirectly. Capabilities first emerged in multiprogrammed computer systems as a way of providing resource protection. The capability provided an intermediary for all operations within the system. The level of granularity of protection was based on the selection of domain size. A domain could be a single process, a group of processes, or an entire system. The desired degree of security provides the key to the choice of domain size.

For capabilities to perform properly, they needed to be discernible from other items in the system. Typically, this has been done in one of two ways, either by the use of a tag or by protected memory segments. The tag version requires that each capability have associated with it a designator (some number of bits) that inform all that this is a capability. The tag bits typically are managed and only by accessible/discernible hardware, thereby providing the protection from tampering. The alternative method is to associate separate address spaces for capabilities and programs. The capability space is accessible only by the operating system's capability manager. The capability manager receives requests from users, processes these, and provides the capabilities to the users. This manager can be simple or quite elaborate, depending on the desired level of protection and checking. A capability format used in contemporary systems is depicted in fig. 6.14.

TAG	OBJECT ID	ACCESS RIGHTS	LOCATION

Figure 6.14 **Example of Capability**

The tag field is provided to indicate if this word is a capability or an ordinary memory word. This field is needed in systems that cannot otherwise discern a capability from other items in the system.

The object identifier field contains a unique bit pattern that identifies the object referenced by this capability. To guarantee proper use of capabilities, the system must provide for a large number of unique identifiers for all possible objects in the system.

The access rights field typically contains flags for each allowable operation on the addressed object. The condition on the flags will indicate whether a user object has rights to perform an operation or not. For instance, in our previous queue example (Chapter 6, Section 6.2.2) there were six operations: append, remove, initialize, destroy, is-first, and is-last. The access file for this object would have to be at least six bits long, one bit for each operation. If a user is allowed to test or examine only the first element in a queue, the access rights field would contain 000010, indicating that is-first--and nothing else--is allowed by the object that possesses this capability.

The location field, which specifies the beginning location of the object and its boundary, is required so that actual usage and execution of the operations on the object can be performed.

To access a capability, a requestor must provide to the capability manager and "address" that is of the form "capability ID," in which the capability identifier specifies the object and the requestor. These, when taken together, form an address to the object's capability list and an offset into this list for the particular requestor. Before this "address" exists, the requestor first (either at system load, requestor initiation, or at the time of need) must request of the capability manager access to some objects. The capability manager either already has the proper accesses built in or will determine via built-in logic if this user can have rights to this item. In some cases, such as general resources, this is trivial; in others, such as specialized code, dynamic binding of capabilities to user objects is practically impossible for protection reasons.

Once a capability has been allocated to a requestor object, it can use it to perform the allowable operations on the server object.

The requestor object operates on the object by providing its "capability identifier" for the object and its operations. This identifier provides, depending on implementation, either an address into the object's capability list (C List), where the actual access rights are stored, or an address to the entry point of the object and its operation via some form of indirection (address to C List and offset, which provides an entry-point address).

Logically, this process can be equated to that shown in fig. 6.15, which provides a requestor/server view of the capabilities and objects in a system.

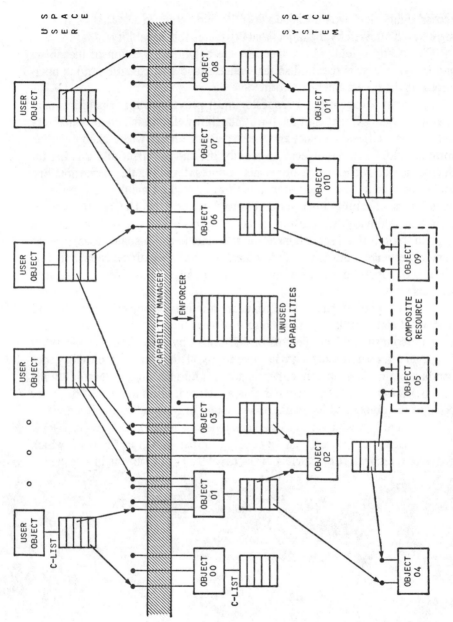

Figure 6.15 Example of Object/Capability Interfacing

The important feature is the control of the accesses via the capabilities. The figure denotes the user objects, server objects, and their associated capabilities. Users and servers collect the capabilities they need to do their job. If the system is comprised of objects that have non-conflicting operations (that is, users do not require the same operations), a simple scheme of allocating capabilities on demand and holding them until done will work. The problem is that resource utilizations and operations do conflict; therefore the object management primitives must control the sequencing of user object operations on underlying objects to guarantee non-interfering operations on the objects. Additionally, to ensure security in actual systems, capabilities are controlled and managed by a singular process and additionally are located in areas of memory protected from any access except from the capability manager. Even though logically each active user object "possesses" (has use of) a set of capabilities, in reality it has access only to the C List via the capability manager using the object and operand nomenclature, for example, Pop(i, stack 1).

The capability manager provides the policies and mechanisms for handling requests for objects, granting capabilities with proper protection, or denying use to a requestor that does not have the right to acquire it. The manager must act for user parent objects by providing to the children objects the rights to parent resources as the parent deems fit. There are typically two levels of objects and privileges in systems: user objects, created, operated on, and deleted by user objects; and system objects, created, operated on, and deleted by the system. User objects will link up via passing of capabilities from one user object to another or via a common global object.

6.2.4 Synchronization

In a distributed system there are complications; objects operating in one machine may need to invoke an operation on an object in another, or may need to invoke many objects on many sites. The object model, if adhered to strictly, would require us to construct a communications object to control and carry out the interobject communications. Synchronization of objects could be performed via operations like semaphores embedded in objects. For example, a signal-and-wait operator embedded in cooperating objects and used properly will provide an adequate level of synchronization in a distributed system. Synchronization techniques for objects (processes) in a distributed system have three main objectives [LELA78]: coordinated broadcasting, serialization of converging flows, and correlation of parallel flows.

Coordinated broadcasting refers to synchronization of the start sequence of N server objects (process). The critical concept in synchronization is that all server objects operations must be initiated and completed. This is similar to data-base transactions that have the requirement that all are performed or none at all. This implies loose synchronization. All the objects used execute, but no particular order is assured, as in a Forth operation.

Serialization of converging flows refers to a synchronization policy in which a number of server objects (processes) are invoked from a requestor object with a known precedence relationship associated with them. This could be as simple as a straight line relationship (fig. 6.16a), a tree structure (fig. 6.16b), or a complex graph, (fig. 6.16c).

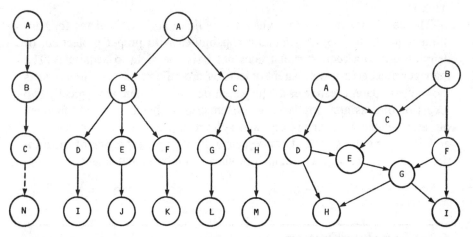

Figure 6.16a, 6.16b, 6.16c **Precedence Relationships for Object Operations**

The important concept for synchronization to derive from these structures is that there exists some serial performance of the operations to construct the proper affect on the underlying objects. The operations and objects may or may not be related in some cases. The assumption is that they must occur in some predefined order to effect the proper change to the data structures. This class of synchronization is converging; that is, computations from multiple sites may need to come together for another to continue (join, rendezvous).

The computations are assumed to be noninterfering; that is, one does not interfere in the proper execution of operations on objects, with another at the same level.

Correlation of parallel flows refers to a synchronization policy in which a number of objects execute in parallel and need service from the same object. For example, if one performs its first operation, then the second performs its first operation on the object, then the first performs its second operation on the object, we could have an error in the consistency of the object's state. A good illustration of this is found in distributed data bases in which we have partially replicated versions of data in a system. The data must be kept current; to do this requires synchronization of reads and writes between the data bases, in particular between the redundant subparts. To write an item, the writer must perform his write on all of the items or none at all. In terms of synchronization, ordering constraints over a number of parallel service requests, some of them interfering with each other, must be controlled.

Many schemes for providing services for object operations' synchronization policies have been designed. One such technique is the physical clock; if hardware could be developed to provide a consistent clock time for all devices, an ordering of a set of operations could be provided through a time-stamp-ordering scheme, which would allow objects to order their operations by time; if my time is less that yours I go first, and you wait.

Another mechanism is explicit control privileges. This scheme provides markers that propagate from one object to another, based on the precedence relationship built into the code. This does not allow for parallel execution and would therefore have poor performance in systems with low synchronization requirements between objects.

Utilization of counters embedded in each object has proven workable. When a synchronization message is issued, all objects increment their counters. When my value equals the counter value, I perform my operation. By setting up the proper sequencing of values in objects and their operations, a proper synchronization of the object's actions can be achieved. Another ordering scheme utilizes the notion of transactions in data-base systems. A set of operations is bounded by a transaction. This transaction will exist in the system with many others that are similar. The transactions operate on the objects in the same manner in which transactions operate on data in data-base systems. All the schemes associated with data-base serializability and atomicity of operations hold. If transactions do not interfere, they can be executed in parallel; if they do, they are serialized based on their interactions.

Serialization is performed in contemporary data-base ways, (that is, using time-stamp ordering, locking, optimistic concurring control, etc.).

This scheme is gaining more support from new systems developers as a tool to aid operating systems designers, particularly in the object-based systems being developed [SHA85].

An example of transaction use in distributed systems will help to clarify the mechanism. In this class of synchronization, processes (objects) are viewed as having two phases, an autonomous phase and a dependent phase. During the autonomous phase, the processes operate separately from each other, and during the dependent phase, their interactions cross. The data-base transaction model provides the synchronization of the autonomous and dependent sections. The autonomous element (like data-base reads) can be performed in parallel, whereas the dependent operations (like data-base writes) must be coordinated to be performed in the proper sequence. There is a problem with this method of synchronization: it can provide synchronization only of logically sequential actions. A further refinement of this model [SHA83] will be discussed in Chapter 8 in the section (8.3.6) on the ARCHONS operating system's synchronization mechanisms.

6.3 Process Management

As in traditional contemporary systems, process management (in this case object management) deals with the policies and mechanisms for controlling the creation, operations, and destruction of objects in the system. To provide the basic mechanisms for building the operating system, the collection of computers must possess a kernel level for providing capability management, object creation, operation, destruction, synchronization, communications, and scheduling. Process management is composed of the kernel level and process management objects.

The capability manager exists on all sites. Each site's capability manager maintains capabilities for objects that reside on it, though they have location information on all capabilities in the system (a directory). The directory is used to steer local requests for capabilities to the site on which they are located. As in the centralized implementation, the capabilities are encapsulated in an object unforgable and unchangeable by requestors. Only the capability manager has the rights and mechanisms to change the state of capabilities under its control.

Addressing of capabilities are by name, and addresses are interpreted by the capability manager. Typically, indirect addressing is used to get into the proper region in memory. The capability manager will then determine if this process has been previously granted rights (a hardware implementation of a mechanism to do this search would be a content-addressable memory). If the requestor has rights, the capability manager grants him the right to access the requested object. Once this is done, the requestor process (object) then directs the requests for service (for example, pop items from stack) to the named object as previously described. If the named object is on another site, the local capability manager will direct the requestor (via a new address computation and message) to the proper capability manager. The capability manager performs the task of granting capabilities in numerous ways. It uses information supplied by the compiler to determine what objects this user object requires and what authority they need to operate on these objects. If they are system objects, the operating system (capability manager) must determine (by the mode of use, past history, operator settings, etc.) how to allocate the system's objects to the requestor(s). Another form of object that must be controlled is the user-defined. The capability reservations and rights of this class of object are provided by the parent object (the creator of the object). The parent or partner object grants the rights to its siblings or pairs as it sees fit. This can be done at run time, load time, or compile time of the objects. The important point here is that the user objects create and migrate their capabilities for themselves to others.

An important job of the kernel is to provide the capacity to create and delete objects dynamically. Creation of objects implies bringing them into the system, making their existence known to all who need to know, and providing them with the level of access and service necessary to ensure their correct operation. The creation action allows the creator to specify where the object will reside, state the object, and the peers it requires for its operation. Operation of objects is performed by the run-time kernel environment. The object scheduled to execute on the device is given control of the device, and it performs its task. Once completed it relinquishes control to the kernel, selects the next object to execute, and so on. This dispatcher, in essence, can be a very simple program or one with many caveats. Its main job, however, is to properly load and unload objects from the operational hardware (a task switch).

Synchronization, as previously discussed, is a very important aspect of operations in any system. In order for an object-based system to operate properly, it, too, requires synchronization. The kernel portion of a distributed operating system must provide some form of synchronization primitive for synchronization to work. Typically, this has been some form of shared variable, such as a mailbox, signal/wait primitives, or serialization policies. Details of this aspect will be shown when example systems are discussed in chapter 8. The kernel must also provide for communications support. The communications between distributed objects can be in the form of shared data objects, message objects, or control interactions. Most systems provide multiple communications primitives to their objects. They typically are either synchronous or asynchronous; that is, either the sender and receiver must be linked up and ready to send and receive, or there is some repository (mailbox, holding bin, queue, stack, etc.) to which the communicated information is sent. The receiver object periodically operates on its receptor to see if anyone has sent anything. This is different from the previous synchronization case, in which the receiver waits, doing nothing else, until the communicated information arrives. There also can be an intermediate level in which the user may have some mix of these on less stringent boundaries. For example, if he is using a repository, instead of him periodically checking it, it could signal him that he has had a communication sent to him. The user then can respond as he sees fit. The benefit is that the receptor object need not periodically check the receptacle (possibly wasting time when nothing is there), it need do this only when something is waiting.

A final major feature of the kernel environment for distributed systems is the scheduler. This kernel primitive must provide a consistent and robust mechanism for scheduling of objects within the system. The goals of the system's operations must be reflected within the policy and mechanisms that implement them; for example, if the scheduler is operating in a real-time environment, it is desirable that the scheduler provide proper schemes to schedule the real-time operations on the objects in response to the system goals. If there is more value to the system in scheduling event Y for operations than event X, event Y should be scheduled; also, scheduling should be based on time remaining in real-time constrained systems. More details on schedulers will be given in Chapters 7 and 8.

Assuming that these primitives exist, process management is comprised of the following tasks:

        Creation of objects
        Synchronization of operations on objects
        Scheduling of objects
        Dispatching
        Deletion of objects
        Communications among objects

The process management object (fig. 6.17) receives requests for operations such as:

> Run X
> Create X
> Abort X
> Block X
> Send X, Y
> Receive X, Y
> Associate X,Y
> Fork
> Join

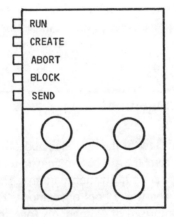

Figure 6.17 **Process Management Object**

It must, using these commands, perform the task required of objects in the running, ready, waiting, and blocked states; that is, the process manager object will take in requests from requestor objects to create new objects, run an object, abort an object, block an object, spawn or join objects, etc. To perform these tasks, the process manager object utilizes the kernel environment that provides the primitives it needs to affect the low-level hardware in the system. For example, to run object Y, the process management object must do the following:

> 1. It must determine if the object is in memory.
> 2. If not, it must find it on secondary storage, allocate

space in memory for it, log it into all the proper locations (capabilities, etc.).
3. It must provide the proper information for scheduling the object in the system.
4. Once it has been scheduled, the object will be pulled out by the kernel dispatcher to place it into the running state.

The same type of process must be performed for each of the other operations required of the process manager.

The similarities between this manager and that of the process model should be clear. The major difference is that the objects being acted on contain all of their state information; it does not need to be stored in some process control block or other data structure separate from the object. We will see some examples of process management in section 8.4.3 of Chapter 8.

6.4 Memory Management

To control the ebb and flow of memory demands, the memory manager object utilizes requests from the process manager to allocate and deallocate space, based on the system's utilization patterns. The memory manager, as in traditional systems, controls a pool of memory. The pool of memory for the entire system is comprised of N subpools (one for each processor). The memory manager has a subpart that exists on each processor. To allocate space to an object, the manager examines his free pool of memory. If the object can fit and the device is compatible (properly attached), the allocation is performed and the pool is adjusted to show the new allocation. To the outside world, the memory manager object has two operations: allocate and deallocate space. The manager also may use internal objects to garbage-collect memory (recover lost memory), to perform compaction (bring used memory together at one end and free memory at the other, forming a larger contiguous space of free memory), to select which objects are the most and the least active, and to determine which objects to remove to provide space for others. This object is a good example of a nested object; that is, it provides a view of how one object utilizes another within itself in performing its task. Figure 6.18 depicts the memory manager object.

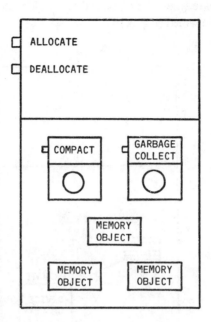

Figure 6.18 **Memory Manager Object**

The linkage to this object will be available only through requests to allocate or deallocate memory. All other memory management functions will be performed oblivious to any other objects in the system. The only object that may need to be involved is the capability manager which needs to have the addresses for the objects being moved adjusted in order to represent the new reality.

6.5 Device Management

In distributed systems controlled by the object model, device management has a very consistent architecture. The physical device is viewed as an object, just as any other item in the system. The physical device is surrounded by a layer of software (the drivers, etc.) that provides the view of the device object to the outside world (fig. 6.19).

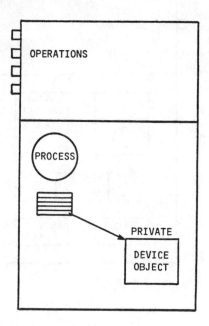

Figure 6.19 **Device Management Object**

The physical device is manipulated by a set of operations, the physical commands that provide the stimulus to the device to perform its designated function. For example, an object to control a tape unit would require operations to rewind, fast forward, and scan (Fig. 6.20). Requestors that wish to utilize a tape drive issue an operation on a tape object, as follows:

> with tape do rewind;
> or
> with tape do fast forward (N) records;
> or
> with tape do scan until record Y;

It is assumed at this point that the operating system has previously granted to the requestor capabilities (authorization for use) to the tape object, to allow access. If this has been done, the previous requests are valid. The requestor can perform the normal tasks associated with tape files.

Another important device that must be manipulated is the disk. This unit is used as a natural extension to the primary memory. As such, there are many requests for input and output to this device. Disk information is stored in the file format; that is, the data stored there is structured as a set of records (files) that are addressable by name. In an object-based implementation of a device manager for a disk, the following operations are important:

    Create file X
    Destroy file X
    Open file X
    Close file X
    Read file X
    Write file X

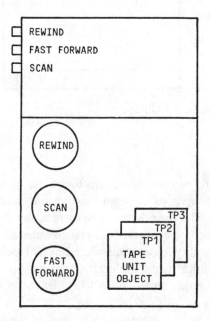

Figure 6.20 **Tape Manager Object**

Using these operations, a disk object can be represented, as in fig. 6.21.

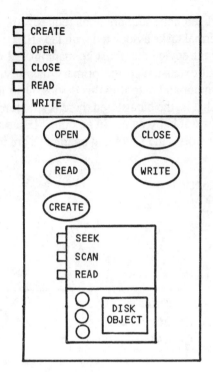

Figure 6.21 **Disk Manager Object**

The requestor would provide operations to the manager to create a new file, destroy an old file, open or close an existing file, read information from a file, or write to it. The user does not have to know the underlying mechanisms that implement the operations, just the operations themselves. This notion aids in the ability to construct mechanisms for control of devices that are devoid of any implementation details. The objects can be constructed to communicate and synchronize with each other to provide a distributed resource network; accomplished by having each object cognizant of its distributed peers, but only from a location view. If the local device manager object cannot meet the need, it is sent to another peer device manager object in the system for services. The user object need not know that the resource it is using is centralized or distributed, only that adequate service is provided to its requests.

Another device encountered in any system is the printer. In an object-based system, the printer, or hardcopy output, object is comprised of a few components: the user object interface, the spooler, and device output/print access controller (fig. 6.22).

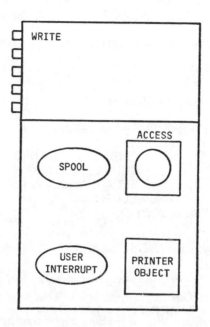

Figure 6.22 **Object/Printer Object**

The user object interface provides the users' view of the entire object; for example, this object could control multiple printers and graphics output devices. The users may view these only as print text, print graphics, or possibly only print with no difference. The object controlling the variety of devices would be required to perform the control of the multiple requests and the management of what device to utilize in meeting the request, based on the information structure provided. For example, if the file provides for output of type text, then a text-quality line printer would be used. Conversely, if what is wanted is type graphics or map or some other iconic abstract type, a graphics-quality printer would be used. This election-type process would hold for other parameters such as color or letter quality. Details of such a control object are shown in fig. 6.23.

```
PACKAGE H-COMP-OUT IS

    TYPE PTYPE IS TEXT, GRAPHIC, COLORG, LETQ;
        (these are defined in detail elsewhere)

    PROCEDURE PRINT (F: IN FILE ; E: IN P-TYPE)

PRIVATE

    SUBTYPE NON-NEG IS INTEGER RANGE
            O .. INTEGER . LAST ;
    TYPE QUEUE (MAX:NATURAL) IS
        RECORD
            FIRST,LAST:NON-NEG:=O;
            CURSIZE:NON-NEG:=O;
            ELT:ARRAY(O..MAX) OF P-TYPE
        END RECORD
END H-COPY-OUT;


PACKAGE BODY H-COPY-OUT IS

    PROCEDURE PRINT (F:IN FILE; E:IN P-TYPE) IS
    BEGIN
        IF P-TYPE = TEXT THEN
            WRITE FILE TO LPT(FREE);
                    WHERE LPT(FREE) IS ANY LINE PRINTER THAT
                    IS FREE;
        ELSE IF P-TYPE = GRAPHIC THEN
            WRITE FILE TO GPT(FREE);
        ELSE IF P-TYPE = COLOR G THEN
            WRITE FILE TO CGPT(FREE);
        ELSE IF P-TYPE = LET-Q THEN
            WRITE FILE TO LQPT(FREE);
        ELSE EXCEPTION RAISED DUE TO INADE-QUATE
            CONDITIONS;
END H-COPY-OUT;
```

Figure 6.23 **Example of Output Hardcopy Object**

The procedure for writing to any of the physical devices require a a spooling-type operation to queue up all files to output to the device, as well as a procedure for controlling the physical transfer of information from the logical files to the device for output.

In the distributed case, the device manager object for each site must contain a directory of device objects on all sites. When a requesting object wishes to have service from an output device to print something, it presents this to its local device manager, which examines it to determine if it can provide the proper service. If it cannot meet the request locally due to inadequate reserve, processing capacity, or not possessing the proper device, it sends the request to a peer device manager on a site that has the proper device. The remote site will then process the request and perform the operation for the requestor.

Details of mechanisms and systems architectures for supporting device management in object systems will be described in Chapter 8.

6.6 I/O Management

Input/output management is concerned with control of the interaction between requestor objects and device server objects, with the goal of maximizing the system's performance in providing for input and output of information. The I/O manager provides the intermediary function, the store-and-forward type operation of files and information in the system. The I/O manager accepts interrupt-type operations for services and from servers, and provides operations to input or output data, and to open or close files, devices, blocks, etc.

The major operations on the I/O manager object are open, close, read, write, wait, block, and signal.

The I/O manager object is the view of the files, devices, etc. that the actual applications objects possess. It provides the interface for them to read or write information. To read or write to a file, for example, the I/O manager typically provides to the user operations and their semantics as follows:

OPEN FILE (FNAME, MODE)

This operation provides a means for users to open a specified file with a given access mode such as read/write, or both.

CLOSE FILE (FNAME)

This operation provides a means to close a file to user use.

READ (FNAME, DNAME, VOLUME)

This operation provides to a user object a means to read information from a file in many forms; that is, you can read byte, word, item, group, or entire file.

WRITE (FNAME, DNAME, VOLUME)

This operation provides a user object with a means to write information from the user object to a file object.

WAIT, BLOCK, SIGNAL

This conditional operation allows a user object to read or write a file, and to either wait in active mode until the operation completes, be blocked and go into a dormant state until the operation completes, or continue on and be signaled when the operation completes.

The operations shown above provide various measures for user objects to synchronize with their I/O operations. Users can use this as one way to perform loose synchronization among themselves. Some additional details of I/O management architectures will be shown in Chapter 8.

6.7 Network Management

A network/communications manager object provides for the inter- and intramode communications facility among cooperating objects. A process (the active code elements within objects) can invoke an operation at a specific instance of an object by sending to it a request message. Knowledge of the location of the receiver is not necessary; only its name needs to be known. The network manager will provide for the proper routing of the message to the receptor. Additionally, a process can invoke a private operation that is enveloped within its local object environment. Generally, in systems built to date, some level of the following operations are included:

SEND (D-OBJ, OPR, MSG)
RECEIVE (D-OBJ, OPR, MSG)
REPLY (D-OBJ, MSG)
REQUEST (D-OBJ, OPR, MSG)

The send primitive allows objects to send a message with operations to any object in the system.

The receive primitive provides a means for objects to ready themselves for communications from any object in the system.

The reply primitive provides a means for objects to respond to requests for communications from another, to respond to a send they were not prepared for, or to indicate to someone that they are ready to accept a send; that is, a message can now be sent in the knowledge that the receiver is awaiting it.

The request primitive provides a mechanism for objects to ask for particular services; for example, they could request for a message to be sent.

The services supplied by this portion of the operating system are typically provided in a kernel level of the object operating system. This is done in response to the number of objects that will use this mechanism and to the requirement for efficient service of the mechanism. Depending on the system, network/communications management may be a basic service using send and receive, or it may be constructed using ports, mailboxes, channels, etc.

The send-and-receive class of system requires that users know the name of the objects they will communicate with, whereas in the port, channel, or mailbox case they need to know only the name of the port, channel or mailbox with which any object is associated. For example, if a communications facility is built on top of a port-object type mechanism, the following view holds:

> Objects are grouped as senders, receivers, ports, and messages. They link together via capability associations.

A typical view of such an architecture and its associations is shown in fig. 6.24. This figure shows a simple sender process, a receive process, a port object, and a message object, Together with the scheme through which the sender and receiver processes can communicate. Clarification of this

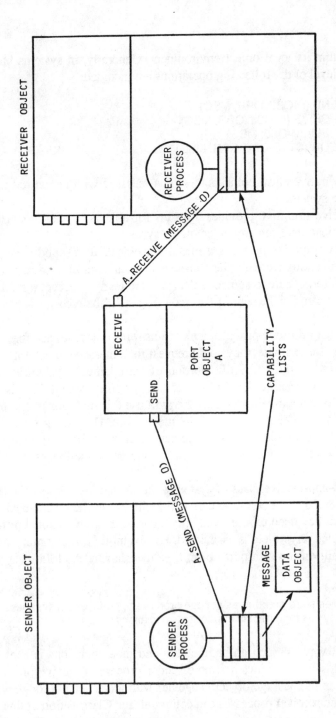

Figure 6.24 Object-based Communications Facility

class of service and details of implementation will be provided when specific systems are addressed in Chapter 8.

Other essential features of operating systems of the object class include: time management, monitoring, and fault isolation services. Time management is an operating system service that provides to objects in the system the capability to determine the system's present time (possibly for synchronization), to instantiate itself on timing boundaries (periods), or to present an alarm to itself on an event (set off a maintenance object every Sunday at 12:00 A.M.).

An operating system should support the means to examine the system's operations and to provide these means to an operator service process. Additionally, it should provide mechanisms to perform fault detection and isolation on itself and its slave or user objects.

6.8 Summary

This chapter provided the reader with a view of what constitutes an architecture for an object-based operating system. The goal was to sketch out the components and workings of such systems without muddling the presentation with unnecessary detail. The details of specific systems, to be shown later, will clear up any gaps in this presentation.

This chapter described the object model in terms of an object that is an encapsulated single processes or a group of processes and data structures, manipulated by operations and controlled through the use of capabilities and their intricate semantics.

Any operating system is comprised of basic management functions, namely: process management, I/O management, memory management, device management, and communications management. The chapter covered these features from an object view.

7. Process-Based Distributed Operating Systems

7.1 Introduction

The previous chapters were concerned with addressing the generic architecture and attributes of distributed operating systems. There was a deliberate intention of only providing upper-level architectural characteristics for the two models discussed. The goal has been to provide an explanation of the basic features and structure of each model so that the reader can approach the following text on specific systems from a knowledgeable standpoint.

The presentation of the process model, described in Chapter 5, stressed two major items:

1. All entities (hardware/software) are controlled and managed by processes.
2. All interaction between these processes is performed via messages.

Most systems, despite variations, have these two basic elements in common. The differences have to do with how stringently a system adheres to either item and how each is implemented; that is, the goals are the same although the policies and mechanisms vary from system to system, as will be seen.

This chapter will provide descriptions of distributed operating systems constructed by utilizing the "process model" of distributed operating system design.

7.2 Chorus

Part of the ongoing efforts of France's Institute for National Research of Information Automation (INRIA) research on distributed systems technology, Chorus is aimed at the understanding of the specifics of distributed applications; that is, it is striving to develop better concepts for control and operation of applications in distributed local area networks.

The Chorus system's designers had specific perceptions on the pros and cons of distributed systems. In particular, the major advantages they stress for distributed systems are security, reliability, simplicity, flexibility, and power. Each of these, in turn, have specific meaning to the Chorus effort.

Security in Chorus is viewed as being realized through physical dispersion; that is, security is provided on a node basis. Each node can lock out others from entering. At the node level, programs and data are protected from each other via a mechanism referred to as an actor. Actors implement a form of monitor exclusion for protection of their given resources.

Reliability is defined as the ability to continue operation in the face of errors and failures. Actors function in sequential steps; therefore their status and results can be checkpointed, and they can facilitate recovery from failures. Through a well-defined set of relationships between its peers and environment, Chorus can readily support reconfiguration.

Simplicity refers to the notion of small and noncomplicated hardware and software. Interactions between these components should be well-defined and few. Chorus is organized around actors and messages. Actors are comprised of sets of sequential processing steps that perform actions on underlying hardware/software or data.

Flexibility refers to the ability of a mechanism to be adjusted or changed without causing undue problems and perturbations on other elements. Traditionally this refers to the concept of modularity. Chorus adheres to this concept religiously, as will be seen.

Power in the context of Chorus refers to the concept of parallel processing. This implies that if tasks can be broken up into many subparts and operated on in parallel (concurrently), the system exhibits more power than do its centralized kin. This, though, is a side effect of distribution use, a goal.

Though the Chorus designers view distribution as the wanted condition, they do recognize its problems, in three categories:

1. Communications overhead and delay
2. Failure rates on components
3. Synchronization problems

Communications in distributed systems have more dimensions than their centralized counterparts. Conversations between elements on one system to another must suffer additional overhead and delay in performing their actions. To address these issues, Chorus has instituted a standard mechanism for interfacing and communicating between actors on the system.

Errors and failures plague all systems, whether distributed or centralized. Distributed systems have a higher overall failure rate because of the volume of elements, although this can be mitigated and even become an advantage if proper mechanisms are put in place to use the additional gear properly.

In Chorus, most controls for error detection and recovery are left up to the user processes to perform.

Synchronization is a crucial item in any operating system. For applications to effectively perform their tasks, they must be able to properly synchronize their actions in some orderly fashion. To do this requires synchronization protocols that could, if improperly chosen and/or implemented, destroy or degrade all the advantages gained by distribution. In response to this concern, Chorus does not provide a specific protocol; it provides a mechanism that allows for a wide range of possible implementations.

Actors represent processes, as in the process model. These actors control and manipulate local objects (passive entities manipulable by actors; for example, data). Actors communicate to each other via ports, using messages. All communication is effected this way. This concept of actors, processes, ports, and messages closely follows the generalized scheme of the process model described in Chapter 5.

Actors in the system control objects (resources), and other actors can access these only via messages to them. Local actors control local physical resources; that is, the site that possesses the physical object resource must have a controlling actor associated with it to effectively provide the controlled manipulation of the object.

As in the process model, distributed applications requiring resources from multiple sites are performed by a set of cooperating processes (actors, in this case). These cooperating processes synchronize and effect control and manipulation of the system's objects via messages. Messages flowing in the system stimulate the action of actors in the system. Cooperating processes set up the mode or type of synchronization they will utilize in their interactions. The operating system does not provide a particular service; it provides a basic capability upon which many schemes can be constructed and utilized in performing synchronization among processes. An example of the concept of actor, ports, and messages will help to clarify the ideas. Two sites, A and B, cooperate in the performance of a task in the system. Site A controls one object, and site B, in conjunction with another actor, controls three objects (fig. 7.1).

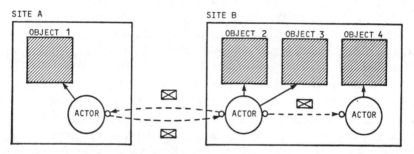

Figure 7.1 **Example of Chorus Concepts**

Through the linkage of actors to objects, ports to actors, and ports to ports, a complete realization of the task's functionality can be constructed. For site A to converse to site B, a port from an actor on one to an actor on another must exist. The cooperating actors set up a synchronization protocol, utilizing message passing. For example, if the actors represent a sales process and an inventory and product line scheduling process, the linkage is to request whether site B's inventory can meet site A's sales. If not, production should be scheduled production via the actor on site B. To make this work, the sales actor (implementing the sales processes) must be linked with the sales data or object, the inventory actor must be linked up with the inventory (object) data on site B and the production scheduling actor must be linked to an object containing all pertinent production data. To work together, ports must be created on each actor and linked to the proper cooperating actor to form the bonds required to realize such a task structure.

7.2.1 Concepts

Some basic notions or concepts relevant to the Chorus structure can now be clarified. Chorus recognizes two distinct process types: local and remote. Local processing is the notion of an actor performing work on its local objects. This type of processing is centralized and can be tightly controlled, whereas distributed processing deals with the interaction of cooperating actors on different sites in performing a single task. Actors are viewed from a systematic view as local sequential processes. Processing is initiated via the reception and interpretation of a message. Once initiated, a Chorus actor can itself send messages to other actors to stimulate requisite processing. An important point is that an actor can perform actions only on local objects. Remote object service requires that a message be sent to the proper actor, linked to the remote object, which then effects the action of the remote object for the requesting actor.

As in the generalized description of the process model, Chorus' actors (processes) utilize a set of primitives within a kernel to support their operations and control in the system. This low-level hardware interface provides the most basic of functions, leaving the actors to implement necessary operating system services.

Kernel functions available to actors for use in building operating systems services and applications processes include:

>   Close-port
>   Create-actor
>   Create-object
>   Destroy-object
>   End-actor
>   Kill-actor
>   Link
>   Open-port
>   Return
>   Select
>   Send
>   Switch
>   Time-out
>   Unlink

This set of kernel primitives represents the core actions necessary to implement an operating system and user application environment. They provide for communications between actors, creation and termination of actors, internal control of actors, linkage of actors to objects, and the creation of objects in the system. When taken together, these give the actors all the power they need to do the system's run-time job.

7.2.2 Communications

As in the generalized view of the process model for distributed operating systems design, the Chorus system employs the concept of processes communicating via conduits (in this case ports) with messages. A message in Chorus is sent from one port (the sending actor) to another (the destination actor's port). The destination can be singular or multiple (broadcast). In addition, ports have no fixed polarization; that is, a port can be used for input of messages or output of messages, though not concurrently. In Chorus, to send a message, the following format is used:

> SEND (SOURCE PORT, DESTINATION PORT(S), MESSAGE);

The semantics of the structure allow for sender and receiver to have full knowledge of the actors involved in transfers. From a system view, the burden of knowing which sites are involved is levied on the kernel that provides the send primitive. Actors view a send to a local actor or a send to a remote actor as equivalent. The kernel will handle transfers through the use of service actors if remote service is required or through the memory, if it is local. The send primitive provides a datagram type service to users. If more resilient and robust service is required, actors must be built on top of the basic send to perform these functions. A mechanism supplied by the kernel provides for some level of error detection in the case of lost messages. This mechanism is the time-out. This primitive provides a means for an actor to time-out or respond to a condition in which a message was not received in the time period expected. This mechanism provides to the actor a capability that allows it to wait for a message, but will not lock up the actor indefinitely. The syntax is:

> TIME-OUT (PORT, TIME);

Port refers to the port name waiting for a message, and time is the period of waiting time from the present time.

Before messages can be sent, a port must exist; that is, it must have been created and associated with an actor before one can send to it. This establishment of the association of a port with an actor is performed by the open port primitive. This primitive allows an actor to open ports only to itself, not to others. Conversely, to disassociate a port and an actor, the kernel provides the close port primitive. This primitive allows the actor who possesses a port to close it (remove it from the system). Ports provide a level of modularity to the actors in the system. Changing an actor's makeup does not ripple into the system; it effects only how the internal object is processed. Outside actors still view the job they want done as being done via port name X, not the underlying actors. This provides a level of encapsulation or hiding of the details. Actors can be created or deleted in the Chorus system through the use of kernel primitives These primitives use information built into parent/child actors to determine the validity of an actor's actions to create or kill another actor.

To create an actor the kernel primitive create-actor is used. Its syntax is shown below:

> CREATE-ACTOR (SITE, MODEL, START-UP MESSAGE, NAME OF ACTOR);

When an actor presents this primitive to the kernel, it examines the validity of this actor's rights to create or delete an actor within this context. The execution of the create command initiates the creation of the actor and the processing of a start-up procedure. The procedure provides the means to establish links to objects, opening of ports, and initiation of conversations with peer actors in the system. Once it has completed this initial start-up procedure, it can act normally in processing requests for services from other actors in the system.

Destruction of an actor can be performed linkwise by the kill-actor primitive. This primitive removes the actor from use in the system and deletes all its links, ports, etc. An actor can likewise terminate itself (suicide) by the end-actor primitive. This provides for a self-destruction mode.

The create construct allows actors to select the site on which they will reside, the group of actors with which they will be involved, start-up messages to actors who will need to know it exists, and the name of the new actor.

7.2.3 Actor Architecture

An actor in Chorus is comprised of a set of sequential processes referred to as processing steps (fig. 7.2). Actors operate by accepting messages that trigger processing steps. Steps are determined via their entry point designations (names).

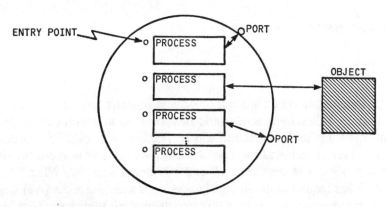

Figure 7.2 **Architecture of an Actor**

Steps are processed sequentially, and an actor can process only one at a time; that is, actors provide only sequential processing of messages. This processing step is an indivisible, uninterruptable unit of work that cannot have any wait operation internally implemented; that is, if a wait is necessary, it must be implemented through use of multiple steps, with the wait being performed by the action of a completed processing step, exit, then dead period (wait), followed by reception of a message that will kick off the next step (fig. 7.3).

[200] Design of Distributed Operating Systems

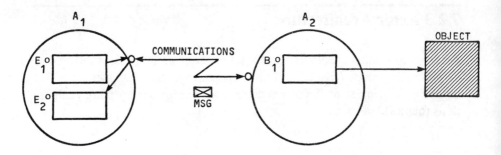

Figure 7.3 **Next-Step Processing**

E1 performs work on an internal object and requests service from an external object. Ordinarily a wait would then be used to prevent anything else from happening until the request was serviced and the result rendered. Chorus, however, does not allow this. The coder would have to break up his job into two steps; a request step, E1, and a response step, E2. When E1 completes, it has requested the service but does not wait. Actor-2,s (A2) step B1 has been requested; it performs this step, then sends a response (request for service) to A1 at step E2. By setting up the actor to accept messages only from A2, we can provide the necessary waiting condition without violating the processing step structure. The problem with this construct is that if multiple messages from many sites are pending, the actor must have a means to specify which of these it wishes to accept next. The kernel provides a means again through a primitive, in this case a select primitive. This primitive either allows for the actors to let the select's procedure choose what message is selected next or provides them the means to dynamically (in line with their code) specify a policy for selection. The format for this primitive is:

SELECT (PORT, CONDITION);

The condition in this case has specific meanings, namely:

All--indicates that any message received on this port
    can be selected
List--indicates that only messages sent from the listed
    port(s) into this port can be selected
None--indicates that this port is being blocked from

receiving any messages

Another modifier of messages is provided through the switch primitive, with the form:

SWITCH (PORT --> ENTRY-POINT);

This primitive provides an actor a means to specifically force a message to a particular port to initiate a specified processing step defined via the entry point.

Once the actor has been entered and a processing step is being executed, nothing can interrupt it until the completion of processing indicated via the return primitive. The significant point here is that the primitives like send will be queued and managed by the kernel procedure but will not actually be executed until the actor executes this return statement. At this time only will the kernel transport the message to the destination.

This mechanism provides a facility that is similar to a data-base transaction; that is, the step completes or does not start at all. This provides a way to organize and synchronize processing steps on atomic action boundaries, about which more will be said later.

The actors do not live alone. They perform their processing steps on objects. Objects are passive entities; that is, they do no work themselves. They need a local actor's processing to affect their state.

To utilize an object, the local actor must possess a link or conduit to it. These links are managed, via the kernel, through the primitives of link and unlink. These provide the capability for an actor to associate or disassociate itself with an object or object in its local realm. The kernel is required to possess the knowledge and capability to determine if an actor can or cannot link to an object. This knowledge is typically associated with the object itself and derived from it. Once the kernel has linked an actor to an object, it does not control the interaction, as is the case in the object model of design. Since control is not lightly performed, Chorus allows actors to directly share an object. Protection or secure use of the object must be worked out with the users. A means to provide security and protection of an object is through the use of a manager actor (fig. 7.4). This share allows for a single actor to control the use of an object by many actors. Additionally, it leaves the partitioning of the actors to sites up for grabs. The actor linked to the object must be on the same site, but all others can be put anywhere.

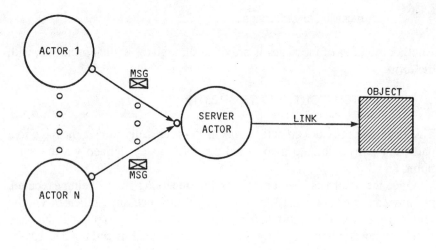

Figure 7.4 **Example of Processing Graph**

Another important aspect or primitive in Chorus is the creation of objects or their destruction. Objects are created via the create-object primitive:

> CREATE-OBJECT (MODEL OF OBJECT, PARAMETERS, NAME);

The model of the object is a structure that describes the structure of the object, creation control procedure, link control procedure, and destruction control procedure.

The structure of the object is similar to the concept of building abstract data types in any programming language. This section of the model of objects provides the specification for the structure of the object. For example, a queue could be defined as follows:

```
TYPE QUEUE IS
    RECORD
        FIRST E, LAST E : NON NEGATIVE : = 0;
        ELEMENTS : ARRAY(0...MAX) OF ELEMENT
TYPE;
    END RECORD;
```

The object-creation control procedure controls who can create this object, whereas the link control procedure of the object specification controls who can associate themselves with this object; finally the destruction control procedure controls how and by whom this object can be destroyed. The destroy procedure is invoked only by the (destroy-object (object name);) primitive.

The other portion of this specification deals with initialization parameters. These are like the unique aspects that delineate one instantiation of an ADA generic from another: parameters such as size or dimension of data structures, access right, mappings of object to physical assets, etc.

7.2.4 Processing Structures

Distributed processing in Chorus maps directly to the graph notion in generic process/message-based environments; that is, any job in the distributed system can be described as a graph, tree, etc., where the nodes represent processes and the arcs or edges represent messages. Pictorially, this is shown in fig. 7.5. The root processing step 1 is initiated via a message received from some other process. The root performs its processing step, then sends messages to trigger processing steps 2 and 3. Processing step 3 does not trigger until it receives the synchronization message from processing step 2.

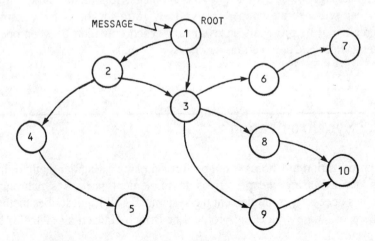

Figure 7.5 **Indirect Sharing**

At this time, processing at step 3 will commence, run to completion, then spawn three other processing steps. These in turn complete, then trigger others, and so on until all complete. Using collections of such steps, designers can structure any processing.

Chorus uses two notions of structures for distributed processing, namely: activities and colloquies.

Activities in Chorus are defined as a group or collection of actors that operate collectively in pursuing a common objective. For example, in a memory management activity, the actors that comprise the activity would collectively pursue the goal of managing the allocation, deallocation, and use of memory in the system. Each of the actors, as part of the activity, has a job that is part of the total function. In memory management, the activity could include an actor on each site that performs garbage collection, one for allocation, one for deallocation, and one for site interaction. All work together under one activity to manage memory for the entire system.

Chorus activities provide a means to organize the administrative aspects of distributed processing. Activities form the basis of recovery and protection in Chorus.

Colloquies in Chorus have a different meaning. They refer to the method by which actors exchange messages and by which they interpret them. The colloquy between actors implements a set of rules for governing how the actors view each other. The run-time realization of the interprocess communications and control protocol governs how the actors will respond to a given message(s). Colloquies provide the means to structure how actors and activities will operate cooperatively. They form the basis for constructing and realizing the protocols necessary for synchronization between operating system actors and applications actors.

7.2.5 Synchronization

Synchronization in Chorus is not performed using a singular method. Instead it is defined using the primitives to implement various synchronization schemes necessary to implement the system. [BANI80] describes methods to implement Hoare's blocking protocol or Brinch-Hanson's [BRIN78] blocking protocol.

For Hoare's method, a "synchronized send" Chorus uses a simple send, switch return combination to set up the sender and a send to set up the receiver. Shown in fig. 7.6 is a framework for the mechanism. Hoare's mechanism will send a synchronization message to the receiver, then block itself until it receives a response. The receiver, upon receipt of the message, will send and acknowledge indicating a successful reception and allowing processing to continue.

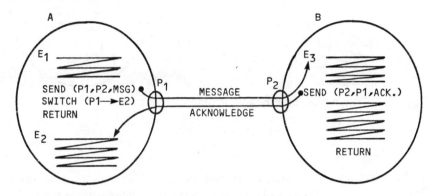

Figure 7.6 **Chorus Notation for Hoare's Blocking Protocol**

The Chorus implementation will act as follows: A.E1 is executing a task that must synchronize with B.E3 before it can continue with its job. To do this, it sends a message to B, then exits this step and waits for an acknowledgment. The wait is set up through the use of the switch procedure which will cause the select procedure to choose only a message on P1 and will switch only to entry point E2, the next step we want. On the receiver side, the message is received, which triggers its processing step. Within the step is a send to port P1 or actor A. This message acknowledges the receipt of the synchronization message and kicks off step E2 in actor A when it is received by A, thus performing the waiting operation on the sender until the processing in B has begun.

Conversely, implementing Brinch-Hanson's method utilizes the same structure, but the send from the receiver is delayed until the end of the processing step (fig. 7.7).

[206] Design of Distributed Operating Systems

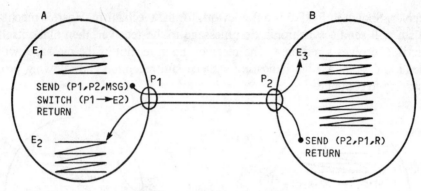

Figure 7.7 **Brinch-Hanson Blocking Protocol**

In this protocol, the sender, A, is blocked until B completes, whereas in Hoare's, the sender is blocked only until the receiver begins processing.

Similar utilization of the send primitive and processing step structuring can allow for structuring of coroutines (fig. 7.8) and fork and join operations/management services (fig. 7.9).

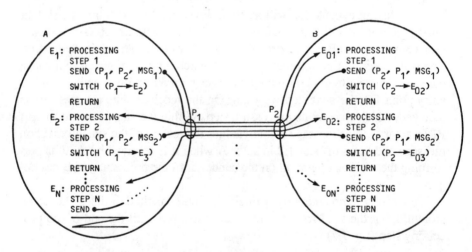

E_1, E_N ARE ENTRY POINTS FOR PROCESSING STEPS FOR CO-ROUTINE A. E_{01}, E_{ON} ARE ENTRY POINTS FOR PROCESSING STEPS FOR CO-ROUTINE B.

Figure 7.8 **Coroutines in Chorus**

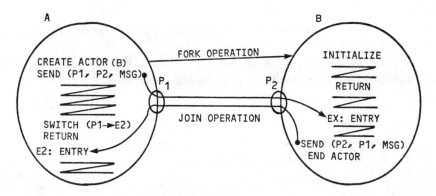

Figure 7.9 **Fork and Join View**

7.2.6 Process Management

Chorus provides primitives to create and delete actors, to create and delete objects, to link actors to objects, and to create, destroy, open, and close ports for actors. Using these, the designers can build an actor manager. This actor has the job of accepting requests for physical assets (CPU) and performing a scheduling of what actor to run, based on the processing structure in place and the protocol for selection. This actor would choose from a list of pending processing steps to determine which should run in what order. Such an actor would have to implement the states of actors as ready, running, or waiting, although the only really important ones are ready and running. Waiting is implemented through synchronization through the scheduler to perform process step $X + 1$ in a sequence of steps. The actor manager implements the requests to create and destroy actors, and to create and destroy or link objects.

The simple fork and join operation shown in figure 7.8 could be generalized to include N forks, all returning back to one site to join. Using these and others, any requisite processing structures for a system could be implemented.

The Chorus architecture provides a basis upon which operating systems can be built; that is, it provides the foundation or primitive structures that allow operating system services such as memory management, process management, I/O management, device management, and network management to create, delete, open, or close ports.

Though far from a regular service point of view, the scheduling and dispatching of actor's processing steps is the most important.

7.2.7 Memory Management

To implement memory management, Chorus uses an actor on each site. The actor performing memory management receives requests from actors who are creating other actors or objects for memory assets. The memory manager actor examines its object (the memory map) to determine if memory is available. If it is, it sends the address to the requesting actor for the new actor or object. Other requests sent to the memory manager are concerned with deallocating memory. When this type of request is received, the actor removes this block of memory from use by flagging it free and inserting it back into the pool of free memory. Additionally, the memory manager actor must provide a processing step that reorganizes memory periodically or on some boundary. This step is compaction and coalescence of holes (free memory), otherwise known as garbage collection. The management of the pages in memory can be performed much as in contemporary systems, using data structures such as free lists to describe it and processing steps in line with processes now used to perform the individual tasks of allocation, deallocation, and garbage collection.

7.2.8 Device Management

The Chorus device managers are viewed as actors in the sense as described in the previous section. They are linked to the physical object (device). They are controlling and have processing steps that mimic the operations of the device. For example, a tape manager actor would possess entry points to rewind, read, and write (fig. 7.10a).

Other actors who need use of a tape unit to read or write files would request service by sending a message to rewind a tape, write a tape file, or read a tape file. Generally, to construct an actor to implement service on a device, the following framework illustrated in fig. 7.10b will suffice.

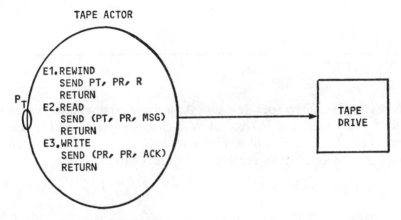

Figure 7.10a **Tape Manager Actor**

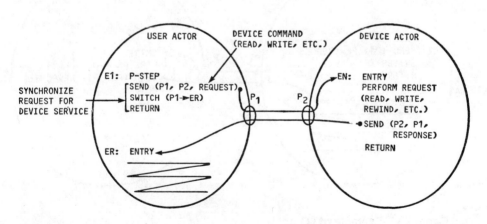

Figure 7.10b **Generalization of Server and Requestor**

This method of having the requestors send a message containing the requests (entry point) provides the means to service the requests for any type service on the objects. Using this structure any type of device can be modeled.

7.2.9 I/O Management

Chorus handles I/O by specific actors. An actor who must perform a read or write operation sends an I/O request message to the appropriate I/O manager actor. Later this sender will receive a response back with the appropriate message from the I/O manager. Fig. 7.11 depicts how this is done.

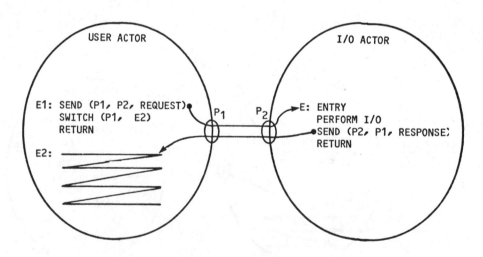

Figure 7.11 **Example of I/O Actor**

7.2.10 File Management

File management is an important aspect of overall systems management. All processes begin by being read in from a storage device as a file, and their outputs are typically ultimately written back to a file. Chorus provides for this need through the use of a file manager actor whose job it is to handle requests for reading or writing items from or to a file. The file manager handles the logical access of files in a system for the users. It will interface with I/O and device managers to acquire the proper file for users.

The user requests a file, via the send primitive; the file manager receives this message and initiates the processing step for a file read. It sends a request for an I/O service to read from a device. The I/O server initiates message transfers with the device manager to retrieve the file. This is then sent back through the response chain to the user. All file management actors seen in contemporary systems (Chapter 2) will be implemented in this way, using the send primitive (messages) to synchronize the processing steps in the proper order to effect the job of file management.

7.2.11 Network Management

Chorus implements network communications management the same way it does all the other operating systems functions. That is, it uses actors and message passing to coordinate this activity.

For local actor-to-actor communications, the simple send primitive suffices; that is, the local kernel will implement the communication between local entities. If the destination port is remote, the kernel passes the message over to a special actor (transport actor) on its local site. This transport actor handles the interaction with the network and its protocols in communicating over the physical lines and with remote transport actors. Once the message is received at the remote destination transport server, it is reformed into a local message that can then be sent through the kernel to the final destination port. The transport servers collectively perform the distributed transport service corresponding roughly to the four lower layers of the open system's interconnection reference model [OSI79]. This is viewed pictorially in fig. 7.12.

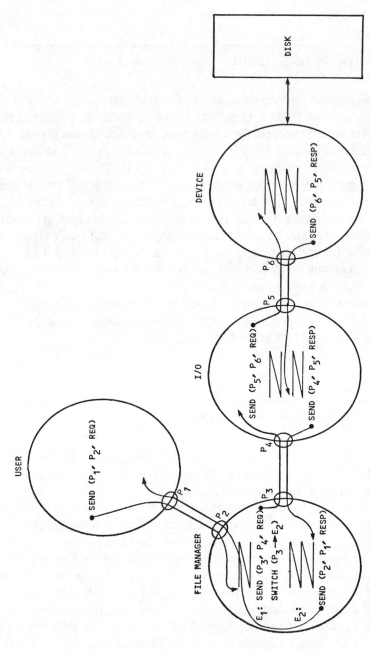

Figure 7.12 Logical Flow for Requests for a File Read

The OSI model entities can be mapped one-to-one to Chorus modules, thereby providing similar services.

The Chorus architecture, as shown, can and has been used to construct a distributed operating system. More will be learned from this system based on experimentation and use as the system evolves. More details of this system can be found in [BANI80], [ZIMM81], [GUIL82].

7.3 Thoth/Hermes

Thoth/Hermes is an operating system developed in the late 1970s at the university of Waterloo and extended to networks by Burroughs Corporation. In Egyptian mythology, Thoth ruled Egypt for 3226 years. Endowed with complete knowledge and wisdom, the inventor of all arts and sciences, Thoth was the all to everyone at all times and for all conditions [LONS68], and his name was thus hopefully attached to this operating system. Thoth uses a message/process-based architecture to implement its services.

7.3.1 Concepts

As in the generic case and in Chorus, Thoth looks at the decomposition of the job in the system into multiple processes. A process is defined as a sequence of actions that can logically (in a data-base sense) execute concurrently with other processes. The use of messages as stimulating events provides a means to synchronize the disjointed processes. The messages being passed in the system provide both data and control through the proper use and interpretation of the mechanism.

The major issues in the Thoth environment, as in Chorus, deal with process management and communications. It has been previously shown that if these basics can be provided, an operating environment can readily be built on top. In Thoth the major mechanisms are:

        Process creation
        Process synchronization
        Process identification

Interprocess message-passing
Process destruction
Process death-detection

In Thoth, the major difference between the needs of the distributed system and the centralized is in its ability to detect and react to death or failure of processes. The use of the process-to-process interaction model provides a means for centralized or distributed interacting processes to view each other as equal, thereby making it easy to move processes around due to failure, death, etc.

The early Thoth system attempted to provide a structure that would form a basis for easily extending the operating system to a distributed environment.

The fundamental component of Thoth is the process. Structuring and interaction occur only via messages. Messages indicate to processes their operations that must occur for the proper organization of actions. The message-passing paradigm utilizes the concept of process blocking to provide the synchronization. As previously shown, a process-blocking protocol prevents the sender from executing until a specific condition (response) is met.

To provide the basic process-structuring, control, and interaction primitives necessary to build an operating system, the Thoth system has defined the following kernel commands or functions.

```
Processes
    ID  =  .Create (funct, stack-size)
    ID  =  .Ready (ID, argument-list)
    VEC =  .Auoc-vec (size)
    VEC =  .Free (Vec)
    ID  =  .Send (Msg,ID)
    ID  =  .Receive (Msg, ID)
    ID  =  .Reply (Msg, ID)
    ID  =  .Forward (Msg, From-ID, To-ID)
    ID  =  .Await-Interrupt (Device-ID)
    ID  =  .Destroy (ID)
    ID  =  .Sleep (Time-and-date)
    ID  =  .Delay (Seconds)
    ID  =  Get-Time (Time-and-date)
    ID  =  .Set-Time (Time-and-date)

I/O
    FCB  =  .Open (Path name,mode)
    FCB  =  .Select-Input (FCB)
    FCB  =  .Select-Output (FCB)
    Data =  .Get ( )
```

```
             Data =   .Put (Data)
             Data =   .Flush ( )
             Data =   .Seek (FCB,where,how)
             Data =   .Close (FCB)
      File system
                      .Set-current-node (Path name)
                      .Make-Node (Path name)
                      .Remove-Node (Path name)
                      .Graft (Path name, device-name)
                      .Ungraft (Path name)
                      .Change-File (FCB<size-in-blocks)
      Position = .Where (FCB)
                      .Mark
                      .Seek-Mark (FCB)
                      .At-Mark (FCB)
```

From this list it can be seen that the basic functions of Thoth are many more than those of Chorus. However, the basic notion still holds. These all are processes and use messages passed between them to effect the control and operations of the system. The following paragraphs will elaborate somewhat on the meaning of each construct above and bring out more fully the global architecture of the Local Area Network version of Thoth and its interactions.

7.3.2 Process Management

Processes in the Thoth environment are part of a program tree. A program tree is comprised of processes which interact with the system via the system function calls or core services. The user processes are therefore part of a system tree that encompasses them and the system processes.

Processes in Thoth are created using the create function. This function creates a process in the system with a unique ID. The process is derived from the function code provided via the function pointer (part of the create semantics). Associated with the process is a stack that is used during run time to manage its state.

This command creates the process in what is called an embryonic state; it does not allow execution, only creation. To operate, the .Ready (ID,Any-list) function is invoked. This system function provides the necessary initialized parameters for the process and provides the process to the scheduler for service. The initial scheduling mechanism described in [CHER79] refers to a simple scheme that selects the process that has been waiting the longest and has the highest priority to go next. Processes run to completion unless preempted by a higher priority process. The create command provides an ID to the process that is then used for all interaction with this process during its life.

The death of a process is accomplished through the use of the Destroy(ID) function. The use of this function provides a means to terminate one's own process or others. The destruction of a process causes all its descendants in its processing tree to also be destroyed.

To aid processing of real-time tasks, a goal in Thoth, the system provides functions dealing with the use of time. In particular, Thoth provides functions to put processes to sleep for some period of time and to awake. Sleep (time-and-date) and .Delay (seconds) functions provide processes a way of suspending processing, pending a scheduled time-driven event, or of entering periodically to perform some test.

Thoth also provides a means to adjust or read the present time in the system using .Get-time(time-and-date) or .Set-time (time-and-date). To interact with other processes, the Thoth environment provides functions to send, receive, or wait for messages and additionally to wait for a specific interrupt to occur. These mechanisms provide the interprocess synchronization and control.

Four basic primitives are provided to implement process communications. They are .Send, .Receive, .Reply, and .Forward. Used together, they provide all the necessary synchronization for processes. The Send primitive

    Status = .Send (Msg, ID

provides a means to send a block of information from the source process to a sending process defined by the ID. When the sending process invokes the Send primitive, it blocks until it receives a reply from the receiving process. To receive a message, a process must have a .Receive primitive. The receiver blocks and waits until it receives a message. The receive process can either perform a dedicated receive:

    Status = .Receive (Msg, ID)

or a generic receive:

Status = Receive (Msg)

These two modes of receives provide mechanisms to implement synchronized send and receive sequences for specific process interactions or generic receives to allow for acceptance of messages from any source. For example, the directed receive would allow for a requestor (user) to synchronize with a server (tape) as follows:

```
Program requestor
    Var server:Process-ID-Type
    Status, Send:Message type
begin
    Do work (processing)
    Read tape file
    Sender:=(send msg, server)
    (*Wait for returned message*)
    Receive (Msg server)
    (*Do noncritical processing*)
end
```

```
Program Server
    Var requestor:Process-ID-Type
    Status, request:message-type
    begin
    While true do
    begin
        Requestor:=.Receive(request);
        .(*Perform critical service*);
        (*Read/write/rewind tape*);
        (*Prepare status message*);
        .Reply (status, requestor);
        (*Perform cleanup*)
    end;
end.
```

Another function used in this sequence is the .Receive primitive. This allows a receiving process to sensitize itself to a requestor's send primitive, followed by the .Reply primitive. The acceptance of this message allows the sending processing to be readied to go on.

In some cases a receiver is not the final destination for a message but just an intermediary (fig. 7.13)

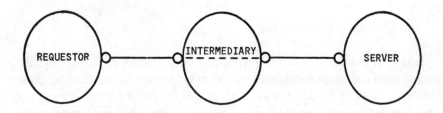

Figure 7.13 Forward Function View

This function blocks all the processes in the path until the reply is sent back through the path.

A final primitive implementation in Thoth to handle specific events (interrupts) is the .Await-Interrupt(Device-ID). This primitive provides the means for processes to await service returns from specific devices. Interrupts in Thoth can only occur when no processes of the same or higher priority are active. The interrupt causes the waiting process to become ready and active.

7.3.3 I/O Management

The Thoth system control paradigm provides specific functions to implement I/O control for the system. It provides a fairly consistent interface for peripheral devices and files, therefore allowing for interchangeability by programs. Devices are assigned specific logical names, and files are represented by their path name (map or list string).

Thoth provides simple constructs to access data stored in either structure. A file or device is accessed (readied) by the FCB=.Open (Path name,Mode) primitive. This primitive returns a pointer to a file control block (Chapter 2) that contains a description of the accessed device or file and any necessary buffer. The descriptor can now be used as an identifier to the file. The mode identifier in the primitive indicates how the file will be used (read, write, append, or read/write). Once initialized, the file control block can be used to transfer data to or from the file or device. To use an opened file or device, a process must perform the .Select-Input(FCB) or .Select-Output (FCB). Once selected a process can input or output data from or to a device or file using the Data=.Get( ) or .Put(data). These transfers occur at a byte at a time.

Other file or device primitives include .Flush( ), which cleans out the buffers of the selected file for output, and .Seek(FCB,where,how) which allows processes to access devices directly. Once finished with a file, the .Close(FCB) primitive flushes out the buffers, removes the rights to access the file, and releases the held resources.

An extension to the basic services described above is provided for file systems. These services provide for more efficient access to files by providing processes to remember the state of a previous access (.Set-current-node(path name)) of the storage tree or to modify the tree (.Remove-node(Path name), .Make-node(Path name), .Graft(Path name, device-name), Ungraft(Path name)).

The .Set-current-node primitive provides a means to access nodes more easily by adjusting the entry point to the tree.

.Remove-node or .Make-node provides a means to prune or grow a tree. Similarly .Graft and .Ungraft provides a way to add or delete subtrees from the file system.

Using these primitives system processes can adjust the operational environment based on file migration, failures, etc. General file manipulation primitives are provided by the change file, where, and mark primitives. The .Change-file(FCB,Size-in- blocks) primitive provides the means to adjust the limits of a file specification. The position=.where(FCB) primitive provides back the position of the current byte position (pointer). The final construct, the Mark, generalizes the concept of end of file by providing a way to set the position of the mark or end of file designator. This aids in the ability to append to files or determine file lengths.

7.3.4 Memory Management

The last basic concept in Thoth is memory allocation. A contiguous vector of memory is allocated by the system call Vec=.Alloc-Vec(size). The function returns to the caller a pointer to a vector of size + 1 words. The allocation of the memory is performed by a next fit algorithm based on Knut's boundary tag method [KNUT69]. To free up memory when, for example, exiting the system, the .Free(Vec) primitive is invoked. This primitive returns the vector to the free list of available storage.

The foregoing constructs described the basic structure available through the Thoth system's architecture. These two facilities can be used to construct services that are distributed throughout the system. Implicit in this is the structuring of this collection of services utilizing higher order protocols to realize a working system.

The basic notion used in Thoth and its extensions is the client/server. In this environment, a "client" is defined as a process that request's the use of shared resources and the server is a process that provides the control and usage of the resources under their control.

Using such a client/server view, resources (printers, CPUs, I/O devices, networks, other processes, etc.) would be controlled by server processes, and processes that need these resources would be controlled in the client process. Clients would request services from servers, who would provide them with some predefined protocol. For example, to implement a printer server, the operating system designer would provide a server process (prints) that provides the printer service to all requestors. To utilize this server, a requestor must:

1. Establish a connection between the client application and the server
2. Transfer data from the client to the server
3. Dissolve the connection when complete

To illustrate the concept of operation a simple generic server (printer) model will be further refined. Initially, the server process is not in use. It has registered with all the remote and local site to indicate its existence. Following this phase, the server process performs a generic .Receive primitive, thereby providing itself for service requests from anyone who wishes it (fig. 7.14).

At this point, any client process which needs the services of a printer can get them by initiating a link to the server. This is performed by creating a client agent (communications server) to provide the distributed network service. Client agent asks to find if a server of the type printer exists. The

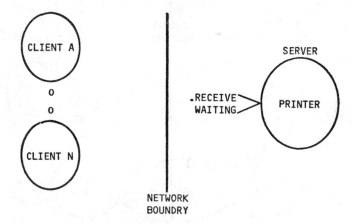

Figure 7.14 **Server Waiting for Requests**

server (printer) process sends back a network identifier indicating its location; that is, it indicates the server's network server (server agent) location. The client agent converses with the server agent to solidify the link. Once that is completed, the client can initiate data transfer by issuing a .Send to its client agent. The client agent performs any necessary packetization (breakdown) of the data and initiates a series of .Sends to the server agent to effect the transfer. Once the server agent has the entire data message sent by the client, it transmits it to the server (fig. 7.15).

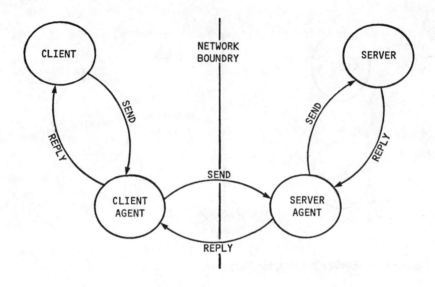

Figure 7.15 **Distributed Communications with Client/Server**

Once the transfer is completed the server sends a status message back through the chain to the client to indicate the success of the operation.

To relinquish use of the server, the client simply destroys its client agent. The server agent ultimately detects this and performs any necessary cleanup before destroying itself. The server now goes back into a wait state, waiting for the next client to request service.

A more complex server could be an administrator type of server. Such a server controls access to N subservers utilizing the same protocol. Pictorially this type of resource controller is shown in fig. 7.16.

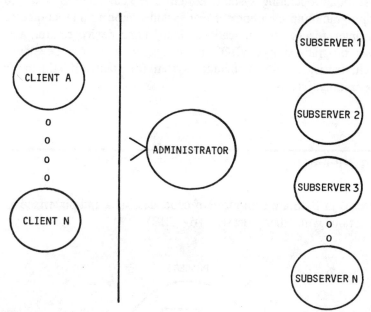

Figure 7.16 **Administrator Servor**

The N subservers, through the administrator, can be accessed to service one of N clients. A representation of such a beast would be a disk-pool controller process that would control the access to N disk units.

Using this type of process of constructing servers to provide control and management of global or local assets, a fully distributed operating system that provides all the necessary functions can be built.

For details on the architecture and use of this operating system see references [CHER79], [CHER82a], [CHER82b], [ANDE82], [HIRSCHY83].

7.4 Basic Operating System (BOS)

Basic Operating System (BOS) was developed for the distributed computer network (DCN) system in the mid to late 1970s. It represents an early effort at distributed operating systems design. The goal of BOS is to provide a multiprogramming environment that includes process and storage management, interprocess communications, input/output device control, and applications program support. BOS is an operating system developed from scratch; that is, it is not an operating system for a network built on top of local operating systems.

7.4.1 Processes

Processes in BOS are comprised of code, data, and and pinterface for communications with other processes, (fig. 7.17).

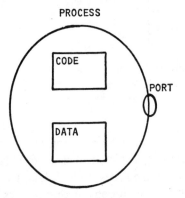

Figure 7.17 **BOS Process**

Control of the interaction between applications processes is performed by a set of kernel processes distributed throughout the system.

BOS architecture consists of three types of processes: supervisor, system, and user.

The supervisory processes are similar to those delegated to a kernel in the previous systems. BOS possesses processes to schedule processes, dispatch device interrupts, coordinate interprocess communications, and provide synchronization to the processes in the system.

The system processes provide mechanisms for I/O management, network management, and device management for the system.

User processes are collections of programs provided by users of the system for execution.

Processes in BOS can be in one of four states (fig. 7.18): running, pending, blocked, or waiting.

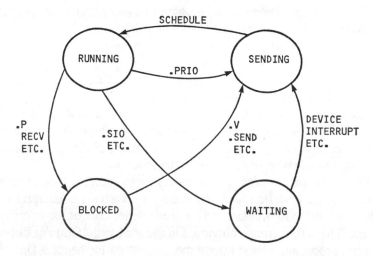

Figure 7.18 **BOS Process**

As in any operating system, a process in the running state has control of the CPU and can execute its code. A process in the pending state is ready to run but is waiting to get access to the CPU via the scheduling mechanism. A process in the blocked state is waiting for a message or a semaphore to release it. Finally, a process in the waiting state is idle, waiting for an event such as an interrupt to occur. When this occurs it is put into a ready to run state (the pending state).

Processes in BOS either run to completion or are interrupted by the supervisor due to an event such as a high- priority interrupt.

7.4.2 Communications

Communications between processes in BOS, whether internal to a site or between sites, are handled via a highly developed message-passing mechanism. The message-passing mechanism is provided via supervisor primitives for sending and synchronizing interprocess communications. As in other process-based architecture, the concept of port is utilized in BOS. BOS allows for one or more ports to be allocated to a process on request. Ports are allocated to only one process at a time, but any process can send to it at any time. Each process, when created, is assigned a system port that is used for system messages. Port addresses in BOS are comprised of two parts: a host ID and a process ID. Such a combination provides a means to efficiently extract out and use host information for routing, etc.

Once a process has access to a port address, it can send messages to that port at any time. Receiving processes can select messages from ports as they see fit. The supervisory process has mechanisms to aid in the reception, enqueueing, and releasing of messages to the processes.

The supervisor provides service processes to accept messages for transfer, formatting, buffering, and translation. Messages are interpreted by a header that indicates whether it is a read, write, control, or acknowledge message. These formatting notions aid in the ability of BOS to quickly interpret what processing is to be performed, based on the header. This aids in the process's ability to decipher the data being received.

7.4.3 Architecture

Processes communicate via ports and use system services to perform the synchronization and control of their interactions. Users are created and provided a system port as described earlier. They then create ports for input and output to other users. To communicate to other processes, the port mechanism provides a means to find out where processes are; that is, user processes can query the port manager to determine the location and port association of any other process with which they wish to communicate. Once they have the port information, the processes can then begin an interactive computing session. They can perform processing and synchronization with each other via messages.

Synchronization in BOS has two dimensions: a local one and a remote one. For local synchronization, BOS defines semaphores P and V. The use of semaphores allows local processes a capability to implement a wide range of synchronization protocols. The basic operation of the mechanisms are as follows:

The P operation causes a process to go into a conditional wait. If the semaphore queue is now empty, the process blocks and places itself in the queue, waiting for the signal operation (V) to release it.

The V operation signals to the waiting queue to resume the waiting process. If no process is waiting, the V operation sets up a queue to immediately release a process when it enters. This implies that a P operation that encounters an empty queue with a pending V operation will not wait, it will stay in the running state.

7.4.4 Supervisor

The supervisor processes provide the mechanisms to user processes for process switching, scheduling, dispatching, message transmission, process creation, destruction, interrupt processing, and storage allocation. The primitives are:

Supervisory
- INIT - Call initialize routine, start up
- PRIO - Reset priority of caller to supplied value
- WAIT - Enter the process wait state
- SKED - Enter the pending state (FIFO scheduling)
- ERRR - Force error interrupt
- SETV - Create device interrupt vector

Timing
- TICK - Suspend caller for number of specified clock ticks
- STIM - Suspend caller for number of specified milliseconds
- CTIM - Remove a timer operation from queue

Semaphores
- PSEM - Perform the wait operation on port specified

VSEM - Perform the signal operation on port specified

Message
- GPRT - Allocate a port to caller
- RECV - Wait for input message on specified port
- RECA - Wait for input message on any port
- SEND - Send message to port
- PUTH - Construct header for message
- GETH - Get header of next message
- CLSE - Terminate output message
- TPRT - Set condition code to specific ports
- BKSP - Delete specified byte from output message
- CNCL - Delete entire current message
- ASYN - Generate an interrupt to specified port

These supervisory primitive processes are used by the system processes to implement the system protocols for user processes. BOS defines four levels of interaction within its architecture. At level O, the supervisory has been described. Level 1 is the message interface; user processes utilize it to synchronize and communicate with one another. This level is a primitive boundary, with synchronization and transfer mechanisms using four constructs:

- MSGBGN - To indicate the start of a message and format the data required
- MSGEND - To indicate the end of a message and suspend the process pending the reception of an acknowledgement
- RDASL - Read the next byte of input message
- PRASC - Write the next byte of the output message

These still are not at the user upper level. Level 2, taken with level 1 provides users with a basic byte-oriented interface with each other. This level provides basic message read ability and port status ability.

The final level, 3, provides full message level transmission and interface. The commands available at this level include:

- READR - Read input message from port
- WRITER - Write output message to port P*
- EOF - Write end of file output message P*
- ATTN - Write attention output message
- CTRL - Write control messageP*
- ASSIGN - Assign physical port (buffer) to logical port name

Level 3 within BOS is the command language interface. This level provides the mechanisms (processes) to create processes, link processes, initiate processes, and communicate with processes. This is more typical of the view shown in the previous presentations and nearer to the process model view of distributed operating systems.

Processes at this level exist to manage logical (physical) devices, to allocate storage, and to create, destroy, and initiate processes, among other functions.

An important point about BOS is that it provides only basic services to read, write, control, and acknowledge messages. Control and processing flow is effected by the interpretation of messages flowing in the system between processes (user and system).

The command language interface provides to users the ability to:

> Associate files and devices with a logical port
>   using the ASG (port, device, or file[s])
> Send a control message to a port using CTRL (port, message)
> Send a message to a port using MSG (port, message)
> Send an interrupt to a port with a message ATTN (port, message)
> Initiate execution of an applications program (process)
>   associated with a port using START (port,   parameters)
> Provide a means to spawn new processes using FORK
>   (port, message)
> Rejoin parallel streams using the Join and End commands

Using this collection of services, users can construct an environment to perform a given task. User processes communicate control, data, and status to each other via the primitives, and can synchronize properly among each other by constructing the proper semaphore mechanisms between themselves.

BOS was an early process-based operating system that provided a model from which others can build. More details of BOS's architecture and its use can be found in [MILLS75a], [MILLS75b], and [MILLS76].

7.5 RTDOS

The real-time distributed operating system (RTDOS) has been developed to provide a hierarchical set of functions that provide applications processes with system management services, controls, and network services for a wide range of real-time processing requirements.

7.5.1 Processes

The hierarchical approach was chosen in response to the processing requirements and structure exhibited in real-time systems (fig. 7.19). Generically, the system's architecture for real-time command and control systems have three major processing categories:

> Real-time processing control
> Information processing and reduction
> Human/machine processing and control

At the lowest level (real-time processing and control), the processing and control is associated with collecting real-world stimuli, processing this to determine its state and effects, and providing an appropriate response (control action or data transfer to steer the real world components), all within a fixed time frame. Such a real-time environment requires a closed loop, deadline-driven, and prioritized processing and control stream to provide the requisite turnaround time. The operating system at this level is rudimentary; that is, it is concerned only with providing service to a few processes and does not require extensive controls, which add overhead. Typically, low-level controllers run one to three processes to control a particular piece of hardware. The processes run at this level perform sampling and detection of the external stimuli, processing and control determination of inputted data, response interaction (control), and data forwarding (monitoring) for control determination of upper-level systems.

The operating system at this level is typically a scheduler and dispatcher that provides deadline-driven, prioritized access to the computer for the limited set of users. The number of processes stays stagnant, and their processing priorities, value relationships, and precedence relationships do not vary much over time. The operating system typically has few states, and most commonly has two: ready and running (fig. 7.20). These states provide the interaction between the active and waiting to run processes; scheduling is the main job of the operating system at this point.

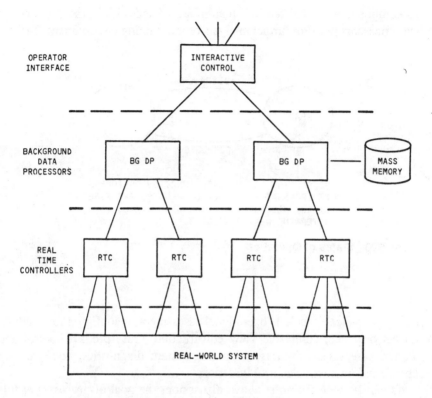

Figure 7.19 **Generic Architecture of Real-Time Systems**

The real-time controllers provide status and reduced data for the background data-processing level. The background data processors are concerned with reception and further processing of low-level reduced real-world stimuli information. For example, in an automated factory, the robotic builders run simple programs continuously, in a loop that allows them to select components and assemble them into a portion of a total product. The job is interactive and very well structured. The real-time controller operating in a robotic assembler's node performs the control programs to effect its motions properly. This device also reports up to a cluster controller (background data processor) with status and information on its actions. The background data processor incorporates many of these inputs from multiple devices to build a composite view of the operations of a section of the production line. Using this composite view and the information associated with it, the background data processors perform further analysis of the running environment. Tasks

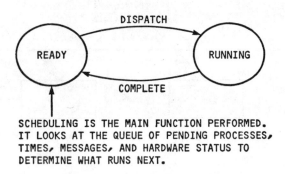

SCHEDULING IS THE MAIN FUNCTION PERFORMED. IT LOOKS AT THE QUEUE OF PENDING PROCESSES, TIMES, MESSAGES, AND HARDWARE STATUS TO DETERMINE WHAT RUNS NEXT.

Figure 7.20 **States of Operation**

performed typically include operational assessment, reconfiguration analysis and performance, composite view construction, cross product control and solution assessment, fault isolation and system diagnostics, configuration control, and interactive control initiation.

As can be seen from the above discussion, the goal of processes at this level is to provide support to the interactive users and the low-level controllers in order to provide a cohesive system for all; that is, these devices perform the continual analysis, modeling, assessment, and tuning of the system's overall running state.

Operating system processes at this level are mainly concerned with a combination of real-time and general purpose applications in the management of processes. Therefore, this level of the system structure exhibits a contemporary view in terms of its structure and performance. The operating system has two main views of this level: management and controls. Management refers to the contemporary management of memory, I/O devices, files, and processing resources, whereas control refers to real-time and system monitoring functions, such as monitoring, localization, assessment, feedback, and communications.

The last level (the operator interface) is concerned with the monitoring of total system process, performance of specific man-in-the-loop processing and control decisions, and system tuning, configuration, and operation. For example, the human operator of the robotics assembly line would be responsible for the control of the initial configuration of processes to processors, the monitoring of their operations, the performance of specific maintenance processes, inventory query or production query, and other higher-level, non-critical, real-time processes. Additionally, the user would be supplied with high criticality, real-time data to allow him to direct the operation of the lower-level controls in order to steer the real-world system's state transitions.

To do such operations, the user applications processes require the aid of an operating system in scheduling processes, utilizing system resources, and directing command processing.

RTDOS is such an operating system. It was developed to operate within an environment as described above, and additionally, it is aimed at distributed real-time command and control systems in which many real-time control devices are linked via networks to multiple distributed domain (cluster) controllers and even to multiple user command consoles.

RTDOS is comprised of a hierarchical collection of processes that, when taken together, provide application processes with system resource management, controls, and network services. The operating system has two components: a local and a global portion. This distinction provides quicker response to local requests than to global ones, in most instances.

The process is the granularity of code and data recognized by the system. All communications and scheduling are performed on a process basis, not lower. A process in RTDOS is comprised of code and data. The code could be one or more programs in conventional terms, but the process is what is seen by all. Processes are created during load time, reconfiguration, and restarts.

Due to the real-time nature of this system, processes are loaded into memory at initialization, and processes are created and provided to the system for recognition. User interactive commands can call up processes from the inactive to the active state, although as far as the system is concerned, it already knows about them (at least about all those relevant to the present load).

When a process is created, it is given a process identifier unique within the system. It must provide to the system services information on what hardware resources it requires, in what file space the source is located for loading purposes, a command argument and environment string to indicate required processes with which it must communicate, requirements for other resources, and a start-up process. Additionally provided are an umbilical port (a port to provide communications access for start-up) and a list of inherited ports from its parent process(es).

7.5.2 Ports

As in all the other models of processed-based operating systems, RTDOS communicates to other processes in the system via messages sent across ports. Ports act as the focal point for all activities in RTDOS. Processes find other processes by requesting look-up from the ports. They communicate control, status, and information via ports. Ports in RTDOS provide global and local interprocess communications. One main difference is the use and types of ports in RTDOS.

RTDOS provides primitives for:

    Creating a port
    Connecting a queue to a port
    Port connection
    Port disconnection
    Port deletion
    Connection queue deletion

Creating a port requires the name of the creating process, its identity number, an external port name (user supplied), transaction role (that is, is this port an initiator or responder), its synchronization type (that is, periodic, aperiodic, or broadcast), and the direction of the data flow for a port (that is, input, output, or both), as an input.

The create port process will provide back a unique internal identifier that the network communications subsystem will use to recognize and address this port and its associated process(es) for the duration of its life.

Connecting a queue to a port is a process that provides a means for processes to allocate queue space for ports to utilize, thereby guaranteeing space available for messages when they are sent.

The port connection process requires as input information the name of the creating process, process identifier, internal port ID number, association type (process, class, any), specific association (process name, class name, external port name), maximum message size (bytes), and message completion time (in milliseconds). This process provides a means for processes to create new ports dynamically and associate these ports with other ports or processes. The port is connected to the creator at this point, but communications cannot be initiated until the connector ports respond, indicating a total connection. This process utilizes other primitives such as process locator, network roster, and logical process element manager process to aid in the location of the resource processes.

The port disconnect process performs the opposite function. It provides the means to disconnect a logical port from the associated process. This command remains the link between source and destination.

The port deletion process provides the mechanism for processes to delete ports altogether; that is, the selected port will be terminated as far as the system is concerned.

The connection queue deletion process removes an allocated queue from the provided port, freeing up physical assets for other devices and processes to utilize.

Special primitives provided by the network component to aid in the linkage and interaction of processes include:

> Process locator
> Network routing
> Path identifier
> Schedulability
> Traffic analysis
> Error logging
> Traffic control (synchronization)
> Channel assignment
> Command blocking
> Real-time, device dependent control

Using the process locator process, any registered (logged-in) process can be located within the network. This process utilizes registration directories at its site and others to return the domain (grouping by bus), processor location, and port that the wanted process is on.

The network routing process is utilized to create a specific route through the distributed system's data bus network. This is performed in support of the logical port control process for setting up links between ports. This process utilizes the path identifier process which, provides unique names for paths as they are created in the network.

The schedulability process for the network provides network flow control; that is, it provides a service to ports that assures them that if a periodic message load is being provided for service (communications), the network can handle it. This process assures that the network can support the load it is being asked to support without saturating at any time. The schedulability process utilizes information provided by the traffic analysis process in its processing of requests. The traffic analysis process periodically senses the load at each node in the network and builds a profile of network link capacity utilizations. This information is used by the network manager and also is reported to the system manager.

For error conditions, RTDOS primitives provide a means to collect, store, and analyze errors encountered during network performance. These reports are sent up to system-level monitoring processes.

The channel assignment process provides a mechanism for ports to request communication channels (buffers) for use in message transfers. This process provides the assets necessary to send and receive data.

The command-blocking process handles the execution of command blocks for the network devices.

The real-time, device-dependent control processes provide network interface and services to low-level, real-time control devices and processes that lack the capacity to perform the functions themselves.

Synchronization in RTDOS is provided through the use of messages being passed back and forth between processors. To begin an active transmission, RTDOS provides processes with a primitive called transaction begin. This mechanism synchronizes the ports on the sender and the receiver to the ready to send state. Once this state is reached, no other processes can interfere with the transaction until it is complete. Once the two ports are sensitized, a series of sends and receives are initiated in order to synchronize the transmission of messages between the processes. Once all communications are complete, the transaction and process terminates the session, thereby releasing the assets for other processes to utilize.

The processes described to this point represent the low-level applications process support, not the entire operating system. Fig. 7.21 depicts the components of RTDOS and their interaction. Each performs a specific service to the user processes.

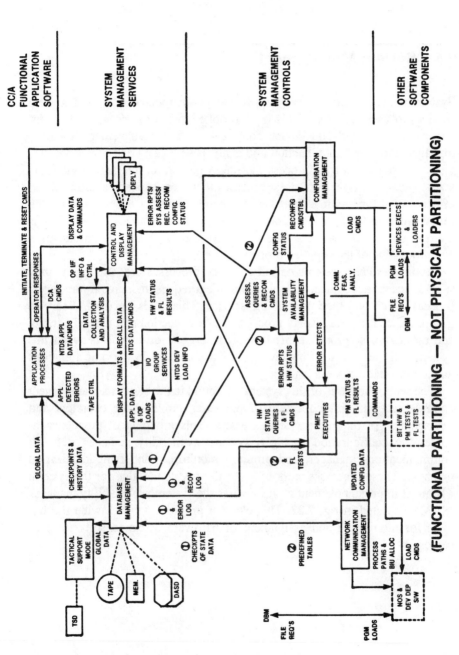

Figure 7.21 System Services Interfaces

7.5.3 System Management

System management services supply the contemporary operating system services to user processes. This level supplies local process scheduling, interrupt services, I/O and device control, data-base management, memory management, and data collection and analysis services. Each one of the services is represented by a process that takes part in an interaction via messages. Messages flow from user processes to system processes and back, to effect system functioning. Processes are loaded into the system to run via the initial program load process. This process takes load sources and distributes them to the nodes specified. The local sites then kick off the initialization and processing of the supplied processes.

As in the other systems described, once processes are running, if they wish to access a resource, they must provide a request message to the server process which will then provide the service. This holds for the I/O service group, the control and display group, the data collection and analysis group, and the data-base group at this level. The biggest difference between this system and the others at this level is the use of built-in periodic functions and a more static process loading.

The unique features of this system are found in the system's management controls section. This collection of processes provides the oversight and management of the entire system's assets. This grouping of processes includes the configuration manager, systems availability manager, network communications manager, and program monitoring and fault localization manager. These processes work together to provide the glue for the system. The most important element at this level is the system's availability manager (SAM), depicted in fig. 7.22. This element provides a systemwide mechanism for monitoring and assignment of hardware assets to software processes.

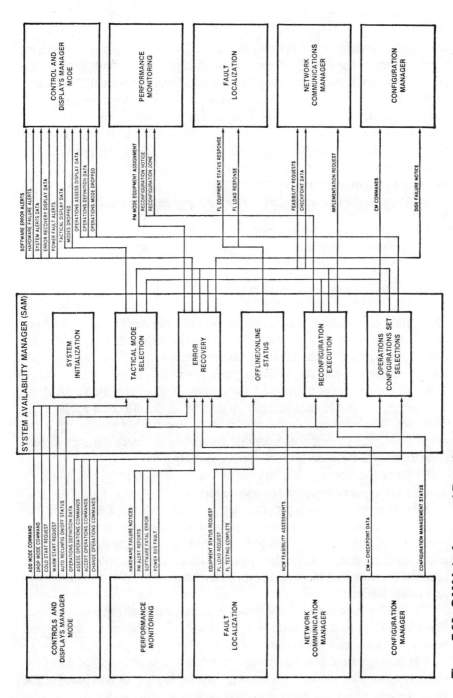

Figure 7.22 SAM Interfaces and Functions

During the running of the system, SAM receives user touch panel actions, reconfiguration requests, performance monitoring status, fault localization status, communications feasibility assessments from the network communications manager, and configuration manager status and configurations. It utilizes this status information to analyze the subsystem's functional capabilities and determines, if necessary, the proper actions to perform in order to maintain the operational integrity of the system. This system service provides the major interface between the operator's processes and the application's and system's processes.

SAM performs five major tasks in performing its primary duties:

>   Initial program load control
>   Recovery control
>   Catastrophic reconfiguration
>   System assessment
>   System status maintenance

The initial program load control process provides the mechanism to load application processes during system start-up. The program load is accomplished through use of the configuration manager and multiple local operating system components that initialize processes to the active state.

Recovery control is a process whose function is to provide to SAM the assessment of error reports in order to determine the effect on applications processes. The recovery control mechanisms report these conditions to the operator interface, along with potential alternative recovery schemes to continue to provide the same level of service to users.

Catastrophic recovery is a process whose job it is to provide a quick reaction recovery service under adverse conditions.

System assessment is a process that provides to SAM the capability to assess the state of the system and to determine if the present state can support the load postulated. This is accomplished by analyzing the current system's hardware usage versus the resources necessary to support a particular phase or scenario and forwarding this information to SAM and to the human supervisor for action.

The final component of SAM is the systems status maintenance manager. The job of this process is to provide SAM with the status of all operational modes and submodes within the system.

The configuration manager component (fig. 7.23a and fig. 7.23b) of the systems management level provides services for loading or unloading of the various applications processes into their host processors under the watchful eye of SAM. This process provides maintenance and longevity between communications, with both application and executive processes to manage the initiation, termination, and deleting of various processes within the hosts. This process is comprised of three subprocesses: the process load subprocess, process control subprocess, and the checkpoint subprocess.

The process load subprocess provides for the initiation of processes in the host processors. This includes preparing the processor for loading (memory reservation, port reservation, etc.), and insertion into run-time queues or, conversely, the deletion of a process from run-time queues and the return of memory to the local memory pool.

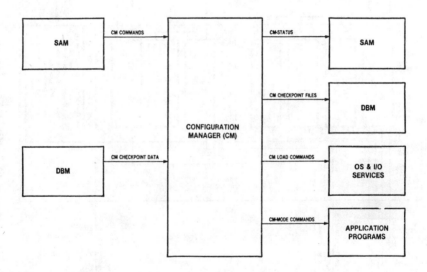

Figure 7.23a **Configuration Manager High-Level Flow Diagram**

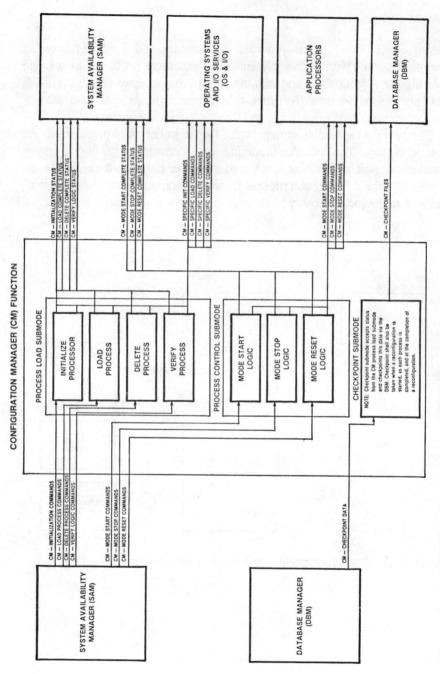

Figure 7.23b Detailed Flow Diagram of Configuration Manager

The process control subprocess of configuration management is responsible for controlling the starting and stopping of software processes.

The final part of configuration management is the checkpoint subprocess. This process is responsible for accepting status from the process load subprocess and checkpointing this information to SAM tables. Checkpoints occur whenever a reconfiguration is started, as each process is completed, and at the completion of a reconfiguration.

As part of the hierarchy of systems management, the network communications manager (NCM) provides systems-level communication resource management in support of SAM. The primary services provided by this process are network feasibility analysis, bridge/bus failure impact analysis, bus interface unit/bridge reset control, and BIU switching control. The NCM is comprised of five major processes (fig. 7.24).

The initialization control process provides NCM with proper initialization during restarts, cold starts, and when directed by SAM. It determines the initial NCM state via data-base information. Using this, it configures itself, then signals this back to SAM for analysis.

Implementation control process is responsible for updating the NCM data files whenever a process is added or deleted from the system. This process provides the communication component with process routes when new processes are added to the system.

Impact assessment is a process responsible for determining whether an applications process can communicate to others with specific loads through the network over predefined links. This is accomplished by checking NCM topology maps and routing status tables. This process is used to determine if communications loads can be supported on the network.

Topology/BIU switch control is a process that provides for updating of topology files due to the insertion or deletion of nodes in the network. NCM additionally provides a capability to reset BIUs and bridges under SAM control.

The last major component of the system management section of RTDOS is the PM/FL section (fig. 7.25). These components provide the capability to constantly examine the operation of the system, construct a view as to its status, and provide this to SAM for action (reconfiguration, reset, etc.). Fault localization provides on-line diagnostics for localizing the areas causing errors in the system. The collection of software described previously provides a total environment for distributed real-time command and control processing.

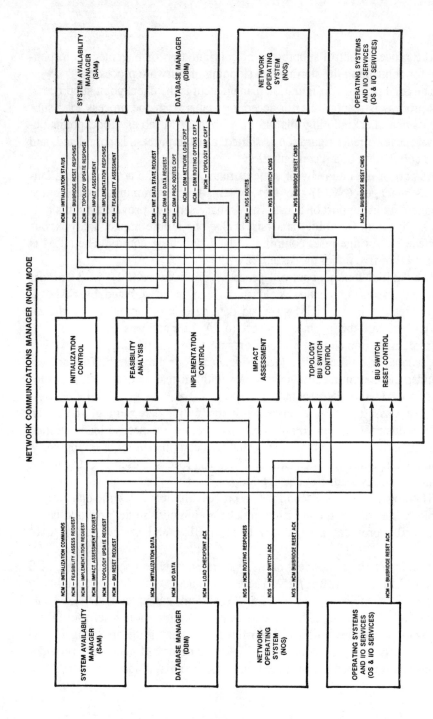

Figure 7.24 Flow Diagram of Network Communications Manager

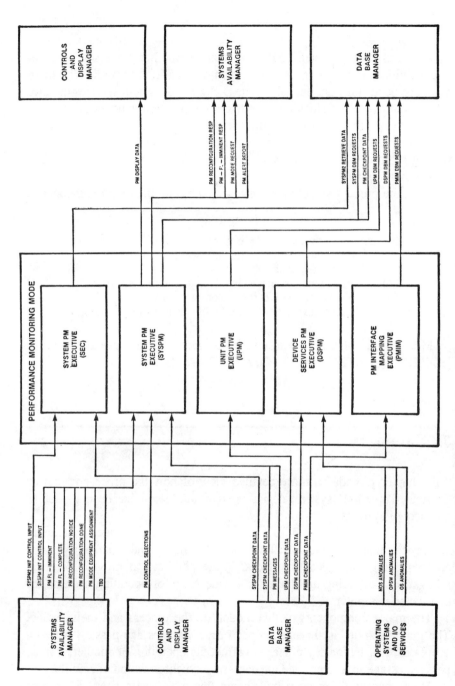

Figure 7.25 Performance-Monitoring Mode High-Level Diagram

Applications processes create ports, associate with other processes, synchronize activities, and perform work in response to real-time stimuli. With these functions occurring continuously in the background, system services monitor actions and assess the situation, and determine if action is necessary to keep the system up to a specified performance level.

This system is less flexible in terms of adding new processes or time-sharing of processors, but it provides high performance processing for real-time computations.

From the process model view, this system has all the major components, namely:

> It is built upon the notion of processes.
> Processes communicate control and data to each other
> via messages.
> Message communications is via a linkage mechanism (ports).
> Processes are grouped as requestors and servers
> (though a process can be one or the other or both).

More details of this system and its operating system can be found in [FORT83], [FORT84], [FORT 85], and [FORT86].

7.6 Summary

This chapter provided a more detailed view of how the process model of distributed operating systems design operates and how it has been applied to a variety of systems.

The process model provides a way of structuring distributed systems in an easy-to-understand fashion. It provides modularity and separability of operations along with clear interfaces. These combine to provide a robust method for describing and building a wide range of operating systems for distributed computers.

The major components of this model are the process and the message. The major activity is that all actions occur via message-passing between processes; that is, for any process to effect the operation of another, it must pass a message to it to provide the necessary synchronization of activity.

Many systems have been built using this model as a basis. Four such systems were described in this chapter. The references provide many more avenues for the interested reader to obtain more specifications on these and other systems utilizing this model.

8. Object-Based Distributed Operating Systems

8.1 Introduction

This chapter provides, through the presentation of example systems, an in-depth examination of the object model of distributed operating systems.

The object model places its emphasis on crisply defining the characteristics and operations of the physical or abstract components of the system being built. The components are defined as objects. Objects have inherent characteristics that cannot be changed; for example, a queue is represented to the outside world through distinct operations. The boundaries of operational characteristics and structure are rigidly defined and unchanging. Users of objects view them as black boxes with switches that can be used to provide some service and nothing else. Objects change state through the innovation of operations on the object's internal structure. For example, the queue object can be inserted into, removed from, or tested, and nothing else. These operations have known results (actions) and do not change. The queue cannot be sorted if it is a FIFO queue, it cannot be reordered, insertions always occur into the tail of the structure, and removed items only come out of the head. The operations and structure are invariant; that is, they do not change over time. Objects are viewed as either active or passive. Active objects are code, while passive objects are data or resources. Operation of the system occurs via the interaction of objects within the systems. Objects can invoke operations on other objects, thereby effecting their state. To perform operations on an object, the requestor must possess the capability or ticket that provides to it the right to use the object and in what fashion. This mechanism protects the individual modules against corruption or abuse by unauthorized objects.

Variations of the basic object model control paradigm and operations are seen in implemented systems, though on the whole there is a close adherence to basic philosophies of object permanence and access, as will be seen. This chapter will present the architectures and mechanisms for four object-based operating systems developed or under development: MIKE, an operating system for the distributed double-loop computer network developed at Ohio State University by Deven-Ping Tsay; ARCHOS, which is being developed at Carnegie-Mellon University under E. Douglas Jensen, as part of the Archons Project; CLOUDS developed at Georgia Institute of Technology by M. S. McKendry, and others; and SODS/OS, a DOS developed by David W. Sincoskie in 1980 at the University of Delaware, Newark.

This is only a sampling. Readers who want more details should consult the references for information on other operating systems developed for distributed systems.

8.2 MIKE

MIKE, in the true sense, is not a distributed operating system, but a network operating system. That is, MIKE is a collection of services built on top of local operating system services at the local sites. Since MIKE does exhibit the qualities seen in an object-based operating system, it was felt that this system would aid in the understanding of the concepts addressed in this model. MIKE has been built to provide the operational environment for the Distributed Double Loop Computer Network (DDLCN), [LIU81]. This network was designed as a fault-tolerant distributed system to interconnect micro-, mini-, and midicomputers, using a double ring structure. This is a local area network that is meant to be used within a small geographical area; for example, a building. The communications networks consists of two loops utilizing twisted pairs to interconnect individual nodes through network interface devices called loop interface units (LIU). Message transfer is implemented using a delay insertion technique performed by the LIUs [FORT85], [LIU75]. Utilizing this technique, the communications path can carry multiple messages simultaneously.

The multiple links (operating in opposite directions) provide a higher level of throughput and reliability for the transfer of messages. This network and its protocols provide the basis for MIKE's operational environment.

8.2.1 Introduction

MIKE's main goals are similar to those for most distributed systems:

> To provide transparent use of network resources; that is, to make the network look like one large system rather than many smaller, disjointed ones
> To maintain the autonomy of local sites while providing cooperative interaction
> To provide an environment that can survive failures (reliability, robustness)
> To provide an extensible and configurable environment

These goals are nothing new and have been expounded in all papers dealing with distributed systems; what they do reflect is the nature of all distributed systems.

As was previously indicated, MIKE is a distributed operational environment built on top of local host systems. MIKE is therefore structured as a hierarchy of software layers similar to the structuring seen in RTDOS (Chapter 7). MIKE has distinct layers that provide a specific class of service to the end user processes. The major layers comprising MIKE are:

> The virtual machine layer (VM)
> The system support layer (SS)
> The interprocess communications layer (IPC)

The virtual machine layer provides to the system's users a view of a singular large "virtual" machine, thereby masking the details of the network architecture underneath it.

The system's support layer provides the glue for the interprocess communications (IPC) and virtual machine layers. This layer provides the system-level controls and primitives for the virtual machine to use in communicating with others in the system. The IPC provides multiple communications protocols for internode communications. These will be described in more detail later in this chapter.

Due to its hierarchical structure built on top of nonobject mechanisms, MIKE needed to extend the basic concept. To provide this extension, the designers of MIKE developed a concept they referred to as a task. A task is defined as a logical grouping of processes (in the contemporary sense) and objects form an autonomous and protected subsystem. Each task has its own resource management policies and controls access to its encased processes and objects, thereby guarding their internal integrity.

8.2.2 Basic Concepts

Basic to the ability of MIKE to use the object model and its structuring is the concept of tasks. Tasks can be thought of as large objects in the pure sense; that is, a task provides an environment similar to that of the pure object in the previous chapter discussions. Objects provide abstraction to system resources, whether logical or physical. Objects additionally provide intrinsic integrity protection because they can be accessed, modified, or related to other objects only through specific sets of operations endemic to the object. Objects, through these characteristics, provide encapsulation of structure and simplicity of interfacing; that is, because of an externally viewed structure (operations) with controlled access, internal structure is hidden from scrutiny or abuse. The task model of MIKE provides such a view, and because of this the object model's capabilities can be wrapped around and used by both the global operating system's level and the local operating system.

8.2.3 Structure of MIKE

MIKE is comprised of a set of objects (resources); some have a direct correlation to hardware (I/O devices) and others do not (processes, semaphores, files, etc.). Objects are defined by a name, type, and representation. The name refers to the unique identifier that delineates this object from others. The type of designator gives information about the data structure and operations possible on this object. The representation is the realization of the object's guts, or internals. This is the portion of the object that possesses the data or programs and that performs the actual processing of the operations supplied.

Tasks are the structuring entity for MIKE. A task is comprised of one or more processes and possibly some objects. The components of the task provide its address domain or sphere of control (fig. 8.1).

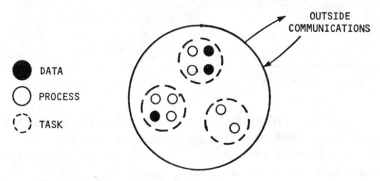

Fugre 8.1 **Mike Tasks in a Node**

Because of the physics of the environment, all components of a task must reside in the same physical computing element. As was shown in discussions of the object model, objects can be requestors of service, providers of service, or both. The same holds true for tasks in MIKE; they can be requestors of service, providers of service, or both. Objects (processes) within a task can directly access other objects, but they must send messages for operations on remote objects.

8.2.4 Objects

Objects within MIKE tasks are either active (called processes) or passive. The task forms a protection domain to the outside world. This protection is provided by a process called a guardian that performs the checking of access to objects (like a capability manager in the pure form). The guardian provides the means to encase and provide the object model qualities to its entrusted processes and data objects. Therefore, in MIKE each task within a node (there can be more than one) has associated with it one process (active object) called a guardian. This guardian provides the qualities of objects to the encased entities. It provides and manages all pertinent information necessary to control, manage, and operate the task. For example, the guardian contains state descriptions for all the objects in its task address space, the synchronization constraints to be enforced, the scheduling policy for active objects, and local resource management polices.

The guardian process is the basis of the task. When a task is created initially, only the guardian process is present. The guardian then will spawn processes (active objects) in response to service requests or to perform some predefined function of the task. Guardian processes are cyclic, and their duration is the entire life of the task. Guardians are used to accept requests for service from the outside, to invoke the necessary functions to provide this service, and to synchronize conflicting requests to guarantee its guarded object's integrity. Access performed by guardians to objects is similar to that provided to a data base by its data-base manager. The guardians additionally provide control and management of local resources through the selective scheduling policies allowed. For example, a guardian could be requested to accept and process requests from task N over requests by any other. From this discussion, we can envision the high-level structure of MIKE as being made up of superobjects called tasks (fig. 8.2). A collection of these across all the sites provides the operating system service to the users.

MIKE provides three main classes of tasks:

    Type tasks
    Service tasks
    Operating systems tasks

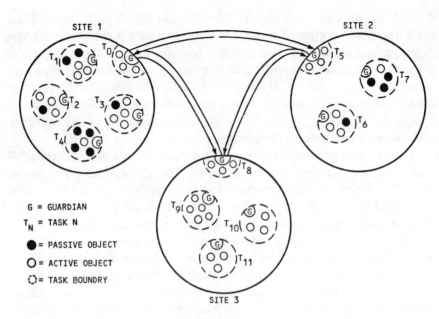

Figure 8.2 **Logical Architecture of MIKE**

The type task provides a structure to realize or bind together objects that comprise an existing data type, such as a process, stack, or file. Such similar objects are bound into types and are encapsulated within a task managed by a guardian or type manager, as the authors call it. The type manager provides the controlled access and integrity of the objects within its associated type. For example, a stack type would possess the following active and passive objects:

> Passive
> > Stack data structure(s)
>
> Active
> > Create
> > Destroy
> > Push
> > Pop
> > Empty
> > Full

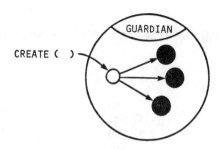

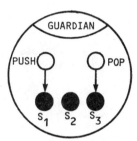

Figures 8.3a-8.3c (*a*) **Stack Task Initiation,** (*b*) **Stack Creation,** (*c*) **PUSH (X_1,S_1), POP (X_2,S_3)**

When the type stack task is initially created, only its guardian exists (fig. 8.3a). Upon receiving a request to create three stacks, the type stack task will spawn the create process, and it will create three stacks for future use (fig. 8.3b). Later on, external tasks issue requests to use the stack and data structures stored and managed by the guardian in the type stack task (fig. 8.3c). The guardian, upon receiving the push and pop requests, will spawn the active object's push and pop in order to perform the operations on the specified object. The guardian will control how the operations will be performed (based on the synchronization constructs) and provide the responses back to the requestor. This simple example illustrates how the type task organization is utilized. This structuring mechanism provides a way to group processes and passive objects into sets acting on the same type, for example, stack. Shown below in table 8.1 are types and their associated operators.

Table 8.1 **Examples of Types and their Operators**

Type	Operators
File	Create Delete Open Close Read Write Append
Process	Create Destroy Fork Join Start Stop
Message	Create Destroy Send-Request Send-Reply Receive-Conditional Receive-Any Wait-Any Abort Status
Tape	Open Close Rewind Read Write Append Erase
Printer	Open Close Write

This level provides a view of the operating system that is more consistent with the classic object model structure discussed in previous chapters.

The service task type exists to organize and provide cohesive system network-oriented services to type tasks. This is similar to the systems services level in RTDOS (Chapter 7). An example of types at this level would be the virtual resource service. This service provides to user tasks the illusion of all hardware and software resources residing on one site, whereas, in reality, they could be stored anywhere. The type managers at this level will create tasks to manage the interaction on the two sites for the user and server so that they need not know or be aware of the actual processes that provide the service. These mechanisms create the illusion that all the distributed network resources are available locally or that all the resource accesses are made by the local users to the local server(s).

The final type task is the operating systems task. An operating systems task resides on each physical site or computer. This task type contains the local operating system for the site and its user processes.

The guardian of the operating systems task is the existing site operating system. The operating system, since it is encased in a task, can have its own personality, scheduling, resource management, etc., but it must interface and react to the rest of the system just as another task would react to its requests. The operating systems task type acts as a resource provider or user within the system. As in the other task types, the operating systems task type provides protection and integrity of the resources it controls.

The systems architecture is structured as a hierarchy, as previously indicated; it consists of three layers: the virtual machine layer, the systems support layer, and the type layer. The operating systems task can reside only in the virtual machine layer, whereas the other task types can reside at any layer. To provide the transparency of location to users, MIKE provides unique names for guardians in the system, which are the only addressable units outside of the task the guardian controls. To access guardians underlying objects, another task must possess the guardian's name, provide and acquire access rights and other pertinent information for the guardian to validate, and allow its access to the objects.

8.2.5 Object Interaction

Due to the distributed environment in which MIKE must operate, there exists a need to provide inter- and intra- computer, or task interaction, mechanisms to provide processes with control and information. Due to the mixed nature of MIKE, a two-level object interaction model was adopted. This model provides MIKE with a message-passing mechanism for intertask communication and either a procedure-invocation or message-exchange mechanism for intertask communications.

The procedure invocation mechanism is similar to that found in most contemporary systems. It uses a simple calling convention with the attendant protocols. This mechanism is used for processes (active objects) within a task that wish to communicate with each other and perform some unit of work. For intratask communications, MIKE can also use message passing with messages stored on a mailbox type of structure.

For intertask communications, MIKE provides a message-based communications facility. All communications among tasks are entirely based on messages. In MIKE there are two types of messages, request and reply.

Request messages contain operation specification in the control portion and parameters for the guardian in the data portion. Reply messages contain information on the results of the requestor's message.

To access and perform some function on a data structure or resource, MIKE tasks must interact with operations and parameters through messages. The two or more interacting tasks perform as requestors and servers. Guardians serve as communications gateways; that is, guardians perform the send request message transfers and the receive reply messages on behalf of their encapsulated objects (processes and data). The messages are controlled by a messenger task(s) that provides all the necessary communications protocols. The guardian at the receiver task intercepts the message for the destined process (active object), and after validating the request, will dispatch the processes to execute the operation(s) on its guarded objects. Once completed, the receiving (destination) task guardian will send back a reply message with the results of the requested operation(s) (fig. 8.4).

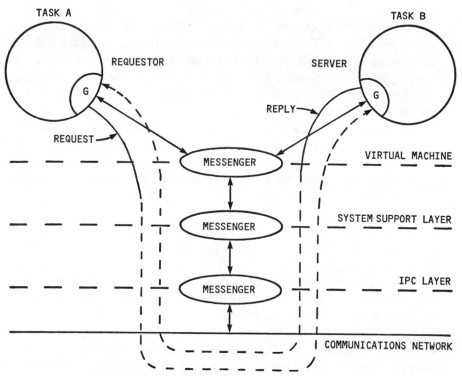

Figure 8.4 **Example of Communications in Mike**

Logically, this sequence of activities is the same as the generic object mode's operation invocation on an object (fig. 8.5).

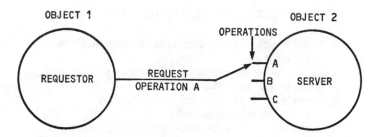

Figure 8.5 **Object Operation Invocation**

The requestor wishes to perform some operation on another object, for example, read X from Y. The server object will provide the operation if the requestor has the rights (capability) to perform this operation. MIKE is performing the same process, but on a larger granularity object called the task. This has allowed MIKE to provide the object model's modularity and clarity on top of existing systems.

For processes in remote tasks to converse, they need to exchange messages. The mechanism to support this is a system support service called the messenger. A messenger is a task that provides the control of communications within the network for requesting and serving tasks. Messengers exist at each layer within the MIKE architecture (fig. 8.4) and trap all messages sent by guardians at this layer. Messengers provide the interface between adjacent layers and to the network communications subsystem. They maintain a set of mailboxes, one for each guardian, to be used for message forwarding and reception.

To provide the protection of an object's integrity when operations are sent via messages from remote sites, MIKE embraces the object model's concepts of authorization via capabilities. To access an object in another task, a requesting process must possess the capability for that object; additionally, it is allowed to perform the operations specified for the requestor only in the access rights field of the capability. Adhering to this structure ensures that only agreed-on access is allowed, thereby isolating the object from unexpected and possibly destructive use. MIKE provides mechanisms to create protection/access domain objects. These objects contain the capability-list entries for accessed objects. When an object is first accessed, the capability list must be examined to see if this process has rights to the requested object. If it does, it is given the capability for the object (this is placed into its protection/access domain object). The guardians on the receiving side of operation requests perform checks to verify the integrity and rights of requests. A guardian performs the following functions:

> It checks the correctness of communications received via checksums.
> It checks the validity of requested operations by seeing if it is one performed under its control.
> It checks if the object to be operated on exists and is therefore manipulable.
> It checks to see if the operation requested is consistent with the state of the object at the present time.

If all checks are met, the operation is honored and the object is manipulated as requested. If, the checks are not met, MIKE will act accordingly to correct them or to signal a problem to the upper levels. For example, errors at the IPC level will be corrected there.

The above discussions present the systems architecture of MIKE. Using these constructs, service applications can be written to provide a wide class of services to user applications, as will be shown.

The operating system MIKE operates as follows. Requests for service are directed first to the local operating system, which controls the node we are on. If local resources can meet the need, the job is performed locally. If it cannot meet the need locally, a remote request for service occurs.

Resources in MIKE fall into two categories: hardware and software. Hardware resources include peripheral devices, main memory, central processing units, and I/O devices. Software resources include file systems, compilers, editors, other system utilities, and applications programs.

Resources located on a site are administered by that site and are sharable with other sites. This sharing is performed via MIKE's communications mechanisms.

Remote service requests are generated via the local guardians when they have determined that the service cannot be performed locally. For example, if we had three sites each performing a subpart of a total task, MIKE could support the effort as follows.

The problem is to manage information in a factory. There are three computer sites: one performing inventory and personnel information and processing, the second performing inventory control and processing, and the third performing floor production information management. The problem is how to coordinate the actions of selling items, determining if they are in stock, shipping them, and scheduling production to replenish stock.

> 1. A user process, sales, is executing inside node one. It is processing sales records for the week. As part of this process, it must request information from the inventory/shipping site to see if all the orders can be filled. If not, it tells the plant management task at site three to take action.
>
> 2. Therefore, the sales task is the requestor looking for now.inventory file. When it determines that it is not in its local task domain, it sends a request via the messenger at the virtual machine layer to the virtual resource service task (VRS) indi-

cating the need to access a remote resource called inventory file (figs. 8.6a,b).

3. After receiving the request from the sales guardian, the VRS will create a dedicated process named sales.inventory to provide for the remote interactions to follow. The VRS task, using the messenger task, will send a broadcast message to all virtual user service tasks (VUS), who will receive this and act accordingly.

4. The receivers create a service process of the same name (sales.inventory) to handle interactions. The request is then conveyed up to the local operating system (LOS) at this site since it controls all local resources.

5. The inventory task, under the local operating system's control, indicates its willingness to cooperate in the request via a reply message to its local VUS.

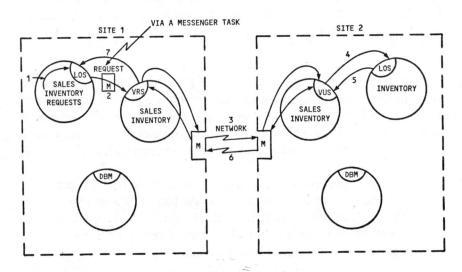

Figure 8.6a **Request for Remote Service**

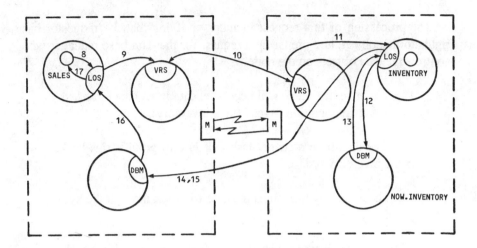

Figure 8.6b **Request for Remote Service (continued)**

6. The VUS in return forwards the reply to the VRS on the sales site, thereby setting up a conversation channel between the two sites.

7. The VRS relays this information to the LOS associated with the sales task to indicate success in setting up a link to the proper service task.

8. The sales task will send an operation to read the inventory file as of today.

9,10 This information will be forwarded to the VRS which in turn sends it to the VUS on the other site.

11. The VUS conveys this request for service to the inventory process, which will process the requested operation read now.inventory.

The processing of this request includes verifying that the requestor has rights to this object, and preparing a request for the data-base manager who controls the data objects on the node.

12. The inventory task will access its data in its data-base task by issuing an operation to read (now.inventory).

13. The data-base manager task will in turn provide this back to the inventory task.

14. The inventory task ships the data file back through the system using the VUS and VRS.

15. The VRS then provides the data-base message with the file to the sites data base for incorporation.

16,17 The data-base task on site in turn provides this to the sales task, which can now use it for processing of the sales records for the week. Likewise, if the job was to schedule more production, the inventory, sales, and production sites and tasks would be involved to perform the jobs of determining how much more inventory to produce, what people need to be brought to bear on the production problem, what production assets need to be configured for the job, and how and when to do it.

This simplistic model exemplifies some of the interactions and tasks necessary for MIKE to provide in order to give the necessary services to the user's processes. The above scenario was involved only with a request for data and a response for data. The other activities were hidden from the user's view by the underlying virtual machine layer, the systems support layer, and the interprocess communications layer.

MIKE provides a framework for designers to construct distributed systems applications. It provides a structuring means that allows for the interfacing of dissimilar machines and operating systems. Additionally, through the use of the task model, it provides a means to construct other services as deemed necessary to support the distributed applications.

8.3 ARCHOS

ARCHOS is the operating system being developed as part of the ARCHONS research initiative in distributed computer systems for real-time systems. ARCHONS' goals are long term, high risk, and potentially high payoff, as indicated by E. D. Jensen in [JEN84]. The environment ARCHONS is aimed at is the real-time command and control environment where timeliness of computation and the meeting of deadlines is of paramount importance. The prime research issues in ARCHONS are decentralized control, team decision making, transaction management, probabilistic algorithms, and architectural support.

8.3.1 Introduction

ARCHOS, the operating system for ARCHONS, has as a primary goal the pursuit of resource control based on decentralized peer negotiation, compromise, and consensus. The main emphasis is on new control paradigms and architectures. ARCHOS is a home-grown, from-scratch operating system that runs on the bare machine. There is no underlying operating system or mechanisms. ARCHOS is all there is.

ARCHONS research is striving to understand the characteristics and costs of decentralization and decentralized operating systems resource management. ARCHONS and ARCHOS will have no centralized implementation of the operating system function at any level.

ARCHOS will neither build upon nor utilize mechanisms based on unfounded assumptions from contemporary systems.

ARCHONS and ARCHOS must possess the ability to change readily (modularity) and be amenable to monitoring for experimentation purposes.

ARCHOS possesses a computational model closely linked to the previously presented object model of systems design. The model ARCHOS embraces includes the structure of the object model and the process model within the objects. Objects in ARCHOS are referred to as arobjects. An environment for a total system is comprised of one or more arobjects working toward the system's operational goals.

8.3.2 Arobjects

In ARCHOS, objects are called arobjects. An arobject is a distributed abstract data type, as in the object model. It is comprised of a specification (externally viewed part) and a body (internal part). Arobjects, once created, exist in the system as unique entities. The extent of their existence is under user control and is potentially unlimited. Uninstantiated arobjects reside on the disk waiting to be brought to life via a create command. Death of arobjects occurs either when a specified duration arises or an explicit kill is performed.

The specification part of an arobject is comprised of a set of operations that other arobjects can use and a set of data types for the arobject.

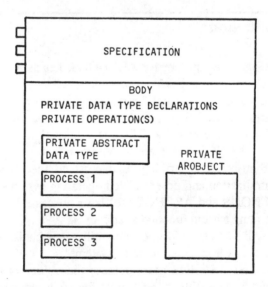

Figure 8.7 **Arobject Body**

Operations in ARCHOS are specified as a name, input arguments and output arguments with invocations, and replies using call-by-value semantics. A call-by-value is a mechanism in which the actual item is passed, rather than an address.

The body of an arobject consists of private data types, private operations, private arobjects, and processes (fig. 8.7).

Arobject Process

An arobject must have, as a minimum, one process. The information associated with the body is visible only to processes within the arobject. Access rules to the encapsulated data are specified and performed via procedures defined in the private abstract data types. This private data can be normative data types (integer, real, boolean, stack, queue, tree, etc.), but it can also be defined as atomic or permanent. Atomic data declaration will force such data to stable storage at the culmination of a transaction. This is the same concept as exists in data-base systems.

The private operations, data types, and nested arobjects are encapsulated within the body and are hidden from access or viewing by any outside arobjects. They are used only by the bodies' internal processes. This is the concept of information hiding and abstraction previously described in sections on the object model's characteristics.

The process internal to an arobject is a sequential execution unit. As indicated before, an arobject is comprised of one or more processes. Processes are invoked only by other internal processes, and are terminated by their own request, by request of another internal arobject, or by extermination of the entire arobject. Processes are "light weight" in ARCHOS terminology. This implies no computational state transferred to a process, only operation and formal input parameters. The process has its own internal state that it maintains. This construct simplifies ARCHOS' ability to locate processes of an arobject anywhere, implying that arobjects themselves can be broken up over multiple sites (fig. 8.8).

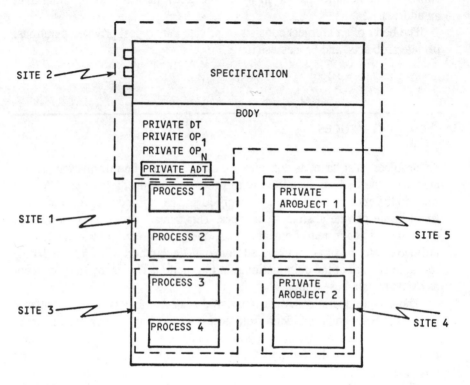

Figure 8.8 **Example of Possible Distributed Object Externals**

This construct of ARCHOS is a research goal, although the actual implementation may possess a limitation on dispersion. Only time will tell as to the success of this construct.

8.3.4 Communications

Communications in ARCHOS are performed via invocation parameters and messages. Communications are closed loop; that is, each involved arobject must agree to the communications for it to be successful. Communication is viewed as cooperating peers rather than as a master/slave situation. Using this cooperating view, ARCHOS can construct many types of cooperating sessions, such as client/server constructs, coroutine type constructs, tightly synchronized cooperating processes, etc. To communicate, cooperating arobjects utilize a request-accept-reply type of interaction in either a synchronous or asynchronous manner. The ARCHOS communications system provides for directed point-to-point, multipoint, and broadcasted (acknowledged) types of communications, to support the potential wide range of interaction seen in real-time computing environments. More will be said in the section (8.3.8) on communications management.

8.3.5 Transactions

To gain more reliability and correctness, ARCHOS has embraced the notion of a transaction for operating system actions. ARCHOS allows the tuning of the system by providing the data-base concept of atomic actions (all or nothing) to the items specified to require this action. This notion is important for real-time systems in which actions on objects either must occur fully as planned or indicate otherwise, in order to allow for corrective action.

Two types of transactions are supported by the ARCHOS operating system: elementary and compound. Elementary transactions are referred to as traditional nested transactions. This notion is consistent with that depicted by Moss in [MOSS81]; compound transactions [SHA84] are different. In Moss's model, commit processing occurs in the future; it is optimistic. In Sha's model, commit processing occurs immediately. The concept of compound transactions described by Sha provides a means of increasing concurrency in applications where such transactions can be employed. Due to the nested capability provided by such transactions, one must be careful in writing such transactions to preserve consistency between transformation or data objects. More details of this mechanism are to be found in [SHA84].

Transactions of these types are defined by the use of ARCHOS' primitives. The constructs associated with these primitives allow them to be easily associated and assimilated into any point in a process.

To guarantee the proper access to shared objects, defined as such, ARCHOS provides a locking mechanism. Clients (requestors) must explicitly request locks on shared objects required for execution of a given transaction. ARCHOS defines and supports two classes of locks: discrete locks and tree locks.

Discrete locks are locks performed on independent, individual data items, whereas a tree lock is a structure of related discrete locks. Discrete locks in the traditional data-base sense require the manipulator to acquire a lock, set it, manipulate the item, and release it. This is the mechanism utilized in ARCHOS. Tree locks are handled differently: the locks are organized as a tree structure, and rules are associated with their use, as follows:

> Clients initially may set a lock located at any point in the tree of locks.
> A client, after this, can set any child lock of presently held locks.
> A client cannot reacquire locks once released until all of the tree locks are released.
> Locks can be released at any time as long as the above are adhered to.

To lock items, the arobject programmer must explicitly acquire them. When commits at the upper true level occur, all locks below are released. Locks held by parent transactions are not automatically acquired but can be acquired through a primitive. Details of these locking mechanisms and references to other details are found in [SHA84]. The interested reader is directed to that document for further clarification since this topic is beyond the intended scope of this book.

8.3.6 Synchronization

ARCHOS provides two levels of synchronization support for processes to utilize, one for controlling access to a single shared object by multiple requestors and the other for controlling accesses from concurrent transactions.

The critical region scheme should be used when the shared object does not need to satisfy some failure criteria. If a truly consistent state is necessary for proper synchronization, the transaction model is necessary. The following section, on process management, will provide more details on this construct.

ARCHOS, as mentioned previously, is an operating system developed for real-time systems. As such, ARCHOS operations must be time driven (that is, have bounded execution times), have precedence and priority interrelationships, and be "fair" in allocating the resources for execution. To provide this, ARCHOS provides primitives tuned for time driven responsiveness. Arobjects can define relative priority (precedence) of one arobject versus others, relative value of the arobject completing within its time to the system, and a fairness doctrine that regulates what happens when deadlines for processing must be missed. These can be extended down into the process level where the real-time component is further broken down. The process level within an arobject looks at periodic scheduling of processes, priority, value or importance of this process versus others, and time required to execute a process in determining how to schedule processes to occur. Using these high level structures, ARCHOS allows distributed systems to be constructed.

The following sections will describe the process management, communications management, file management, I/O and device management, time management, and policy management of primitives for ARCHOS.

8.3.7 Process Management

ARCHOS provides primitives to create or destroy instances of processes or arobjects within the system. The process/arobject management primitives available include:

       Create arobject
       Create process
       Kill arobject
       Kill process
       Self AID
       Parent AID
       Self PID
       Parent PID
       Bind arobject name
       Bind process name
       Unbind arobject name
       Unbind process name
       Find AID
       Find PID
       Find all AID
       Find all PID

These primitives provide the basic mechanisms necessary to create and utilize arobjects and processes at run time.

The create arobject primitive, when invoked, creates a new instance of the named arobject. The creating arobject can specify where this arobject is to reside; the system will decide if it is not specified. The syntax for the primitive is:

                                Name of Arobject

AROBJECT-ID = CREATE AROBJECT (AROBJ-NAME,[INIT-MSG], [NODE-ID])

Unique identifier

                                Location, if wanted

                                                  Pointer to initial parameters for initialization

Likewise, to create a process with a given arobject, we would use:

PROCESS-ID = CREATE PROCESS (PROCESS-NAME,[INT-MSG], [NODE ID])

This primitive creates processes only within the arobject from which it is invoked.

Conversely, to snub out an arobject or process, the kill primitives are used. They are shown syntactically as:

VAL = KILLEROBJECT(AROBJECT-ID)
VAL = KILLPROCESS(PROCESS-ID)

An arobject can be killed only by one of its own processes (suicide), not by another arobject.

The determination of one's process or arobject identifier is important at times in order to perform some task within the system. To acquire this information, four primitives are provided:

        Arobject = SelfAID()
        ProcessID = SelfPID()
        ParentAID = ParentAID(AID-X)
        ParentPID = ParentPID(PID-X)

These provide arobjects or processes a means to determine their own process or arobject identifier or their parent process or arobject identifier.

To provide a way of binding unique names to one or more reference names, ARCHOS provides the following primitives:

> True, if successful
>
> VAL = BINDEROBJECT NAME(AID,AROBJECT-REF-NAME)
> VAL = BINDPROCESS NAME(PID,PROCESS-REF-NAME)
>
> Unique identifierNew name

Conversely, ARCHOS provides unbind primitives to remove run-time names from the association with unique identifiers for the arobject or process. These reference names provide a more logical means to associate a title for an arobject or process making for easier understandability of the code that requires the use of naming.

ARCHOS provides a way, via the find primitives, for processes or arobjects to acquire the unique identifier for other processes or arobjects in the system. Arobjects can find a single arobject or process, or acquire all the process and arobject identifiers for all in the local domain or remote domains within the system. These primitives provide a way for the local arobject or process to gain knowledge of who is active within the system. The syntax for these follow:

> Local or remote search
>
> AROBJECT-ID = FINDAID (AROBJECT-REF-NAME,[PREFERENCE])
> PROCESS-ID = FINDPID (PROCESS-REF-NAME,[PREFERENCE])
> AROBJECT-IDLIST = FINDALLAID(AROBJECT-REF-
>   NAME,[PREFERENCE])
> PROCESS-IDLIST = FINDALLPID(PROCESS-REF-
>   NAME,[PREFERENCE])

Mentioned above was the concept of parent and children arobjects and the nested arobject. ARCHOS additionally provides to users the ability to create and manage private (internal to any object) objects. Private objects are instances of abstract data types defined within an arobject. To create an instance of a private abstract data type, one uses the allocate primitive.

> OBJECT-POINTER = ALLOCATEOBJECT(OBJECT-
>   TYPE,PARAMETERS,NODE-ID)

To deallocate or free up storage, ARCHOS provides another primitive called free object. This primitive deallocates storage for an abstract data type.

Finally, if the abstract data type is designated as permanent (therefore requiring that if actions are the result of this object, they must be guaranteed to be saved), ARCHOS must provide a means to ensure atomic actions on the object. This is provided via the flush permanent primitive:

FLUSHPERMANENT(OBJECT-POINTER, SIZE)

When invoked, this primitive guarantees that it will not allow any more access to this object until it is saved in nonvolatile storage.

The above primitives provide a way to create and delete abstract data types such as stacks, queues, trees, etc., as needed by the arobjects within the system.

Synchronization of access to objects in ARCHOS is handled by primitives to create, delete, and manage locks within the system, and to create and manage transactions within the system.

ARCHOS provides a way to set up variables on which to synchronize, using the Region primitive:

REGION (EVENT-VARIABLE,TIME-OUT)

This construct delivers a simple means to provide a synchronization mechanism to interacting arobjects.

ARCHOS provides the primitives

NEWLOCK-ID = CREATELOCK([PARENT-LOCKID])

and;

VAL = DELETELOCK((LOCKID)

For users to create a lock for use in synchronization, the lock identifier returned is used to provide the variable for synchronization. To use the created lock, ARCHOS provides the following primitives:

SVAL = SETLOCK (LOCK-TYPE,LOCKID,LOCK-MODE)
SVAL = TESTANDSETLOCK(LOC-TYPE,LOCKID,LOCK-MODE)
TVAL = TESTLOCK(LOCK-TYPE,LOCKID,LOCK-MODE)
RVAL = RELEASELOCK(LOCK-TYPE,LOCKID,LOCK-MODE)

These primitives are used in the same way one would use them in a centralized system; that is, we would test a lock; if it is available, we would set it; once we are done with it, we release it for others to use. If the testing and setting must be atomic, the test and set would be used to guarantee that no one else gets in to set the variable while one is testing it.

For interactions that require a more robust mechanism that guarantees the operation and sequencing of actions, the transaction mechanism is provided. This scheme provides to clients a traditional data-base type of nested transaction mechanism for their interactions. The main benefit to users is the ability to access objects in an atomic fashion (that is, as if one were secluded from all others). The primitives provided for this include:

    (T(TIMEOUT){....TRANSACTION STEPS....}

or

    ET(TIMEOUT){....TRANSACTION STEPS....}

These constructs provide the mechanism to build elementary transactions or compound transactions [SHA84].

To manage the operation of these transactions, ARCHOS provides primitives to:

    Determine the identifier of a transaction
    Access the state of a transaction
    Abort a transaction

Details of this mechanism can be found in [SHA84].

8.3.8 Communications Management

ARCHOS is an object-based operating system. As such, its main function is to provide mechanisms to perform operations on objects (local or remote). To provide this capability, ARCHOS supplies a communications management object. This object provides inter- and intranode communications among cooperating arobjects. Using this capability, a process within an arobject can invoke an operation at a specific instance of an arobject by sending it a request message. ARCHOS does not require that processes know the location of an arobject to invoke an operation; it needs only to know its name and to possess the rights to perform the given operation on the named arobject. ARCHOS provides three primitives to provide the cooperative interaction between arobjects: request, accept, and reply. Using these primitives, ARCHOS can provide service to allow interaction between arobjects.

The request primitive provides the mechanism to trigger an operation at another arobject through the transfer of a message. The sending arobject blocks until the receiving arobject returns a reply message. A process also can send a request for an operation to its own arobject, which invokes a local operation. Upon reception of a reply, the requesting process is unblocked and can continue on.

The syntax for the request primitive is:

```
TRANS-ID = REQUEST(AROBJECT-ID,
            OPERATION, MESSAGE, REPLY MESSAGE)
```

ARCHOS provides extensions to the basic request primitive that are non-blocking protocols; that is, they need not block (stop processing) to wait for a reply from the receiving arobject. The primitives provide a one-to-one and a one-to-many communications capability, allowing an arobject to initiate an operation on one or more arobjects. The syntax for these primitives are:

```
TRANS-ID = REQUESTSINGLE(AROBJECT-ID,
            OPERATION, MESSAGE)
TRANS-ID = REQUESTALL(AROBJECT-ID, OPERATION,
            MESSAGE)
```

The invocation of any of these operations is bundled into a transaction, thereby providing the failure-safe performance of the actions.

The accept primitive provides a means for a process within an arobject to receive a message from some other process. Using the selection criteria built into it, the operating system selects a message and provides it to the process that must perform the operation. This process then performs the requested service and formulates a reply to the initial request once it has completed its service.

The process that is executing an accept primitive blocks until it receives a request for service message. ARCHOS again provides an extension to the basic primitive. This extension provides for acceptance of any operation or some subset of operations. The syntax for these primitives are:

    ACCEPT(REQUESTOR, OPERATION, MESSAGE)
    ACCEPTANY(OPERATION(S), MESSAGE)

To help manage the servicing of requests, ARCHOS provides a primitive to check the status of the arobject's incoming message queues. This allows processes to see if work is pending without the necessity of blocking.

The reply primitive provides the means for the servicing arobject to signal to the requesting arobject the status and result of the servicing operation requested. The syntax for this primitive is:

    REPLY(REQUEST-ID, REPLY-MESSAGE)

8.3.9 File Management

ARCHOS provides mechanisms to manage the storage and use of files within a defined system. Files are viewed as a set of long-term persistent data. Files are represented in ARCHOS as arobjects with the file name bound to them. Reading, writing, and control actions are handled as operations on the file objects. The data stored in the file is represented as the arobject's private data object. ARCHOS provides a set of primitives to control and manage files. They are:

    FD = OPENFILE(FILENAME,MODE)
    VAL = CLOSEFILE(FILEDESCRIPTION)
    NR = READFILE(FD, BUF,NBYTES)
    NW = WRITEFILE(FD, BUF,NBYTES)
    VAL = CREATEFILE(FILENAME, FILETYPE)
    VAL = DELETEFILE(FILENAME)
    POS = SEEKFILE(FD, OFFSET, ORIGIN)

There is nothing novel about this feature other than its integration into the total distributed environment. The mechanisms are similar to those one would see in any file system today. Additionally, ARCHOS allows the file creator to determine the type of the file as atomic, permanent, or normal, thereby providing different levels of protection and constancy to users.

8.3.10 I/O and Device Management

The designers of ARCHOS wanted a simple device management protocol for users. They provided primitives to open, close, read or write a device, and special commands to wait on the I/O action and provide device dependent information, if necessary. All hardware dependencies, etc., are handled at the servicing object, which manages the actual transfer from the device to the requestor. The primitives are shown below:

```
(DD)DEVICE DESCRIPTOR = OPEN DEVICE (DEVICE-
                       NAME, MODE)
VAL = CLOSE DEVICE (DD)
NUMBER READ = READ DEVICE (DD, BUFFER ADDR, NBYTES)
NUMBER WRITTEN = WRITE DEVICE (DD, BUFFER, NBYTES)
EVENT COUNTER = IO WAIT (DD, TIMEOUT)
VAL = SET IO CONTROL (DD,IO-COMMAND, DEVICE BUFFER,
      TIMEOUT) WHERE IO COMMAND IS A DEVICE SPECIFIC
      CONTROL COMMAND, LIKE REWIND FOR A TAPE.
```

8.3.11 Time Management

ARCHOS provides a means to access the system real-time clock and to utilize this in time-driven process scheduling. The primitives provided include:

```
RTC = GET REAL (TIME()
(TIME, DATE) = GET TIME DATE()
(TIME, DATE) = DELAY (DELAY TIME, DEADLINE, UTILIZATION,
               FLAG)
(TIME,DAY) = ALARM (ALARM TIME, DEADLINE, UTILIZATION,
             FLAG)
VAL = SET TIME DATE (TIME, DATE)
```

The first two primitives are self-explanatory. They get the time of day and time and date respectively. Delay is a primitive that provides a means to set a time at which a process should begin execution, a deadline at which it must complete execution, and a processing delay. Delay is utilized to determine when to schedule the process so that it begins either at or after its set delay time and finishes before its deadline.

Alarm, a means to wake up a process at some predefined time, is very useful for periodic processes that must occur at fixed intervals. This construct utilizes real time plus expected processing time and a deadline time to help schedule the process to occur.

Details of the research into scheduling algorithms for ARCHOS is beyond the intent of this chapter; the interested reader is directed to [LOCK86] for details.

8.3.12 Policy Management

Collections of arobjects grouped together into a distributed program must be controlled via a given management policy. ARCHOS provides primitives to group a given set of arobjects into a policy set. This is used by ARCHOS in fulfilling the execution goals of the set. Research and publication on this topic continues, and the author suggests that the interested reader refer to the appropriate journals.

ARCHONS, as a research project, requires the ability to monitor all aspects of its operation for future reference. ARCHOS has been tasked to provide this service to the researchers. Primitives to be built into the operating system include:

> FETCH AROBJECT STATUS (AROBJECT ID, DATA OBJID, BUF, SIZE)
> STORE AROBJECT STATUS (AROBJECT ID,DATA OBJID (BUFFER, SIZE)
> FETCH PROCESS STATUS (PID, DATA OBJID, BUFFER, SIZE)
> STORE PROCESS STATUS (PID, DATA OBJID, BUFFER, SIZE)
> CAPTURE SOMM AROBJECT (AID, COMM TYPE, REQUESTOR, OPR)
> CAPTURE COMM PROCESS (PID, OPR)
> WATCH COMM AROBJECT (AID, COMM TYPE, REQUESTOR, OPR)
> WATCH COMM PROCESS (PID, OPR)

Using these primitives, an arobject monitor can be built that will run periodically or on a time boundary to test the condition of arobjects and their interactions.

8.3.13 System View

Using the primitives provided and ARCHOS object model view of the systems, any operating system service can be constructed. For example, a distributed data base can be constructed utilizing ARCHOS primitives as follows.

The data base is viewed as a collection of data objects spread across the system (fig. 8.9) but encased in one arobject.

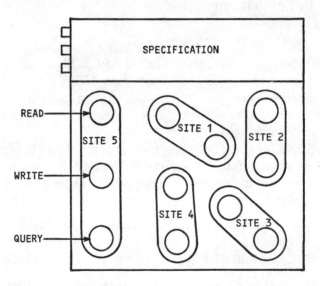

Figure 8.9 **Data Base**

To access the data, another arobject would issue a query (data-base read/write request). The query process would process the query to see how to best perform the user's request. It would then issue the appropriate read and/or writes to implement the query. The transaction subsystem of ARCHOS would be utilized to maintain consistency, atomicity, and integrity of actions and data in the system.

An example of a distributed directory, from [JENS84], is shown in the Appendix.

8.4 CLOUDS

The goals of CLOUDS researchers is to design and construct a reconfigurable, fault-tolerable distributed operating system. Their design goal is to hide the decentralization of the resources from the users to relieve them from needing to know what resource is performing their task for them, while grouping resources for purposes of autonomy and protection into protection domains (objects). This autonomy is viewed in CLOUDS as an issue of operating systems policy rather than structure. The clustering of resources and service for them provides a structure where work can be assigned to the sites best able to perform the job, which enhances the service to all users. Concepts embraced in CLOUDS closely mimic those of the ARCHOS operating system. As does ARCHOS, CLOUDS, embraces the concept of a global operating system in which all resources are managed and allocated globally. The locality of a resource does not play a significant part in allocation. CLOUDS stresses that the decision process is based on logical constraints such as value to the system. For example, determining how to run a process might include considering the location of the file, I/O requirements, CPU utilizations, and network loading.

8.4.1 Introduction to CLOUDS

The environment for CLOUDS has been characterized by Enslow [ENSL78] as a fully distributed processing system. The characteristics exhibited by this system include a multiplicity of resources, physical distribution, unity of control, network (location) transparency, and component autonomy. The primary goal of the architecture is to support a reliable, unified computing environment. Secondly, it must provide the same type of services seen in contemporary systems. Finally CLOUDS research is aiming at providing tunable disjoint elements of the whole system, or "tunable autonomy."

Like ARCHOS and MIKE, CLOUDS is an object-based distributed operating system. The primary components in CLOUDS, as in the others, are objects and actions on these objects. Objects in CLOUDS are instances of abstract data types. Objects are comprised of a data part, representing the objects "state," and a procedural part, which specifies the changes that can be made to the data (fig. 8.10).

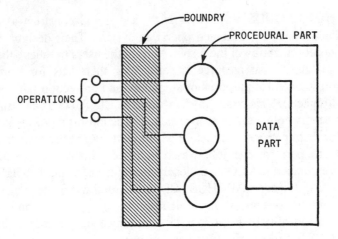

Figure 8.10 **CLOUDS Objects**

CLOUDS utilizes a concept called actions to structure operations (ordering of operations). As in ARCHOS, CLOUDS has embraced a data-base transaction view of operations on objects to protect consistency and reliability within the system. This concept is to provide the data-base-like feature of actions occurring completely (commit) or not at all. This implies the protection of the state changes on objects to either occur totally as planned or to return to the start state upon failure. Actions in CLOUDS correspond to transactions in ARCHOS and provide the fundamental computation mechanism for the system.

To program the system, CLOUDS utilizes a concept referred to as an action network. The action network (viewed as a petrinet) corresponds to action executions; traversing the network constitutes changing the "state" of the machine (objects).

To facilitate recovery and performance, CLOUDS utilizes multiple job schedulers to provide assignment of actions to machines and backup of actions to facilitate recovery upon failure.

CLOUDS is represented by a hierarchy of services. All of them consist of objects. Pictorially, the CLOUDS hierarchy is shown in fig. 8.11.

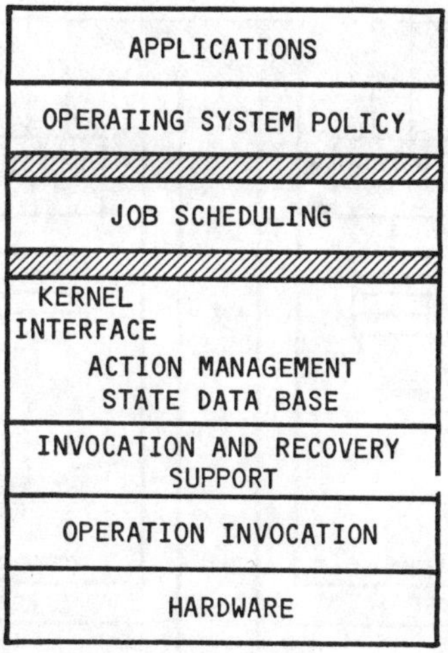

```
+-------------------------------+
|         APPLICATIONS          |
+-------------------------------+
|    OPERATING SYSTEM POLICY    |
+///////////////////////////////+
|         JOB SCHEDULING        |
+///////////////////////////////+
|  KERNEL                       |
|  INTERFACE                    |
|      ACTION MANAGEMENT        |
|      STATE DATA BASE          |
+-------------------------------+
|  INVOCATION AND RECOVERY      |
|            SUPPORT            |
+-------------------------------+
|     OPERATION INVOCATION      |
+-------------------------------+
|           HARDWARE            |
+-------------------------------+
```

Figure 8.11 **CLOUDS Hierarchy**

An applications view of the system is as a collection of objects with associated operations allowable. Additionally, not all applications have the same view; views depend on the rights granted via the capability list (fig. 8.12).

The policy management layer provides the primitives necessary to implement cooperation between objects and to determine the qualifiers that will actually control job scheduling, etc. The scheduler implements the provided policy (FIFO, least time remaining, least memory wasted, minimize communications, etc.) in performing the allocation of jobs to physical devices. Action management provides the services shown in the previous example

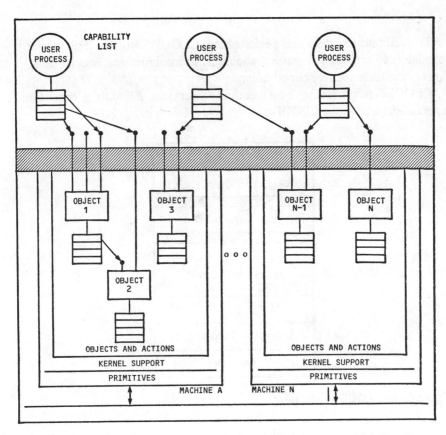

Figure 8.12 **Conceptual View of CLOUDS Architecture and Applications**

systems, encased on the action (transaction) model to provide location transparency and reliable execution. Parts of this layer are the data or object manager and the resource management components, to be discussed later.

The invocation and recovery support layer provide the virtual machine services, communications management, and file management type services. This layer provides the simple primitives, such as create, delete objects, move files, change type, create action, destroy action, delete action, invoke operations. The lowest level in the system is the operation invocation layer, which provides the necessary mechanisms to execute the object operation on the machine supporting the data portion of the object. For example, if one wished to invoke an insert operation or a tree file on some other device, this layer would provide the actual address necessary and the slave processes to carry out the operation on the remote data structure (fig. 8.13).

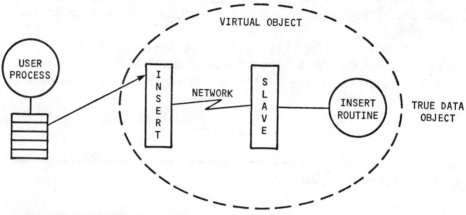

Figure 8.13 **Example of Invocation**

To provide such a service requires that the invocation manager possess tables and mechanisms to search tables to find the actual data object.

User processes utilize the system by requesting service from objects. The underlying services provide the transaction view of the system and the execution of such a mechanism. The key to such a view and implementation is an object manager (data-base-like, in this system). The primary components of this manager are objects and actions. Objects are passive entities accessible only via interface procedures that define and implement operations on the objects. Actions are ordered collections of these operations on objects that require failure atomicity for the entire action. The object management system provides a complete means to bound operations into actions, invoke their operation, synchronize these actions, and block others from acting on these objects until the entire action set is committed (completed). This implies the existence of primitives to bound actions (a begin and end action primitive) to precommit, commit, abort, or recover an action, in the traditional data-base sense for an action with one operation. For example, the following would hold in executing an atomic operation: the system must provide primitives to request service, acquire the service, guarantee that the service is irreversibly complete, and signal back to the requestor that this is true. Assuming that this mechanism is in place, reliable invocation of objects on any site can be ensured.

Using the above mechanisms, the object model, and reliable invocation and control, any operating system or user-required operation can be constructed.

The basis model for CLOUDS is ordered invocation of operations on objects. Using this simple notion, one can postulate how CLOUDS would implement memory management, process management, and network management as follows.

8.4.2 Memory Management

Memory management deals with how to allocate storage assets to active processes. In CLOUDS the scheduling mechanism implements the storage of the most active objects on any site in prime memory and keeps a virtual view of all others on any secondary devices. When requestors wish to utilize more memory to load a new object into memory, they request this via a create primitive, which determines, based on the policy at hand (site of call, least loaded site, etc.), where to place the object. The site chosen could, using a heap-based view of free pages, allocate the largest page to the object (worst fit algorithm) and remove this page from the free list.

For I/O device management, an object would be written that provides the necessary operations consistent with the I/O or device object under its control. For example, if a tape unit manager is needed, the tape unit would be the "data object" (the structure being manipulated) and the operations supported would be read, write, append, and rewind (fig. 8.14).

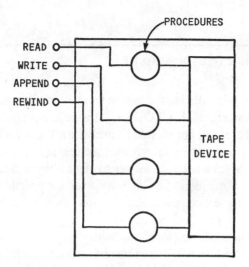

Figure 8.14 **Tape Object**

To operate on the tape objects, an object would require a capability to the tape object. Once it has this, it would invoke the operation within an action set to actually perform the operation reliably. The same holds true for other devices, such as disks, displays, keyboards, etc.

8.4.3 Process Management

Likewise, process management in CLOUDS is performed by process management objects. An object of this type can create, destroy, and provide for operation objects in the system. The structure of such an object would be similar to that shown in Chapter 6 on object-based arbitrations for distributed operating systems.

8.4.4 Network Management

Network control is handled at the lowest level, with all upper levels kept free of location dependencies in CLOUDS. User objects view all objects in the same fashion; that is, all are viewed as locally available for service. Network requirements are handled by the virtual machine layer, which would handle communication of invocation messages to other objects and responses to the invocations. To implement the intercomputer communications, CLOUDS would need to implement some form of low-level primitives for send, receive, and reply, although these can be hidden from user view to keep the transparency of network and location clean.

More details on CLOUDS architecture and its control environment can be found in [ALLC83a], [ALLC83b], MCKE83], [MCKE84b], and [SPAF84].

8.5 SODS/OS

The Series/1 Distributed Systems Operating System (SODS/OS) and its environment are parts of an experimental system for research in distributed computing at the University of Delaware. The SODS researchers have aimed their research at producing a decentralized computer system with distributed control. SODS/OS provides to users a transparent virtual machine. Users of the system need not know where they are running or where any servicing or cooperating processes are operating. Processes in SODS/OS can and do migrate from site to site, depending on conditions. SODS/OS has similarities to conventional time-sharing systems, in the way it allows swapping of jobs and sharing of the resources in the system.

8.5.1 Introduction to SODS/OS

The SODS operating system is based on an environment in which entities interact by sending messages (messages are used to request services from others); transparency is achieved by hiding location information from the interacting active objects. SODS is loosely comprised of objects. Objects are controlled by capabilities, and operations on these objects provide the state transitions within the system. The operations are carried out by active objects, or entities, as SODS/OS calls them. These active objects are processes. They can change themselves, other processes, and data, based on rights granted to them via capabilities. The passive component of objects in SODS is data. Data cannot change itself or anything else. It can be changed only by the actions of a process upon it.

The objects in SODS/OS are broken down into four types:

>
> Processes
> Exchanges
> Messages
> Capabilities

Processes in SODS/OS represent active computational entities comprised of code and state or context information (fig. 8.15).

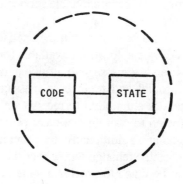

Figure 8.15 **SODS/OS Process Object**

The code portion contains the executable instructions and associated data. The context portion contains the capability list along with characteristics of the implementation. The context portion maintains the state of the process; that is, it maintains tables as to who can utilize this process and specific information that defines the process at a point in time. This context part must be maintained separate from the process in order to guarantee its integrity.

Access to this context is the responsibility of SODS/OS, and processes can only act on context information through system calls provided by SODS/OS.

Exchange objects provide the communications subsystem and mechanisms for processes in SODS/OS. An exchange resides outside the address space of a process and is composed of a first in, first out mechanism for message exchanging. This mechanism is similar to the port notion in process-based architectures, although there are some differences in its concept and uses. An active object (processes) either requests or sends messages to exchanges. When requesting a message from an exchange, it always receives the first message in the queue. To utilize an exchange, a process must possess a capability that has the proper permission. Additionally, SODS/OS mandates that all interprocess communications be handled through these exchanges. This allows SODS/OS the ability to regulate, as in the traditional object model, access to the operations on an object.

The use of exchanges as opposed to direct process-to-process communications provides a higher level of transparency to user processes. Processes need not know the names of other processes, only their associated exchange. Such a mechanism provides for more reliable service to users. One can move processes or routing without effecting the senders.

Synchronization is also achieved within the exchanges. An exchange can have varying numbers of queue locations available for sending and receiving messages. If a process sends a message to a full exchange, it blocks until another process comes around and removes a message from that exchange. Conversely, if a process is attempting to receive something from an empty exchange, it will be forced to wait until another process in the system sends a message to that exchange. Additionally, by providing multiple processes, and access to an associated exchange with either the same or varying capabilities, the system can be tuned to provide a wide range of service. The access to exchanges can be adjusted dynamically through the presentation of different or modified capabilities, providing a means for exchanges to dynamically alter their modes of operating. For example, if an exchange is set up to provide linkage to processes for servicing various raw data devices, the first message received could be used to alter the type of service necessary. Later, during its run time, another change can be instituted by again realtering the capabilities. Exchanges do not have to serve a single process. They can be set up to serve multiple processes, providing a means to grow or shrink the number of active processes based on the exchanges loading. Exchanges provide the conduits for job execution and information flow. They encase, control, and manage the processes within their control. This is similar to the concept of the guardian in MIKE, although the underlying processes in SODS/OS do not have to reside on the same node (fig. 8.16).

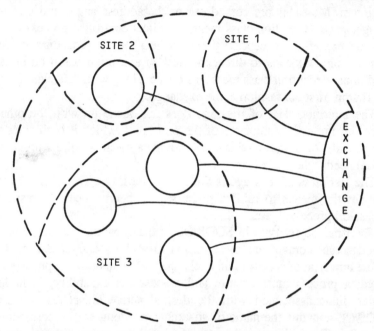

Figure 8.16 **Relationship of Processes to Exchanges**

The ability to have processes associated with an exchange on various sites aids in the ability to provide parallel execution of multiple requests for service. For example, if there are multiple line printers in the system, all managed by one exchange, the processes (active objects) servicing these printers could all access the exchange and remove and service multiple jobs in parallel. The same would hold if we had one exchange servicing process scheduling in the system; the multiple servers could go in, get work, and process it in parallel. As work is received, any waiting server would process it immediately.

To set up an interactive session with another process, the initiator needs to send the capability to the other process so that it can communicate with the initiator's exchange. The processes could then communicate via each other's exchanges.

Messages in SODS/OS come in four flavors; data, exception, interrupt, and control. Data messages are the simplest form. They are comprised of information with a variable size, from zero to an implementation-dependent maximum. Messages are copied out of the address space and into the exchange space. Exception class messages direct control of process execution to some predefined exception point, as in a remote procedure invocation. This provides a means to direct the flow of execution based on predefined conditions. Exception class messages queue, along with data class messages, in a first in, first out fashion at the exchange.

The interrupt class of message does not queue up with the others but causes an immediate stoppage of the process to which it is directed (via a system call). Messages of this class provide a means to direct processing to critical needs when necessary.

The last class of message is the control message. This class of message provides the means to initiate processes, suspend processes, resume processes, kill processes, etc.

The final object type in SODS/OS is the capability object. This object provides the storage and mechanisms to address and access exchanges. Before any type of access to an exchange and its underlying processes is allowed, a process must acquire and possess the capability, including the proper rights associated with the desired active object. A capability in SODS/OS contains the name of an exchange, along with access-control information. Capabilities can be moved around the system through the use of system primitives.

8.5.2 Architecture

The SODS/OS is constructed with six major components:

        Nucleus
        Process manager
        Exchange manager
        User memory manager
        Agent manager
        Network manager

SODS/OS runs in the machines as a set of cooperating tasks, with the nucleus providing for the sharing of the processor with the tasks. These operating systems tasks are totally separate and different than the objects previously described. Tasks are entities utilized inside the operating system only (like a kernel in the traditional sense), whereas processes are objects supported by the operating system and utilized by users. The nucleus provides the services necessary to support intertask communications and interrupt control within the system.

The process manager provides the control, creation, and destruction of processes in the system. It is distributed in each site and maintains a data base of processes off-line and on-line. This process controls the states of operation for the processes in SODS in a way similar to that of services that would exist in contemporary systems.

The exchange manager provides the management of the exchanges in the system. Requests for service from an exchange are directed to this process to provide the actual primitives for the operation of the exchange. The exchange manager maintains the tables of information required by the exchanges in a data base.

The agent is a task of the operating system that provides the coordination among the process manager, exchange manager, and user memory manager in performing system calls initiated on the behalf of user processes. The function of this process is similar to that of the service agents in MIKE; they provided the "hidden" services necessary to perform a given task. The final module or task in SODS/OS is the network manager. This module is responsible for providing the routing of messages between exchanges and processes in the network. This portion provides the total virtual machine crew to all the other components. The function of this module is to determine where an exchange resides, and to exchange the information to the network manager on the other site, which communicates this to the proper exchange to complete a remote transfer. The agents, exchange managers, and process managers are aware not of the distribution, but only the results.

8.5.3 System Calls

As mentioned in the above sections, users interface to SODS/OS via a set of system calls. These calls are roughly grouped into five major categories·

    Privileged
    Process-oriented

Exchange-oriented
Message-oriented
Capability-oriented

Privileged system calls are reserved for the operating system tasks to use when conversing with each other.

Process-oriented system calls in SODS/OS are simple and few. SODS/OS provides two system calls to manipulate processes: CRPROC and EXIT. CRPROC provides a means for a process to create a child process. When the call is performed, SODS/OS must first provide space for the process in the system. The instructions are placed into the allocated memory, and its context is created and initialized. The operating system creates a control exchange for the process in which vectors for all control class message types. Finally, a capability to the control exchange is returned to the creating process for its use.

The EXIT system call provides the means to terminate a process. When the system call is executed, the process is halted. The memory allocated for the process is returned to the free pool, and a death certificate is sent to the control exchange of the destroyed process, where all other processes having capabilities for this process can receive it.

Exchange-oriented system calls provide mechanisms to create an exchange and clear out an exchange's queue. The two system calls are CREXCH and FLUSH. CREXCH creates a new exchange and provides back a capability to the calling process. The calling process sets the type of access it wishes to have to the exchange. The FLUSH system call is used to remove any messages queued at the exchange.

Message-oriented system calls provide a means to send messages, receive messages, and capture particular classes of messages. The system calls are SNDMSG, RCUMSG, and TRAP. SNDMSG will transmit a message to an exchange. To use this system call, a user must specify a capability for the destination exchange, a message class and type, the size and location of the message, and a time for completion of the transfer. RCVMSG indicates to the system to remove a message from the exchange's queue into the caller's space. The calling process can specify a time that it will wait for a message. If none arrives, an error occurs, and the message is returned to the calling process. TRAP is used to provide a means to specify vector addresses for various types of exception, control, and interrupt class messages.

The final type of system call is the capability class. These include DLCAP, SNDCAP, and GETCAP. These system calls provide means to delete capabilities from the capability list of a process, to send a capability to a specified exchange, and to acquire a capability and insert it in the requestor's list.

8.5.4 Process Management

Process management in SODS/OS provides operations on the active and passive objects controlled by the exchanges via the setting of traps at exchanges. Once a trap is set, any message of that type (operations object) will trigger the wanted action to be performed. This mechanism, an early form of object invocation, provides a means for processes to set up sequences of operations for user process to access.

8.5.5 I/O Management

SODS/OS provides basic I/O operations of read, write, get status, and set status. These calls provide the means to implement a wide range of control to device drivers utilizing the setting and unsetting of status indicators. Details of SODS/OS use and design can be found in [SINC80a], [SINC80b], and [CROC79].

8.6 Summary

The thrust of this chapter was to introduce work in the area of distributed operating systems design that utilizes concepts from the object model described in Chapter 6. CLOUDS and ARCHOS have strictly adhered to the object-based approach, whereas MIKE and SODS/OS utilize concepts from the model but have not rigorously adhered to all of them. Discussions displayed mechanisms that were utilized to realize the concepts of the model and showed the methods used to encapsulate data and programs into objects. Additionally, discussion was provided on how systems interpret and utilize the concept of access rights granted via capabilities.

8.7 Other Systems

There are many other distributed operating systems, as the following list suggests:

    Accent
    Amoeba
    BFS
    Cronus
    Crystal
    Dinos
    DOSK
    E10.S
    Eden
    ELXSI
    GALAXIE
    Herbert-II
    HXDP
    KOCOS
    LOCUS
    MEDUSA
    MICROS
    MIMAS
    MuNet
    Phidias
    REBUS
    RIG
    Shoshin
    Sirius-Delta
    STAROS
    V-System
    XOS
    ZCZOS
    ZMOB-OS

One of the more interesting of these systems, conceived on the object model, is EDEN, a distributed research system developed at Washington State University. Its computational model is comprised of a set of distributed objects referred to as Ejects, each of which is comprised of a process and shared data encapsulated into a single unit. Ejects cannot span nodes, they must reside totally at one site. They communicate via remote procedure call semantics. More information on this system can be found in [ALMES83].

Another interesting project, similar to MIKE, is ARGUS. ARGUS is a research vehicle developed at Massachusetts Institute of Technology. Its computational model resembles that of MIKE in DDLCN. It is comprised of a set of guardians, or abstract data types consisting of processes and encapsulated data. Guardians invoke actions that are classical transactions (as in CLOUDS), including nested transactions. Guardians provide for the serializability of these actions on their objects. Again, guardians must exist in one site; they cannot be dismembered and distributed.

The goal of this text has been to introduce readers to the concepts involved in the development of distributed operating systems. Extensive research has developed sound concepts and mechanisms for the realization of operational distributed systems. The main obstacle in making these systems more widely available and desirable has been the lack of good operating systems for these machines. Only recently have real products in this area begun to emerge into the market place as a result of early research.

Future work will strive to finely tune these systems concepts and to add to them in order to increase their functionality and service to the user community. It is hoped that this text will provide insight that will help in these new endeavors.

Appendix

This section presents a sample application involving a distributed data object, along with two potential solutions employing arobjects and the ARCHOS system primitives.

In this example, the problem is to implement a distributed directory, where the directory data is physically spread among several processing nodes, with each directory entry replicated at multiple nodes in order to improve reliability. (There is no guarantee that every node has a complete copy of the directory information.)

In particular, the problem is to construct a distributed directory of a fixed length, in which each entry associates a name (a string of characters) with a value (in the examples, the values used are assumed to be integers). The data in the directory must be partially replicated at several different processing nodes, and directory users must always have a consistent view of the directory.

This type of distributed directory represents a class of data object that will be common in an ARCHOS client's distributed program. It is highly robust (due to the presence of multiple copies of each critical data item at physically separate nodes) but does not require that the user of this data object be aware of the physical distribution involved in the implementation. (In fact, this implementation is invoked by the user in exactly the same manner as a centralized data object.)

The directory data is contained in several different arobjects (called directory-copy arobjects), located at different processing nodes. These arobjects each contain some portion of the total directory state, but it is unlikely that any two of them contain exactly the same data or that any one of them contains all of the current directory data.

Another entity (called the directory arobject) is provided to consistently access and maintain the directory-copy arobjects so that the directory user "sees" a single directory object. In the example, one or more directory arobjects accepts directory operation invocations and then services them by making the appropriate invocations on the directory-copy arobjects. Since all of the arobjects in this solution are separate entities, this solution views the organization of arobjects as being quite "flat."

The solution manages the coordination of the multiple directory copies by applying the notion of using only a quorum [GIFF79], [HERL84] of directory copies in order to carry out any operation on the distributed directory. Using this method allows the directory to continue operating smoothly, even if several directory copies are unavailable at any given time. Each directory operation (lookup, add, delete) requires that only a quorum of directory copies be involved to perform that operation. In order to determine the latest value of a given name, the directory-copy arobjects also maintain a version number with each entry name. (The current value of a given name corresponds to the entry for that name with the highest version number in any directory copy.)

Notice that the transaction facility has been used in order to guarantee the consistency of the directory information at all times. Elementary transactions have been used for the most part, since the directory operations invoked by a user of the directory arobject may be part of a larger transaction: in that case, if compound transactions had been used, the consistency of the directory could no longer be guaranteed.

This solution uses several separate directory and directory-copy arobjects distributed throughout the system. The code for these arobject types is assumed to be contained in two files: "directory.arb" contains the code for the directory arobject and "dir-copy.arb" contains the code for the directory-copy arobject.

```
**********************************************************
*                                                        *
* This code is contained in the file "directory.arb"     *
*                                                        *
**********************************************************

#define DIR-COPIES 2*N+1
#define READ-QUORUM N+1
#define WRITE-QUORUM N+1
#define DEL-QUORUM 2*N+1
/*      If a DEL-QUORUM cannot be formed, NULL can be written
        to the value field of a new version of the desired
        name. Later, when all copies are available, a
        delete can again be attempted. */

arobject directory specification
```

```
{
        char *name;
        int value
        STATUS result

        operation add(name, value) --> (result);
        operation delete(name) --> (result);
        operation find(name) --> (result, value);
}

arobject directory body
{
        ***** insert message type declarations here *****

        /* Private Abstract Data Type Definitions */
        private-abstract-data-type DCNAME = {
        permanent AROBJ-REFNAME dir-copy-name;

        /* Procedures to Operate on Atomic Data Items */

        procedure store(dcname)
        AROBJ-REFNAME dcname;
{
        dir-copy-name = dcname;
}

        AROBJ-REFNAME function get()
{
        return(dir-copy-name);
}
}       /* end of private-abstract-data-type DCNAME */

        DCNAME dcname;

        process INITIAL(dircopyname)
        AROBJ-REFNAME dcname;
{
        MESSAGE *requestmsg;
        OPERATION opr;
        dcname.store(dircopyname);

        while(TRUE) {
        AcceptAny(ANYOPR, requestmsg);
        opr = msg-header-operation(requesting);
        -CreateProcess(opr, requestmsg);
        }
}
```

```
process add(add-requestmsg)
{
        char *name;
        int value;
        int 1;
        STATUS rd-result;
        int val[READ-QUORUM];
        int version[READ-QUORUM];

        TIME timeout = TIMEOUT;
        TRANSACTION-ID ted, trans-id;

        PID pid;
        struct add-replymsg {
        STATUS result;
}

        strcpy(name, requestmsg.body.name);
        value = requestmsg.body.value;


        pid = msg-header-caller(add-requestmsg);
        tid = msg-header-tid(add-requestmsg);

        ET(timeout) {
                trans-id = SelfTid();

                read-quorum(name, val, version, rd-result);
                if (rd-result ! = OK) {
                        Reply(pid, tid, {FAIL});
                        AbortTransaction(trans-id);
                }
                max-version = -1;
                for (i = -1; 1< = READ-QUORUM; i++)
                        max-version = max(max-version, version[i]);
                write-quorum(name, value, max-version+1. wr-re-
sult);
                add-replymsg.body.result = wr-result;
                Reply(pid, tid, add-replymsg);
        }
        if (isaborted(trans-id)) {
                        /* handle error condition hers */
        }
}
procedure read-quorum(name, value, version, result)
char *name;
int value[READ-QUORUM];
```

```
        int version[READ-QUORUM];
        STATUS result;
        {
                int count;

                TRANSACTION-ID tid;
                FIND-REPLYMSG find-replymsg;

                count = 0;
                /* initiate timeout */
                tid = RequestAll(dcname,get(), find, {name});
                while (count < READ-QUORUM) {
                        GetReply(tid, find-replymsg);
                        if (find-replymsg.body.result == OK) {
                                count++;
                                value[count] = find-replymsg.body.value;
                                version[count] = find-replymsg.body.version;
replymsg.body.verson;
                        }
                }
                /* Need to fix case where quorum cannot be
                   established. */
                AbortIncompleteTransaction(tid);
                result = OK;
        }

        procedure write-quorum(name, value, version, result)
        char *name;
        int value, version;
        STATUS result;
        {
                int count;

                TRANSACTION-ID tid;
                struct add-replymsg ...
                count = 0;
                /* initiate timeout */
                tid = RequestAll(dcname,get(), add, {name, value
                        version})
                if (add-replymsg.body.result == OK) count++;
                while (count < WRITE-QUORUM) {
                        GetReply(tid, add-replymsg);
                        if (add-replymsg.body.result == OK) count++;
                }
                /*  Need to fix case where quorum cannot be found. */
                AbortIncompleteTransaction(tid);
```

```
        result = OK;
}
    }/* End of directory arobject body */
```

```
*********************************************************
*                                                       *
* This code is contained in the file "dir-copy.arb"     *
*                                                       *
*********************************************************

arobject directory-copy specification
{
    char name[MAXSIZE];
    int value;
    int version-no;
    status result;

    operation add(name, value, version-no) --> (result);
    operation delete(name) --> (result);
    operation find(name) --> (result, value, version-no);
}

arobject directory-copy body
{
    /* Private Abstract Data Type Definitions */
    private-abstract-data-type TABLE = {
        TREE-LOCK-ID t-lock[TABLESIZE];
            /* define tree lock structure as a "linear" tree,
                t-lock[1] is the root and has child
                t-lock[2];
                t-lock[2] has child t-lock[3];
                and so on. */
        atomic struct table[TABLESIZE] {
            char *name;
            int value;
            int version;
        }
    }

    /* Procedures to Operate on Atomic Data Items */

    procedure init-table()
    {
        int 1;
        TIME timeout = TIMEOUT;
        TRANSACTION-ID tid;

        /* define tree lock structure */
        t-lock[1] = CreateLock(NULL-LOCK_ID);
        for (1=2; 1<TABLESIZE; 1++) {
            t-lock[i] = CreateLock(t-lock[i-1]);
        }
```

```
CT(timeout) {
        tid = SelfTid();
        for (i=1; 1<=TABLESIZE; 1++) {
                SetLock(TREE-LOCK, t-lock[i], WRITE);
                table[i],name = NULL;
                ReleaseLock(TREE-LOCK, t-lock[i],
                    WRITE);
        }
}
        if (IsAborted(tid)) {
                /* handle error condition */
        }
}
procedure lookup(name, index)
char *name;
{
        int index, i;

        TIME timeout = TIMEOUT;

        index = -1;
        ET(timeout) {
                for (i-1; 1<=TABLESIZE; i++) {
                        SetLock(TREE-LOCK, t-lock[i],
                            READ);
                        if (strcmp(table[i],name, name) ==
                            NULL) {
                                index = i;
                                breakfor;
                        }
                        ReleaseLock(TREE-LOCK, T-lock[i],
                            READ);
                }
        }
}
STATUS function enter(index, name, value, version-no)
char *name;
int index, value, version-no;
{
        TIME timeout = TIMEOUT;
        TRANSACTION-ID tid;

        ET(timeout) {
                tid = SelfTid();

                SetLock(TREE-LOCK, t-lock[index],
                    WRITE);
```

Appendix [305]

```
                        if (table[index].name ! = NULL //
                                table[index].name ! = name)
                                AbortTransaction(tid);
                        strcpy(table[index].name, name);
                        table[index].value = value;
                        table[indes].version = version-no;
                }
                if (IsCommitted(tid)) return (OK);
                else return(FAIL);
        }
                procedure get-fields(index, name, value, version-no,
                result) char *name;
                int index, value, version-no;
                STATUS result = FAIL;
                {
                        TIME timeout = TIMEOUT;
                        TRANSACTION-ID tid;

                        ET(timeout) {
                        tid = SelfTid();

                        SetLock(TREE-LOCK, t-lock[index], READ;
                        strcpy(name, table[index].name);
                        value = table[index].value;
                        version-no = table[index].version;
                }
                if (IsCommitted(tid)) result = OK;
        }
}               /*end of primate-abstract-data-type TABLE*/

        TABLE tab;

                process INITIAL()
                {
                        OPERATION opr;

                        tab.init-table()

                        while (TRUE) {
                                AcceptAny(ANYOPR, requestmsg);
                                opr = msg-header-operation(requestmsg);
                                CreateProcess(opr, requestmsg);
                        }
                }

                process add(add-requestmsg)
                ADD-REQUESTMSG add-requestmsg;
                {
```

```
        char *name;
        int value, version-no;
        int index;
        STATUS stat, enter();
        TIME timeout = TIMEOUT;

        struct add-replymsg {
                STATUS result = FAIL;
        }

        strcpy(name, add-requestmsg.body.name);
        value = add-requestmsg.body.value;
        version-no = add-requestmsg.body.version;

        ET(timeout) {
                index = lookup(name);
                if (index < 0) index = lookup(NULL);
                if (index <0) AbortTransaction(selfTid());
                stat = enter(index, name, value, version-no);
                if (stat ! = OK) AbortTransaction(SelfTid());
                add-replymsg.body.result = OK;
        }
        Reply(msg-header-caller(add-requestmsg),
                msg-header-tid(add-requestmsg),
                add-replymsg);
}
        process find(find-requestmsg)
        FIND-REQUESTMSG find-requestmsg;
        {
        char *name;
        int index, value, version-no;
        char *entry-name;
        STATUS stat;

        struct find-replymsg ...;
        PID pid;
        TRANSACTION-ID tid;

        strcpy(name, find-requestmsg.body.name);
        pid = msg-header-caller(find-requestmsg);
        tid = msg-header-tid(find-requestmsg);

        index = lookup(name);
        if (index < 0) Reply(pid, tid, {NOT-FOUND});
        else {
                get-fields(index, entry-name, value,
                        version-no, stat);
                if (strcmp(name, entry-name) == NULL)
```

```
                    Reply(pid, tid, {OK, value, version-no});
              else Reply(pid, tid {FAIL});
        }
    }
}/*End of directory-copy arobject body */
```

References

[ALLC83a] Allchin, J. E., and M. S. McKendry. "Synchronization and Recovery of Actions." Proceedings of the Second ACM SIGACT-SIGOPS Symposium on Principles of Distributed Computing. Montreal, 1983.

[ALLC83b] Allchin, J. E., "An Architecture for Reliable Decentralized Systems." Ph.D. diss., Georgia Institute of Technology, 1983.

[ALME83] Almes, G., et al, "The EDEN System: A Technical Review." TR 83-10-05, University of Washington, October, 1983.

[ANDE82] Anderson, A. "Hermes: A Message Passing Operating System for Real Time Applications." Burroughs Corp., ATD/SDRC, San Diego, Ca., 1982.

[ANDR78a] Andre, E. "On Providing Distributed Application Programmers with Control over Synchronization." Computer Network Protocols, 1978.

[ANDR78b] Andre, E. "On Providing Distributed Applications Programmers with Control over Synchronization." Proceedings of the Symposium on Computer Network Protocols, 1978.

[BAER80] Baer, J. *Computer Systems Architecture*. Computer Science Press, Rockville, MD, 1980.

[BANI80] Banino, J., et al. "Chorus: An Architecture for Distributed Systems." *INRIA Technical Report*, No.42. Nov., 1980.

[BEHR84] Behr, P., et al. "Object Orientation in High Performance Fault Tolerant Distributed Systems." Proceedings of the Seventeenth

Hawaii International Conference on Systems Sciences. Honolulu, 1984.

[BERE85] Berets, J., et al. "Cronus: A Testbed for Developing Distributed Systems." *IEEE MILCOM*, October, 1985.

[BLAI82] Blair, G., et al. "Mimas: A Network Operating System for Strathnet." IEEE, 1982.

[BRIN78] Brinch, H. "Distributed Processes: A Concurrent Program Concept." *Communications of the ACM* 21/11 (1978).

[BRUI83] Bruins, T., et al. "A Layered Distributed Operating System." Proceedings of Local Net 83. Minneapolis, Mn., 1983.

[CASE77] Casey, L. and N. Shelness. "A Domain Structure for Distributed Computer Systems." Proceedings of Sixth ACM Symposium on Operating Systems Principles, 1977.

[CHER79] Cheriton, D., et al. "Thoth: A Portable Real Time Operating System." *Communications of the ACM* 22/2 (1979).

[CHER82a] Cheriton, D., et al, "A Local Area Network Architecture Based on Message Passing OS Concepts. Seventh Conference on Local Area Networks. Minneapolis, Mn., 1982.

[CHER82b] Cheriton, D. *The Thoth System: Multiprocess Structure and Portability*. Elseviere, New York, 1982.

[CORS84] Corsini, P., et al. "The Implementation of Abstract Object in a Capability Based Addressing Architecture." *The Computer Journal* 27/2 (1984).

[COX84]   Cox, B. "Message/Object: An Evolutionary Change." *IEEE Software* 1/1 (1984).

[CROC79] Crocker, D., et al." An Architecture to Support a Distributed File System." UD-IBM-SODS-TR3, Dept. of Electrical Engineering, University of Deleware, 1979.

[CYPS78]   Cypser, R. *Communications Architecture for Distributed Systems*. Addison-Wesley, 1978.

[DATE83]   Date, C. J. *An Introduction to Database Systems*, Vol. 3. Addison-Wesley, Reading, Mass., 1983.

[DAVI73]   Davies, D. *Computer Networks and Their Protocols*. John Wiley and Sons, New York, 1973.

[DEIT84]   Deitel, H. *An Introduction to Operating Systems*. Addison-Wesley, Reading, Mass., 1984.

[DIJK65]   Dijkstra, E. "Cooperating Sequential Process." Technological University, Eindhoven, Netherlands, 1965.

[DIJK75]   Dijkstra, E. "Guarded Commands, Nondeterminacy, and Formal Derivation of Programs." *Communications of the ACM* 18/8 1975.

[ENSL78]   Enslow, P. "What is a Distributed Data Processing System?" *IEEE Computer* 11/1 (1978).

[FABR74]   Fabry, R. "Capability Based Addressing." *Communications of the ACM* 17/7 (1974).

[FLES83]   Fleisch, B. "Operating Systems: A Perspective on Future Trends." *ACM Operating Systems Review* 17/2 (1983).

[FLOR72]   Flores, I. *Peripheral Devices*. Prentice-Hall, Englewood Cliffs, N.J., 1972.

[FLYN79]   Flynn, M. *Operating Systems: An Advanced Course*. Springer-Verlag, New York, 1979.

[FORT83]   Fortier, P. "Generalized Simulation Model For Evaluation of Local Computer Networks." Proceedings of Hawaii International Conference on Systems Sciences, Honolulu, 1983.

[FORT84]   Fortier, P. "A Reliable Distributed Processing Environment for Real Time Process Control." ACM Northeast Regional Conference. Lowell, Mass., 1984.

[FORT85]   Fortier, P. *Design and Analysis of Distributed Real Time Systems*. Intertext/McGraw-Hill, 1985.

[FORT86]   Fortier, P. "A Real Time Distributed Operating System (RTDOS)." IEEE, Third Workshop on Real Time Operating Systems, Boston, 1986.

[GEHR82]   Gehringer, E. *Capability Architectures and Small Objects*. UMI Research Press, Ann Arbor, Mi., 1982.

[GIFF79]   Gifford, D. "Weighted Voting for Replicated Data." *Operating Systems Review* 13L5 (1979).

[GRAY82]   Gray, C. "Object Representation on a Heterogeneous Network." *ACM Operating Systems Review* 16/4 (1982).

[GREE80]   Green, M., et al. "A Distributed Real Time Operating System." Distributed Data Acquisition, Computing, and Control Symposium. Miami, 1980.

[GUIL82]   Guillemont, M. "The Chorus Distributed Operating System: Design and Implementation." In *Local Computer Networks*. North Holland Publishing Co., New York, N.Y. 1982.

[HERL84]   Herl, B. "Replication Methods for Abstract Data Types." Ph.D. diss., Massachusetts Institute of Technology, Cambridge, Mass., 1984.

[HIRS83]   Hirschy, E. "Hermes: an Operating System for a Modula-2 Environment." ACM Conference on Personal and Small Computers, December, 1983.

[JENS82]   Jensen, E.D. "Decentralized Executive Control Of Computers." Proceedings of the Third International Conferece on Distributed Computing Systems. Ft. Lauderdale, Fl., 1982.

[JENS84]   Jensen, E.D. and N. Pleszkoch. "ARCHOS: A Physically Dispersed Operating System." Computer Science Department, Carnegie-Mellon University, Pittsburgh, Pa., 1984.

[JONE79]   Jones, A."StarOS: A Multiprocessor Operating System for the Support of Task Forces." Computer Science Department, Carnegie-Mellon Univiversity, Pittsburgh, Pa., 1979.

[KNUT68]   Knuth, D. *The Art of Computer Programming*, Vol.1. Addison-Wesley, Reading, Ma., 1968.

[KNUT69]   Knuth, D. *The Art of Computer Programming*, Vol. 2. Addison-Wesley, Reading, Ma., 1969.

[KNUT73]   Knuth, D. *The Art of Computer Programming*, Vol. 3. Addison-Wesley, Reading, Ma., 1973.

[KUTT84]   Kutti, S. "Why a Distributed Kernal?" *ACM Operating Systems Review* 18/4 1984.

[LARS79]   Larson, A. *Distributed Control Tutorial*. IEEE Computer Society Press, Piscataway, N.J. 1979.

[LAUE79]   Lauer, H. "On the Duality of Operating Systems Structure." In *Operating Systems: Theory and Practice*. North Holland Publishing Co., New York, N.Y., 1979.

[LAZO81]   Lazowska, E. "The Architecture of the EDEN System." Eighth Symposium on Operating Systems Principles, 1981.

[LELA78]   Le Lann, G. "An Analysis of Different Approaches to Distributed Computing." Proceedings of the First International Conference on Distributed Computing Systems. Huntsville, Al., 1978.

[LIU75]   Liu, M. "The Design of the Distributed Loop Computer Network." Proceedings of the 1975 International Computer Symposium. vol.1, 1975.

[LIU81] Liu, M. "Design of the Distributed Double Loop Computer Network (DDLCN)." *Journal of Digital Systems* 4/4 1981.

[LOCK84] Locke, C. D. et al, "Archons Operating System (ArchOS); Top Level Requirement, a Working Paper." Carnegie-Mellon University, Sept., 1984.

[LOCK86] Locke, C. D., "Time-Driven Scheduling for Real-Time Systems." IEEE Computer Society Workshop on Real-Time Operating Systems. Boston, Ma., 1986.

[LONS68] Lons, V. *Egyptian Mythology*. The Hamlyn Publishing Group, 1968

[LYNC81] Lynch, N. et al. "On Describing the Behavior and Implemention of Distributed Systems." *Theoretical Computer Science* 13 1981.

[MCKE84a] McKendry, M. S. "Ordering Actions for Visibility." Technical Report GIT-ICS-84/05, School of Information and Computer Science, Georgia Institute of Technology, Atlanta, Ga., 1984.

[MCKE83] McKendry, M. S. "Architecture for a Global Operating System." *IEEE Infocom*, April, 1983.

[MCKE84b] Mckendry, M. S. "Clouds: A Fault-Tolerant Distributed Operating System." *IEEE Distributed Processing TC Newsletter* 6/SI-2 (1984).

[MILL75a] Mills, D. "The Basic Operating System for the Distributed Computer Network," Technical Report AD-A021 989, University of Maryland, 1975.

[MILL75b] Mills, D. "The Virtual Operating System for the DCN." Computer Science Technical Report, University of Maryland, 1975

[MOSS81] Moss, J. "Nested Transactions: An Approach to Reliable Distributed Computing," Ph.D. diss., Massachusetts Institute of Technology, 1983.

[NEED77] Needham, R. et al. "The Cambridge CAP Computer and Its Protection System." Sixth Symposium on Operating Systems Principles, ACM, 1977.

[OUST80] Ousterhout, J. "Medusa: An Experiment in Distributed Operating Systems Structure." *Communications of the ACM* 23/2 1980.

[PASH84] Pashtan, A. "Operating System Models in a Concurrent Pascal Environment: Complexity and Performance Considerations." IEEE Transactions on Software Engineering SE-11/1 (1985).

[PETE61] Peterson, W. *Error Correcting Codes*. The MIT Press and John Wiley, Cambridge, Ma. and New York, 1961.

[PETE83] Peterson, J. *Operating Systems Concepts*. Addison-Wesley, Reading, Ma., 1983.

[PRAS79] Prasad, K. "Physical and Logical Abstractions in a Kernal." In *Operating Systems: Theory and Practices*. North Holland Publishing Co., New York, N.Y. 1979.

[RASH81] Rashid, R. "ACCENT: A Communication-Oriented Network Operating System Kernal." Proceedings of the Eighth Symposium on Operating Systems Principles, December, 1981.

[SALT78] Saltzer, J. "Naming and Binding of Objects." *In Operating Systems: An Advanced Course*. Springer-Verlag, New York, N.Y., 1978.

[SCHA84] Schantz, R., et al. "CRONUS, A Distributed Operating System: Functional Definition and System Concept." BBN, RADC-TR-83-254, 1984.

[SCHW77] Schwartz, M. *Computer Communications Network Design and Analysis*. Prentice-Hall, Englewood Cliffs, N.J., 1977.

[SHA83]   Sha, L. et al. "Distributed Co-operating Processes and Transactions." Proceedings of the ACM SIGCOMM Symposium 1983.

[SHA84]   Sha, L. "Modular Concurrency Control and Failure Recovery." Ph.D. diss., Dept. of Electrical Engineering, Carnegie-Mellon University, 1984.

[SINC80a] Sincoskie, W. "SODS/OS: A Distributed Operating System." Ph.D. diss., University of Delaware, Newark, 1980.

[SINC80b] Sincoskie, W. "SODS/OS Programmers Manual. "UD-IBM-SODS-TR4, Dept. of Electrical Engineering, University of Delaware, 1980.

[SOLO79]   Solomon, M. "The Roscoe Distributed Operating System." Proceedings of the Seventh Symposium on Operating Systems Principles. December, 1979.

[SPAF84]   Spafford, E.H. and M.S. McKendry. "Kernal Structures for Clouds." TR GIT-ICS-84/09, School of Information and Computer Science, Georgia Institute of Technology, Atlanta, Ga., 1984.

[STAN81]   Stankovic, J. "An Adaptive, System Wide, Decentralized Controlled Operating System." University of Massachusetts Technical Report. Nov., 1981.

[STON72]   Stone, H. *Introduction to Computer Organization and Data Structures*. McGraw-Hill, New York, 1972.

[STON80]   Stone, H. "Introduction to Computer Architecture." SRA, Inc. 1980.

[SVOB84]   Svobodova, L. "Resilient Distributed Computing." *IEEE Transactions on Software Engineering* SE-10/3 (1984).

[TAFT82]   Taft, S. "An Object Based Virtual Operating System for the ADA Programming Support Environment." *ACM Operating Systems Reviews* 16/1 (1982).

[TANE81] Tanenbaum, S. "An Overview of the AMOEBA Distributed Operating System." *ACM Operating Systems Reviews*.15/3 (1981).

[TOKU83] Tokuda, H., et al. "Shoshin OS: A Message Based Distributed Operating System for a Distributed Software Testbed." Proceedings of the Sixteenth International Conference on Systems Science. Honolulu, 1983.

[TSAY81] Tsay, D. "MIKE: A Network Operating System for Distributed Double Loop Computer Network." Ph.D. diss., Dept. Computer and Information Science, Ohio State University, 1981.

[WALK83] Walker, B. "The Locus Distributed Operating System," Proceedings of the Ninth Symposium on Operating Systems Princples. October, 1983.

[WARD80] Ward, S. "Trix : A Network Oriented Operating System." IEEE Compcon, San Francisco, 1980.

[WEGN80] Wegner, P. *Programming With Ada: An Introduction by Means of Graduated Examples*. Prentice-Hall, Englewood Cliffs, N.J., 1980.

[WEIT80] Weitzman, C. *Distributed Micro/Minicomputer Systems*. Prentice-Hall, Englewood Cliffs, N.J., 1980.

[WILK51] Wilkes, M. V. "The Best Way to Design an Automatic Calculating Machine." Manchester University Computer Inaugural Conference, July, 1951.

[WITT80] Wittie, L. "MICROS: A Distributed Operating System for Micronet, A Reconfigurable Network Computer." *IEEE Transactions on Computers* C-29/12 (1980).

[ZIMM81] Zimmermann, J., et al. "Basic Concepts for the Support of Distributed Systems: The Chorus Approach." Second International Conference on Distributed Computing Systems. Versailles, France, 1981.

Index

access list, 169
access matrix, 168
active processes, status of, 120
addressing, 74-75
allocation, 42-47
ARCHOS, 265
    arobject body, 266
    arobjects, 266-267
    communications, 268-269
    communications management, 275-277
    data base, 280
    file management, 277
    I/O device management, 278
    policy management, 279
    possible distributed object externals, example of, 268
    process management, 271-275
    synchronization, 269-270
    system view, 280
    time management, 278-279
    transactions, 269-270
ARGUS, 297
arithmetic logic unit (ALU), 15-19
associations, 138

basic operating system (BOS), 223-224
    architecture, 226-227
    communications, 226
    processes, 224-225
    supervisor, 227-229
batch operating system, 28-29
Brinch-Hanson Blocking Protocol, 206
buffers, 61-62

capabilities, 167-173
capability, example of, 170
CDC Cypher 70 computer, organization of, 26
channels, 61
Chorus, 193-195
    actor architecture, 199-203
    communications, 197-198
    concepts, 196-197
    coroutines, 206
    device management, 208-210
    file management, 211
    I/O management, 210
    memory management, 208
    network management, 211-213
    notation for Hoare's

blocking protocol, 203
process management, 207-208
processing structures, 203-204
synchronization, 204-207
CLOUDS, 281-286
  architecture, 284
  hierarchy, 283
  invocation, example of, 285
  memory management, 286-287
  network management, 288
  objects, 282
  process management, 287
  tape object, 287
coalescing holes, 46
communications and synchronization actions, 147
compaction, 47
complex objects, 165-166
components of operating systems, 15
concept of kinked ready process, 38
cooperating objects, 164
coroutines, 136

deadlock condition, 11
device management, 57-61
distributed computing, 66-68
  addressing, 74-75
  control protocols, 68-69
  data-flow model, 82-83
  federated model, 81
  flow control, 73-74
  hierarchical model, 79-81
  homogeneous model, 82
  local area networks, 83
  models of computation, 79
  real-time system hierarchy, 80
  reliability, 76
  resource network, example of, 67
  resource sharing and distributed processing, 77-79
  resource-sharing model, 81-82
  routing, 69-72
  routing: static by table, 71
  security, 77
distributed operating systems (DOS), 32-33, 97-101
  basic functions of, 131
  communications management, 104-105
  design of, 212
  device management, 106-108
  event management, 112-113
  file management, 108-112
  memory management, 108
  models of DOS design, 113
  object-oriented model, 115-118
  process management, 101-104
  process-oriented model, 114-115
  view, 6, 98
disk manager object, 184
dispatching, 41

early communications services, 4
early network, 126
EDEN, 296
event management, 112-113

federated model, 81
file control block, attributes in, 64
file directory system, 63
file management, 62-65
flow control, 73-74
fork and join view, 207
free list for best fit, 45
full adder, 17

graph topology, 88

hardware architectures, 15-26
hierarchical model, 82
history of operating systems, 1-6
homogenious model, 82

IBM 370 CPU central architecture, 24
indirect sharing, 203
I/O actor, example of, 210
I/O and device management, 54, 56
I/O management, 150-151
I/O management, object model, 187-188
irregular topology, 88

kernal placement on device, 102

LAN, possible configuration of, 139
languages, 93-95
local area networks, 83
logical net of arpanet, 127

mapping of virtual to physical space, 52
mapping physical to logical, 47-49
master/slave computer system, 12
memory allocation, 43
memory hierarchy, 19
memory free block list, 43
memory management, 42
messages, 141-142
MIKE, 249-250
    basic concepts, 251
    example of communications, 259
    introduction, 250-251
    logical architecture of, 254
    object interaction, 258-264
    object operation invocation, 259
    objects, 252
    request for remote service, 262-263
    structure, 251-252
    tasks in a node, 252
models of computation, 79
multi-level time slice, 39
multiple circuitry, 18
multiple processor server, 150
multiple resource server process, 149

multiprocessing operating systems, 31

network manager process, 152
next-step processing, 200
NOS hierarchy, 5
NOS representation, 97
NOVA system, typical configuration, 25

object, 9
object-based communications facility, 190
object-based distributed operating systems, introduction, 248
object/capability interfacing, example of, 172
object model, 8, 11, 154-156
    capabilities, 167-173
        device management, 181-187
        introduction, 154
        I/O management, 187-188
        memory management, 180-182
        network management, 188-191
        objects, 156, 157
        operations, 157-167
        process management, 176-180
        synchronization, 173-176
object operations, precedence relationship for, 174
object-oriented model, 115-118
object/printer object, 185
operating systems, 91-92

operating systems, traditional, 26-27
output hardcopy object, example of, 186

page table addressing, 50
paging address, 49
PDP-11 bus central structure, 23
physical allocation of holes, 46
ports and association, 136
ports and processes, example of, 105
print server process shell, 133
process associations, plant management example, 140
process-based distributed operating system, introduction, 192
process creation, 37-41
process interaction, example of, 8
process management, typical tasks, 144
process management, 101-104
process model, 7-8, 119-124
    basic elements of, 134
    device management, 147-150
    history and motivation, 125-130
    I/O management, 150-151
    memory management, 151
    messages, 141-142
    network management, 151-152
    ports, 134-141

processes, 132-134
process management, 34-35, 144-147
synchronization, 142-144
process-oriented model, 114-115
process server interactions, 148
process state transition system, 35
processing devices, 91
processing graph, example of, 202
processing structures, 203-204
processor states, 35-36
producer/consumer with semaphores, 123
programming languages for distributed computing, 93-94
protection, 53-54
protocols, 89-90
protocols, examples of, 90-91

queue, 155
queue object example, 161
queue object representation, 162

real-time distributed operating systems (RTDOS), 29-30, 229-230
  configuration manager, detailed flow diagram of, 242
  configuration manager high-level flow diagram, 241
  generic architecture of, 231
  network communications manager, flow diagram of, 244
  performance-monitoring mode high-level diagram, 245
  ports, 234-237
  processes, 230-234
  SAM interfaces and functions, 239
  states of operation, 232
  system management, 238-246
  system services interfaces, 237
reliability, 76
requests for a file read, logical flow for, 212
resource network, example of, 67

security, 77
Series /1 Distributed Systems Operating System (SODS/OS), 288-292
  architecture, 292-293
  I/O management, 295
  process management, 295
  process object, 289
  relationship of processes to exchanges, 291
  system calls, 293-295
server and requestor, generalization of, 209
services, 92-93
sharing, 49-50
sharing in a paging system, 50
simple object, 165

simple resource server process, 149
single user operating systems, 27-28
stack, 155
stack object, 10
structure, 54-57
synchronization, 95-96, 142-143
synchronization in a distributed system, 146

tape manager actor, 209
tape manager object, 183
tape storage format, 60
text overview, 11-14
Thoth/Hermes, 213
    concepts, 213-215
    I/O management, 218-219
    memory management, 219-223
    process management, 215-218

timed processes, 36
time-sharing operating systems, 31-32
topology, 84-89
    basic bus topology, 86
    basic ring topology, 84
    basic star topology, 88
    DDLCN, 85
    hybrid bus tiered topology, 87
    irregular topology, 88
    multiloop, 85
traditional operating systems, components, 33-34

unique system path address for User N file, 63

virtual address format, 51
virtual storage, 51-53
Von Neumann architecture, basic, 16
Von Neumann computer, basic structure, 21